Postmodern Poetry and Queer Medievalisms: Time Mechanics

New Queer Medievalisms

Volume 2

Postmodern Poetry and Queer Medievalisms: Time Mechanics

Edited by
David Hadbawnik

DE GRUYTER

WESTERN MICHIGAN UNIVERSITY
MIP
MEDIEVAL INSTITUTE PUBLICATIONS

ISBN 978-1-5015-1882-9
e-ISBN (PDF) 978-1-5015-1118-9
e-ISBN (EPUB) 978-1-5015-1123-3
ISSN 2701-1143

Library of Congress Control Number: 2022931156

Bibliographic information published by the Deutsche Nationalbibliothek
The Deutsche Nationalbibliothek lists this publication in the Deutsche Nationalbibliografie; detailed bibliographic data are available on the Internet at http://dnb.dnb.de.

Cover image: Jess, *The Mouse's Tale*, 1951/1954, gelatin silver prints, magazine reproductions, and gouache on paper, 47 5/8 x 32 in. (120.97 x 81.28 cm), San Francisco Museum of Modern Art, Gift of Frederic P. Snowden, © JESS – The Jess Collins Trust, photograph: Ben Blackwell
Printing and Binding: LSC Communications, United States

www.degruyter.com

Table of Contents

Acknowledgments

I would like to thank Daniel Remein, with whom I first discussed this volume at the New Chaucer Society conference in Toronto in 2018. Next, thanks are due to Christopher Roman, the series editor we approached with the idea at that same conference; his initial enthusiasm encouraged me to craft a formal proposal. I must thank the other series editor, Will Rogers, and the editorial board: Michelle Sauer, Anna Klosowska, Gabrielle Bychowski, and Bill Burgwinkle, for their guidance and suggestions; also Ilse Schweitzer VanDonkelaar of MIP; Matthias Wand and Christine Henschel of De Gruyter; and Andrew Ascherl, indexer extraordinaire.

I must also extend my gratitude to the "research group" at American University of Kuwait: Katherine Hennessey, Ben Crace, and Abid Vali, who gave valuable feedback on this and other projects during my time there; all of the contributors, without whose patience and dedication this volume wouldn't have been possible; the readers who made excellent suggestions during the revision process; Margaret Sloan and Christopher Wagstaff of the Jess Trust; The San Francisco Museum of Modern Art; friends and fellow travelers Micah Robbins, Dale Smith, Chris Piuma, and Kent Johnson; and my wife Tina Žigon and son Elliott. Finally, a huge thank you to Scott Gunem, the graduate assistant who was assigned to this project during my time as Visiting Professor at University of Wisconsin-Eau Claire. Scott was absolutely invaluable during the busiest part of the project: coordinating among editorial staff and contributors, communicating with external reviewers, and doing early copy editing on the chapters.

https://doi.org/10.1515/9781501511189-001

David Hadbawnik

Introduction: The Opening of the Field

Often I am permitted to return to a meadow
as if it were a given property of the mind
that certain bounds hold against chaos,

that is a place of first permission,
everlasting omen of what is.

– Robert Duncan[1]

An edited volume has many origins, some of them quite distant from and different than the finished product. In this case, I must trace the thread all the way back ten-plus years to my days as a student in the PhD program at SUNY-Buffalo. Beginning to attend conferences and explore the field as it were, casting about for a project for my dissertation, I made the acquaintance of like-minded graduate students who were frustrated by the rigid distinctions enforced by periodization and the academic-literary genre. Buffalo's storied Poetics Program—still extant though buffeted by attrition and entropy—has a proud tradition of encouraging non-traditional projects. But the academic job market, as if entrenching itself against the economic catastrophe unfolding throughout higher education, seemed to many of us as conservative as ever, if not more so. As a result, my dissertation wound up being a largely risk-averse study of the poetic diction of medieval through early modern poets, anchored on the twin foundations of Geoffrey Chaucer and Edmund Spenser. I'm proud of the research I did and happy I wrote and finished the project, though the market proved difficult to solve regardless.

Closer to my heart were the engagements with medieval material undertaken by contemporary poets. For those of us who also followed current conversations in poetry and translation, such engagements held much more than merely academic interest. They were vital, even political, as competing visions of what poetry is and was, what it should be doing and where it should be headed, playing out around us in real time. This awareness of the contested matter of poetry lent an urgency to every conference paper, every publication. We understood that even the act of editing became a statement of purpose, a move to add context to a given body of poetry and spread the gospel about the importance of the medieval to contemporary poets, and conversely the ways in which attention to con-

1 Robert Duncan, "Often I Am Permitted to Return to a Meadow," in *The Opening of the Field* (New York: New Directions, 1960), 7.

https://doi.org/10.1515/9781501511189-002

temporary poetry could help illuminate medievalist scholarship. Early breakthroughs in this vein included the discovery and publication of selections from Jack Spicer's *Beowulf* translation (CUNY's Lost and Found Document Series, 2011) and Thomas Meyer's *Beowulf* (punctum books, 2012).[2] Spicer had been a key figure in the so-called "Berkeley Renaissance" along with Robert Duncan and Robin Blaser in the late 1950s, a precursor to the Beat movement. Meyer emerges from the "New American" cadre of poets that includes Gerrit Lansing and Robert Kelly and traces its lineage to figures like Basil Bunting and Charles Olson, among others. Both queer, somewhat under-studied "poets' poets" (especially in Meyer's case), their medievalist engagements struck us as fresh, bold, and incredibly central to their work. In short, they became the perfect exemplars of the rich cross-currents in these respective fields that we wished to unearth and explore.

There were many others. With a classmate from University at Buffalo—Sean Reynolds, a fellow poetics student with a strong interest in older forms of literature—I presented at the International Congress of Medieval Studies at Kalamazoo in 2011 on Spicer's *Beowulf*, also mentioning and showing some images from Meyer's more fully fleshed out and experimental version. The strong interest in this material led to our guest-editing a special issue of *postmedieval.*[3] Contributors covered a wide range of poets and topics including, among others, Arabic lexical monographs in translation; Patience Agbabi's *Telling Tales*; Caroline Bergvall's "Shorter Chaucer Tales"; the Black Mountain poets and "Caedmon's Hymn"; Alice Notley and her *Descent of Alette*; Pier Paolo Pasolini's film adaptation of *The Canterbury Tales*; and of course the Berkeley Renaissance poets who'd provided the impetus for the project. Our emphasis was on experimental, more or less consciously avant-garde and edgy projects that pushed beyond updating medieval material and sought to extend boundaries and shed new light on their sources. We hoped this would be another milestone in a series of projects, involving ourselves, the contributing authors, and many others. How naïve we were! With Daniel Remein and Chris Piuma—eventually, also, Lisa Ampleman—I started eth press, a subsidiary of punctum books meant to publish medievalist-inflected creative projects. While there were plenty of writers whose work excited us, about whom we felt there was much to be written and whose work we wanted to publish, maintaining momentum and actualizing these

---

2 David Hadbawnik and Sean Reynolds, eds., *Jack Spicer's Beowulf*, Lost and Found, The CUNY Poetics Document Initiative (New York: The City University of New York, 2011). Thomas Meyer, *Beowulf* (New York: punctum books, 2012).

3 David Hadbawnik and Sean Reynolds, eds., "Contemporary Poetics and the Medieval Muse," *postmedieval* 6, no. 2 (2015).

plans proved elusive. In retrospect, the difficulty of corralling enough scholars ready and willing to contribute to the special issue of *postmedieval* should have been a sign.

The problem that we encountered at that time is the same one that haunts this volume, articulated in the introduction we wrote for *postmedieval:* "What we found as we proceeded to call for, and in some cases solicit, pieces for this issue was a sort of double-edged bewilderment that cut between medievalist scholars and scholars of contemporary poetry (a bewilderment that we, at times, admittedly shared)."[4] While both my medievalist and poetics-oriented colleagues are highly curious and well-read people, there is still a level of hesitation in delving into multiple discourses for a hybrid project, one that additionally proposes to approach its subject matter under the aegis of a series entitled "New Queer Medievalisms." In many ways, I found myself once again confronted with academia's artificial boundaries between time periods and disciplines. Clare A. Lees and Gillian R. Overing describe a similar issue in the introduction to their recent volume, *The Contemporary Medieval in Practice*, which they write is "informed by the three disciplines of medieval studies … the contemporary arts and creative-critical work."[5] The authors sketch a series of questions they find themselves facing:

> Are we literary scholars, historians, medievalists, feminists, cultural theorists?, we are often asked. How can we speak through and across these categories or environments? And, to whom are we speaking?[6]

Lees and Overing are somewhat reassured on the question of audience, as they feel confident that there is strong interest among the public for creative contemporary engagements with medieval material, and indeed, the continuing proliferation of medievalist creative works, and the positive critical and popular response to them, would seem to confirm this.[7] In many senses, the only way forward in the face of such questions is to accept that failure is inevitable. As Lees and Overing add, "We are acutely aware of the incommensurability of our knowledge about early medieval culture on the one hand, and the contem-

---

4 Hadbawnik and Reynolds, "Contemporary," 116.

5 Clare A. Lees and Gillian R. Overing, *The Contemporary Medieval in Practice* (London: University College London Press, 2019), 5.

6 Lees and Overing, *The Contemporary Medieval*, 6.

7 Maria Dahvana Headley, *Beowulf: A New Translation* (New York: Farrar, Strauss and Giroux, 2020). This "new, feminist translation" of *Beowulf* was published during the editing of this volume in summer 2020. Headley also wrote *The Mere Wife*, a retelling of *Beowulf* published in 2018.

porary on the other. Moving across times, disciplines and practices is a risky business." What makes the risk worth it is that there are "also possibilities of new ways of thinking and different directions."[8] Like them, I hope that the work of the authors collected in this volume helps create new audiences for contemporary, creative-medievalist projects, sparks interest in their medieval source material and languages, and sheds new light on both contemporary and medieval texts.

Although not explicitly "global" in scope, I hope this volume also contributes to a discourse guided by two of its contributors: the ongoing "Global Chaucers" project of Jonathan Hsy and Candace Barrington. As they write in the introduction to their special issue of *Literature Compass*,

> A pervasive "normative monolingualism" has long informed Chaucer Studies—and medieval studies writ large—from the time of the field's origins, and a long-standing Anglophone and implicitly nationalist bias (be it deliberate or unintentional) has determined what materials Chaucerians deem worthy of study or inclusion in academic discourse.[9]

Though focused on global reception, interpretation, and translation of Chaucer into various cultures, there is yet a good deal of complementary content and critique in that project and this one. As Hsy and Barrington note, one of their aims is to "expand the 'Inner Circle' of scholars typically considered as 'proper' medievalists or Chaucerians."[10] In part they hope to accomplish this by reorienting not only the "who," but the "where" (and in what language) Chaucer's poetry lives and thrives, away from English and the Anglophone West. While the latter is not, again, an aim necessarily shared by this volume, it does hold in common a desire to broaden the field and to re-define notions of expertise and authority in approaching poets like Chaucer. Further, although Anglophone in nature, many of the poets considered in this volume write in English as a second or even third language, and otherwise stretch the limits of English by mixing and mingling with various tongues and dialects in their texts.

As for "queer medievalism"—what is it, and in what way does this project contribute to it? Some of the oldest definitions of critical queerness, like this one from David Halperin, seem to serve well:

---

8 Lees and Overing, *The Contemporary Medieval in Practice*, 7.

9 Candace Barrington and Jonathan Hsy, "Editors' introduction: Chaucer's global orbits and global communities," *Literature Compass* 15 (2018): 2.

10 Barrington and Hsy, "Editors' introduction," 3.

> Queer is by definition whatever is at odds with the normal, the legitimate, the dominant. There is nothing in particular to which it necessarily refers. It is an identity without an essence. "Queer" then, demarcates not a positivity but a positionality vis-à-vis the normative.[11]

More recently, queer theorist and experimental poet Sophie Robinson writes, "The move away from a fixed and binary set of gender and sexuality identities … towards a more relative, mobile and oppositional group politicizes sexuality as a tool for critique and enables a more dynamic discussion and thinking through of the available models for living." She adds, "Queer theory marks part of a poststructuralist move away from identity politics as fixed positions, and towards a general view of identity as culturally constructed and performative, rejecting notions of authenticity of self."[12] Queer forms of engagement—for the purposes of this volume, queer medievalisms—would tend to make the personal political; they would be oppositional to received norms; and they would involve the performative. In the illuminating introduction to her book *Queer Phenomenology,* Sara Ahmed writes, "To follow a line might be a way of becoming straight, by not deviating at any point … To say that lines are performative is to say that we find our way and we know which direction we face only as an effect of work, which is often hidden from view."[13] Ahmed adds,

> For a life to count as a good life, then it must return the debt of its life by taking on the direction promised as a social good, which means imagining one's futurity in terms of reaching certain points along a life course. A queer life might be one that fails to make such gestures of return.[14]

Following Ahmed, a queer medievalism might be one that deviates from the expected and linear in terms of its relationship to its source material, with a foregrounded awareness of the performative in terms of how it adapts, translates, appropriates. If it also "fails to make … gestures of return," it might do so in the name of challenging readers' expectations for more or less political aims. Following from the above, "a disturbance of temporality" is one of the key

11 David Halperin, *Saint Foucault: Towards a Gay Hagiography* (Oxford: Oxford University Press, 1997), 62.
12 Sophie Robinson, "Queer Time & Space in Contemporary Experimental Writing" (PhD diss., University of London, 2012), 7, 11.
13 Sara Ahmed, *Queer Phenomenology* (Durham: Duke University Press, 2006), 16.
14 Ahmed, *Queer*, 21.

ways that queer medievalism might deviate from the expected.[15] Instead of thinking in terms of a linear progression from past to present—a progression that any medievalist worth their salt already knows to view as suspect—a queer medievalism would consider such a timeline "preposterous." As Glenn Burger and Steven F. Kruger write, the implications are far-reaching:

> might we need (preposterously) to rethink what we have come to know as the Middle Ages not as preceding modernity but as the effect of a certain self-construction of the modern, which gives itself identity by delimiting a "before" that is everything the modern is not?[16]

All of the authors considered herein, however experimental and whatever element of the personal resides in (or is absent from) their work, maintain a queer medievalist poetics that upsets temporal and disciplinary boundaries, in ways that are inherently, if not explicitly, political in nature. They all have something to say about politics. Their writing makes political interventions, whether about ecological disasters, or the plight of queer and trans bodies, or the vicissitudes of migration, or the injustices of postcolonialism, and so on. This in itself, I believe, seems very much in the spirit of what a queer medievalism could and should be. Beyond that, however, these political interventions fall along a spectrum of poetic approaches that I will describe in the following terms—keeping in mind that some of the writers in this collection clearly fall under more than one category. First, religion. At least two authors examined in this volume channel medieval material to explore religious questions: Anne Sexton and Robert Glück. To some extent, the work of Jos Charles also engages in religious motifs, albeit in an indirect way, as it traces the contours of a highly personal transformation that seems akin to the journeys described in saints' lives, which are also present in the writing of Sexton and Glück. Next, translation; in many ways, all of the writers under consideration could be said to translate, however loosely or creatively, from medieval source material. Yet translation per se is most directly addressed in the case of two poets, W. H. Auden and Peter O'Leary, who take very different approaches to translating and altering their source material, shedding new light on that material and the translation process itself.

Beyond the two above-mentioned, fairly easily identifiable categories of queer medievalist interventions, things get a bit more nebulous, but no less interesting. "Adaptation" seems an appropriate, though instantly inadequate, ru-

---

15 Glenn Burger and Steven F. Kruger, "Introduction," in *Queering the Middle Ages* (Minnesota: University of Minnesota Press, 2001), xii.
16 Robinson, "Queer Time," xiii.

bric under which to consider the work of Patience Agbabi and Caroline Bergvall, as well as that of Medbh McGuckian. All three adapt medieval source material—updating and recasting poetic content—in their creative work, although they do so in startlingly different ways. In a certain light, what these authors do with their source material could be described as translation, even appropriation (this is especially true in the case of Bergvall and McGuckian). Having lighted on this category, however, I am immediately tempted to add a fourth: experimentation, particularly of the linguistic variety. Bergvall has long drawn the attention of literary critics who write about avant-garde, experimental writing in English; viewed in this light, I must circle back to Jos Charles, who like Bergvall makes experiments in Middle English itself a central feature of their work.

I sketch the above groupings to preview the particular types of queer medievalisms explored in this volume, and to help explain its organization; a fuller description of individual chapters can be found below. The queer medievalist interventions and "new vantage points" on medieval material represented by these authors are desperately needed, today more than ever; not only in terms of temporal, but also linguistic and cultural hegemony, and the way in which all of these "constructions" are wielded to foreclose on possibilities and oppress people. David M. Perry has written extensively on the "alt-right" and its appropriation of a narrow-minded version of the medieval.[17] As Perry writes, "White supremacists explicitly celebrate Europe in the Middle Ages because they imagine that it was a pure, white, Christian place organized wholesomely around military resistance to outside, non-white, non-Christian, forces." Such a misperception must be countered, and I hope that the writers and texts examined by the contributors to this volume help demonstrate the ways in which marginal voices can lay claim to the medieval, both then and now. Even so, modern poets' engagements with older forms of literature and language have often been problematic, and contemporary poetry (like the field of medieval studies) has dealt with issues of racial and gender bias.

Here I must address the long shadow that Ezra Pound casts over this particular line of inquiry, as he does over Anglophone modernism in general. Pound's translation of "The Seafarer"—with its archaisms and alliterative, stress-heavy lines—is central to the "break" with previous English verse that he championed. "To break the pentameter, that was the first heave" he writes in *The Cantos*.[18]

---

17 See David M. Perry, "What to Do When Nazis Are Obsessed With Your Field," *Pacific Standard*, September 6, 2017, https://psmag.com/education/nazis-love-taylor-swift-and-also-the-crusades.

18 Ezra Pound, "Canto LXXXI," in *The Cantos of Ezra Pound* (New York: New Directions, 1950), 538.

Elsewhere Pound praises "The Seafarer" as the finest example of Old English poetry and one of the greatest poems of all time;[19] he also points to the poem as one of his "required texts" from the Middle Ages in the didactically titled "How to Read."[20] As Christopher Jones argues, the entire modernist aesthetic was more indebted to the "primitive" verse of the early Middle Ages than to later periods such as the Romantic and Victorian.[21] Pound's "Seafarer" and other medieval-inflected experiments were hugely influential, to the extent that it becomes difficult to imagine almost *any* modernist (or even post-modernist) gesture towards older forms of literature in English without them. In light of this, one must also reckon with Pound's avowed fascist and anti-Semitic background.[22] Nor can one excuse the problematic side of Pound or compartmentalize it from his poetry, indeed from the entire project of modernism. Violence is written into the phrase "MAKE IT NEW" that first appears in "Canto LIII," Pound's translation from the Chinese, which was destined to be taken up as credo and rallying cry for waves of avant-garde artists ever since. The poetic addendum to the phrase is worth reproducing: "Day by day make it new / cut underbrush, / pile the logs / keep it growing" (*Cantos* 265). The poet's further comment on the Chinese characters, as quoted by Carroll Terrell's authoritative guide, is even more revealing: "Pound said of this ideogram: '[It] shows the fascist ax for the clearing away of rubbish.'"[23] As Richard Owens notes, starting with the Chinese characters,

> Pound extrapolates the "fascist axe" that allows him to identify newness and innovation with the violence necessary for creating the space that might allow new growth to flourish. To this end the Poundian axe of newness shears away undesirable trash and all gestures toward anteriority—toward a meaningful future—are identified with violence, strength, and power.[24]

---

19 Ezra Pound, *ABC of Reading* (New York: New Directions, 1960), 51–52.

20 Ezra Pound, *Literary Essays of Ezra Pound* (New York: New Directions, 1968), 28.

21 Christopher A. Jones, *Strange Likeness: The Use of Old English in Twentieth-Century Poetry* (New York: Oxford University Press, 2006), 6. Jones writes about Pound, W. H. Auden, Edwin Morgan, and Seamus Heaney. See also David Hadbawnik, "Differing intimacies: *Beowulf* translations by Seamus Heaney and Thomas Meyer," in *Dating Beowulf: Studies in Intimacy*, ed. Daniel C. Remein and Erica Weaver (Manchester: Manchester University Press, 2020), 232.

22 See Evan Kindley, "The Insanity Defense: Coming to Terms with Ezra Pound's Politics," *The Guardian*, March 28, 2018, https://www.thenation.com/article/archive/coming-to-terms-with-ezra-pounds-politics/.

23 Carroll F. Terrell, *A Companion to the Cantos of Ezra Pound* (Berkeley: University of California Press, 1993), 621.

24 Richard Owens, "Finance Innovation Commodity Culture," in *SAUVAGE: Essays on Anglophone Poetry* (Buffalo: BlazeVOX, 2019), 172.

The unpacking of the phrase "make it new" provides a neat summary of the inherent contradictions in Poundian modernism: a fascination with and reliance on the past, even as he advocates (violently) clearing it away in favor of the new. The "fascist" thread woven into the phrase also reveals how inextricable Pound's troublesome tendencies are to his life and work. While there are no chapters in this volume that directly address Pound, as mentioned above, it is impossible to pursue the line of inquiry proposed herein without at least acknowledging his far-reaching influence.

Nor is Pound the only problematic poet to have engaged with medieval material. This volume takes part of its title from a statement by Spicer: "A poet is a time mechanic not an embalmer ... Words are what stick to the real. We use them to push the real, to drag the real into the poem. They are what we hold on with, nothing else."[25] Though he died at 40 of advanced alcoholism in 1965, Spicer went furthest among the other Berkeley School with medieval studies, completing coursework and progress towards a PhD under philologist Arthur Brodeur at Berkeley. Yet he was also a misogynist and anti-Semite.[26] As with Pound, Spicer is not the main subject of any chapters herein, but in addition to the title of the volume, in many ways his spirit infuses this work as a whole. Anne Sexton, meanwhile, whose medievalist turn is addressed in Christopher Roman's chapter, suffered from mental illness all her adult life and sexually abused one of her daughters.[27]

The importance of mentioning all of the above should be apparent, but beyond that, what is my responsibility as editor? I make no excuses for any problematic issues associated with the authors whose work is explored herein. As a medievalist, I understand quite well that many of the authors I study—Chaucer and Spenser primary among them—are likewise problematic, for different but often overlapping reasons (racism, sexism, religious bigotry ... and in Spenser's case, endorsement of wholesale genocide).[28] As with my brief sketching of Pound's history with fascism and how it intertwines with his work as a whole,

---

25 Jack Spicer, "Dear Lorca," *My Vocabulary Did This to Me: The Collected Poetry of Jack Spicer* (Middletown, CT: Wesleyan University Press, 2008), 122–23.

26 See Lewis Ellingham and Kevin Killian, *Poet Be Like God: Jack Spicer and the San Francisco Renaissance* (Hanover, NH: Wesleyan University Press, 1998), 66, 72.

27 The sexual abuse is detailed in the biography *Anne Sexton* by Diane Wood Middlebrook, published in 1991, and controversially relies on recorded sessions with Sexton's therapist. See Alessandra Stanley, "Poet Told All; Therapist Provides the Record," *The New York Times*, July 15, 1991, www.nytimes.com/1991/07/15/books/poet-told-all-therapist-provides-the-record.html.

28 See Katarzyna Lecky, "Irish Nonhumanness and English Inhumanity in *A Vewe of the Present State of Ireland*," *Spenser Studies* 30 (2015): 133–50, https://doi.org/10.7756/spst.030.009.133-50.

I believe in embarking on a study of any poet with eyes wide open about the circumstances surrounding their work. I also understand that we are learning more all the time about the poets and poetry we study, and shifts in consciousness are constantly putting what we've learned into new and different light. This holds true even of a long-dead author like Chaucer.

When I first began pursuing medieval studies, the matter of Chaucer's involvement with the possible rape of a woman named Cecily Chaumpaigne was often noted but rarely discussed in depth in the classroom.[29] Remarkably, even within the past few years, new evidence has come to light.[30] At the same time, attitudes about Chaucer have changed considerably; rape in Chaucer is no longer confined to an uncomfortable conversation centered on "The Wife of Bath's Tale," but for many scholars, issues of power, gender, and sexualized violence color the entire scope of the poet's work.[31] To be sure, Caroline Dinshaw and other scholars had long been focusing criticism on this thread in Chaucer, but the shift in consciousness that has resulted from their work as well as developments in society such as MeToo have raised the volume, to the point where it would seem inconceivable to study *The Canterbury Tales* without serious, prolonged consideration of the above-mentioned issues.

To conclude, it is my hope that the "new queer medievalisms" explored in this volume contribute to re-evaluations of medieval source material, in every way. For example, engagements with Geoffrey Chaucer's *The Canterbury Tales* by contemporary poets such as Caroline Bergvall and Patience Agbabi not only update Chaucer's experiments in poetic diction and speech registers, but also point the way for careful readers to understand more about the regulatory function of the vernacular language project (in terms of gender, class, race) undertaken by Chaucer. Such recent projects invert the usual transactional nature of engagements with older forms of literature, in which readers are asked to exchange some small measure of bewilderment at archaic language or forms for a sense of having experienced a medieval text, a text that remains safely tucked away in a distant and qualitatively different past. The poets under consideration

---

29 See Susan S. Morrison, "The Use of Biography in Medieval Literary Criticism: The Case of Geoffrey Chaucer and Cecily Chaumpaigne," *The Chaucer Review* 34, no. 1 (1999): 69–86.
30 See Alison Flood, "Document Casts New Light on Chaucer 'Rape' Case," *The Guardian*, June 7, 2019, www.theguardian.com/books/2019/jun/07/document-casts-new-light-on-chaucer-rape-case#:~:text=A%20cloud%20of%20suspicion%20has,%3A%20%E2%80%9CDe%20raptu%20meo%E2%80%9D.
31 See for example *The Chaucer Review* 54, no. 3 (2019), titled *New Feminist Approaches to Chaucer*. Essays in the volume address Chaucer's *The Legend of Good Women* as well as many of *The Canterbury Tales*; www.jstor.org/stable/10.5325/chaucerrev.54.3.issue-3.

in this volume demand that readers grapple with the ways in which we are still "medieval"—in other words, the ways in which the questions posed by their medieval source material still reverberate and hold relevance for today's world. They do so by challenging the primacy of present over past, toppling the categories of old and new, and suggesting new interpretive frameworks for contemporary and medieval poetry alike.

The title of this introduction, *The Opening of the Field*, is shared by the debut collection of poet Robert Duncan, yet another appropriation that seems especially, well, appropriate. Duncan was, as mentioned above, one of the trio of queer poets who formed the Berkeley Renaissance; an image of a collage by his lifelong partner, the artist Jess, graces the cover of this volume. That collage, "The Mouse's Tale," in turn shares its title with an essay on Jess written by Robert Glück, whose medievalist work is explored herein; the title also provides a fortuitous allusion to a frequent topic in the volume, Chaucer's *Canterbury Tales*. And thus the circle comes back to the medieval and medievalisms with which we are concerned. This is the field we, and so many others, are trying to open.

Chapters

Robin Tremblay-McGaw tells the story of a queer writer's refashioning of *The Book of Margery Kempe*, which necessarily delves into the story of the "New Narrative" avant-garde creative movement against the backdrop of the AIDS crisis in the Bay Area during the 1980s–1990s. The writer is Robert Glück, whose *Margery Kempe* originally appeared in 1994 and was reprinted in a new edition in 2020. As Tremblay-McGaw argues, "Glück's *Margery Kempe* uses transtextuality and collaboration/community to interrogate gender, appropriate the already-made, and to reveal and revel in the paradox, the *punctum* of the 'real fictional depth' at the heart of 'the made-up.'" In her chapter, Tremblay-McGaw compares the collaborative nature of *The Book of Margery Kempe*—famously created by the author along with two scribes—with Glück's own intertextual, often "crowdsourced" project. She explores how Glück's adaptation of the story to that of "an obsessive gay love affair" further queers Kempe's already queer text, and elaborates on the tropes of obsession in Kempe's account. Along the way, Tremblay-McGaw provides a brief but fascinating account of the "Poetry Wars" that Glück and other writers found themselves taking sides in, with Glück adopting a "heretical" recourse to narrative at a time when "Language Writing" had gained supremacy in avant-garde circles. Ultimately, Tremblay-McGaw finds that both Kempe's *Book* and Glück's project based on it are "predicated on risk," still having fresh and important things to say to us about queer love and embodied, religious obsession.

What does the touch of God feel like? From where does it come and what part of the body does it reach? These are some of the questions suggested by Anne Sexton's work as explored by Christopher Roman. A "confessional" poet in the mold of Robert Lowell and Sylvia Plath, Sexton nevertheless persistently channels medieval mystics, such as Julian of Norwich, throughout her poetry. Roman makes use of Queer Theology to trace this thread, asserting that Sexton arrives at a "queer, theophanic materiality" in her book *The Awful Rowing Toward God*, published in 1975, wherein "Christ is no man." The theology Sexton develops, according to Roman, allows for "embodied, lived experience, a critique of the Church," and presents the body as "containing pieces of God that are everyone." Sexton speaks as a prophet, but the prophet of a queer body that challenges the heteronormative dictates of the Church; in her poetry, as Roman outlines, she recovers a sense of relationship with God that is physical, heretical, even blasphemous, but entirely real and necessary.

Candace Barrington contributes a chapter on *feeld*, a finalist for the Pulitzer Prize published in 2018 by trans poet Jos Charles. Similarly to Caroline Bergvall—though with strikingly different aims and outcomes—Charles's work seems attracted to Chaucerian Middle English precisely because of its unfamiliarity and inherently unstable nature. Barrington argues that Charles successfully constructs a "transpoetics," wherein the semantic and linguistic challenges of Middle English become a powerful tool for the author in working through a process of transformation, and confronting the limitations in expression for describing that transformation, with various features of Middle English making it a particularly appropriate tool. As Barrington notes, the "weave of possible meanings" that derive from Middle English diction and syntax encourages us to "loosen up our readerly habits." The complex diction and forms in Charles's *feeld* offer a way to read back into Chaucer's own linguistic instability and, as Barrington argues, the Wife of Bath's tendency to "queer" language and meanings in her Prologue and Tale.

Daniel C. Remein's chapter opens with a contemplation of a "queer" performance of the Old English *Judith*, which could itself be said to queer its Latin source material. The concept of "performance" is key to Remein's chapter, as it "provokes questions worth asking about the relationship between translation and performance in the queer medievalisms of modern and contemporary poetry." The chapter focuses on W. H. Auden and Thomas Meyer, two poet-translators of Old English who approach their material from different backgrounds. Both queer poets, Auden was also a traditionally trained medievalist, while Meyer set out to translate the entire Old English corpus despite a lack of formal training. Remein updates his previous essay on Auden, elaborating on what he calls "a certain kind of potentially queer translation of the medieval as an economic 'queer mixing of times and languages *as a mixing of sexualities.*'" Explaining Spicer's description of the poet as a "time mechanic," Remein insists that "instead of being a 'maker,' the poet's role is essentially performative," and the act of translation is key to this role. Drawing on Eve Kosofsky Sedgwick and Judith Butler, he points out performativity is foundational to Queer Theory; thinking in terms of performativity helps put translation practices on a spectrum that includes speech acts, citation, theatricality, and intertextuality—in other words, reframing translation away from what Carolyn Dinshaw calls the "false dilemma" between identification with and alterity from the past. Both poets, in different but related ways, craft projects that propose a queer translation of the medieval.

The way we manage our relationship to the past—with the translation process itself and its concern with "source text" and "translation" offering an illustrative model—is the subject of Sean Reynolds's chapter on Peter O'Leary. We don't often think of translations of old poems in the context of ecology, but Reynolds makes a compelling case, by way of O'Leary's *The Sampo*, a reworking of the Finnish epic the *Kalevala* published in 2016, for doing just that. Reynolds explores Peter O'Leary's "mycopoetics," "a poetics modeled on mushrooms," one that seeks to find a form and language to respond to the ecological devastation wrought on the earth by humans. This is a question primarily of waste management: "The question mycopoetics addresses is this: what do we do about all of this toxic waste we have created? How do we get rid of it? Mycopoetics is about getting rid of existing material." In this creative translation, O'Leary takes a number of risks and liberties, condensing the epic, which is itself cobbled together from a range of sources and forms, altering some elements and emphasizing others, "cultivat[ing] a covert ecological plot" that runs alongside the narrative. O'Leary draws out, and in some ways adds, this element to the poem by focusing on ecological shifts within the text—differing climates, environmental destruction, and recuperation. He also accomplishes a "mycopoetic" approach by means of stylistic choices in meter and syntax, adapted from other poets. In this way, though not a Queer Theory reading per se, Reynolds carefully traces the means by which O'Leary challenges readers and puts the act of translation itself under his ecological microscope.

Almost all of the poets whose work is examined in this volume confront the issue of appropriation in various ways, as they freely translate and adapt source material, the attribution of which is often murky at best. So long as that material is drawn from a shared medieval tradition, such appropriation seems fine, even expected; what happens, however, when the critical apparatus that accompanies such sources finds its way into a contemporary poet's text? This is the situation that Katharine Jager looks at in the work of Northern Irish feminist poet Medbh McGuckian, who frequently borrows and translates from medieval sources. Jager argues that McGuckian's 2007 poem "The Good Wife Taught her Daughter" "occupies an intertextual, queer, post-structural, and postcolonial space that can accommodate at once the present and the past." McGuckian writes in English, which she claims is not her "mother tongue" but an "empire of signs" that she necessarily uses instead of Irish for her verse. Partly for this reason, she has garnered considerable critical discussion of her intertextual approach, mostly through the lens of postmodern criticism, but few or none have discussed her work through the lens of medievalism. Jager's chapter proves the value of the latter approach, as she carefully teases out the threads of appropriation in McGuckian's poem. Jager finds that not only does McGuckian pull from a range of medieval "conduct" texts, as well as Margery Kempe and others, but she also includes material from contemporary feminist critic Sarah Salih. In this way, though McGuckian's appropriative verse queers the relationship between source and translation, past and present, Jager argues that it does so in part by exacting unwarranted "payback" from the work of Salih.

Patience Agbabi is a London-based poet who finds *The Canterbury Tales* a generative locus from which to explore issues of race, gender, and language in contemporary Britain; her *Telling Tales* first appeared in 2014. Jonathan Hsy and Candace Barrington expand on a previous essay to look closely at Agbabi's versions of Chaucer's "Tale of Melibee" and "Man of Law's Tale." In Agbabi's hands, these poems resist narrative conventions and "use medievalism to explore nuanced desires that move across bodies, borders, and time." One simple but profound way that Agbabi accomplishes this is through altering race and gender among the tales and their tellers, a move that challenges readerly assumptions about modes of personal, national, and racial desire in *The Canterbury Tales*. Agbabi's reimagining of Chaucer is thus not only contemporary and fun but also deeply provocative; her modernized versions of the tales "cede no authority to the fourteenth-century poems," and go so far as to insist that such adaptations are hardly "derivative" but deserving of authority in their own right. As Hsy and Barrington argue, Agbabi is neither an "amateur" or a "nerd" when it comes to approaching Chaucer, but a well-trained spoken-word poet who approaches her subject with passion and creativity, first and foremost as a poet. Therefore, her nuanced reworkings of Chaucer's language and versification also contribute to her project of critically reorienting the *Tales*.

Caroline Bergvall is one of the most prolific and prominent experimental artists working on medievalist material today; as I note in my chapter, her work has drawn a great deal of critical attention from contemporary critics, although it is only beginning to be taken up by medievalist scholars. What draws Bergvall to Geoffrey Chaucer—as well as the other medieval source material she works with, such as the Old English *Seafarer*—is her own multilingual background; she has said that writing "began" for her when she started writing in English, her third language after French and Norwegian. A queer multimedia artist, Bergvall seeks to preserve the "friction" between languages, never settling wholly on English either temporally or linguistically, but constantly destabilizing utterance in her texts. Since the rough edges of language are foregrounded most obviously by voice, Bergvall often makes performance part of her process for creating a finished piece, and in the chapter I attend closely to recordings of her readings for important clues regarding Bergvall's interactions with medieval language and material. Drawing on the critical theory of thinkers like Édouard Glissant, Gilles Deleuze, Félix Guattari, and Mikhail Bakhtin, Bergvall's texts upset the usual hegemony between older source material and more recent translations and adaptations; unlike a number of poets who worked from such sources, such as Edmund Spenser, Ezra Pound, and Seamus Heaney, she does not seek "linguistic origins" or "foundations" in English, but to discover the multilingual possibilities and powers within and beyond English. Such possibilities lead her to a stunning recuperation and further development of Chaucer's "Wife of Bath" in *Alisoun Sings*, the most recent of Bergvall's "medievalist trilogy," published in 2019. In that book, the poet builds on previous experiments with a voice that cuts across time and space to comment on contemporary issues.

Robin Tremblay-McGaw

"A Real Fictional Depth": Transtexuality & Transformation in Robert Glück's *Margery Kempe*

> The actual forms we take are a kind of extremity we are driven to in a quest for love
> – Robert Glück[1]

While working on this essay, I heard the exciting news that *The New York Review of Books* is reprinting Robert Glück's 1994 *Margery Kempe.*[2] It came out in spring 2020. What timing! Subverting the genre of the historical novel, Glück's *Margery* is comprised of two parallel stories that quickly travel into and across one another. There is the third-person past-tense retelling of Margery Kempe's fifteenth-century unorthodox spiritual life and pilgrimages and a first-person present-tense twentieth-century narrative of a 40-year-old gay man, "Bob," and his desire for "L," a younger man whose "relatives are the legendary robber barons."[3] Glück's *Margery Kempe* is written against the backdrop of, on the one hand, the American experimental poetry community's suspicion of narrative and self, and on the other, Robert Duncan's framing of self as ""a made-up thing."[4] Taking inspiration from Kempe's audacious experiment, Glück's *Margery Kempe* uses transtextuality[5] and collaboration/community to interrogate gender, appropriate the already-made, and to reveal and revel in the paradox, the *punctum* of the "real fictional depth" at the heart of "the made-up."

---

1 From Robert Glück, "My Margery, Margery's Bob," in *Communal Nude: Collected Essays* (South Pasadena, CA: Semiotext(e), 2016), 79.

2 As a shorthand, I will sometimes refer to Glück's *Margery Kempe* as *Margery*, or Glück's *Margery.* See Robert Glück, *Margery Kempe* (New York: Serpent's Tail, 1994). Any reference to Kempe's autobiography will cite her book's title: *The Book of Margery Kempe.* See Margery Kempe, *The Book of Margery Kempe*, trans. Anthony Bale (New York: Oxford University Press, 2015). All references to Glück's essays refer to the versions published in his *Communal Nude.*

3 Glück, *Margery,* 40.

4 Robert Duncan, *The Years as Catches: First Poems (1939–1946)* (Berkeley: Oyez, 1966), x.

5 Transtextuality, a term coined by Gérard Genette, includes the intertextual (presence of a text within another text), the paratextual (elements important to audience—titles, subtitles, prefaces, epigraphs, etc.), the metatextual (commentary linking one text to another without citation), and finally, hypertextuality (a relationship between texts not based on commentary). See Gérard Genette, *Palimpsests: Literature in the Second Degree*, trans. Channa Newman and Claude Doubinsky (Lincoln and London: University of Nebraska Press, 1997).

https://doi.org/10.1515/9781501511189-003

Glück's *Margery Kempe* begins with a paratextual epigram from *The Garden of Prayer*, "written for young girls in 1454." It exhorts its female readers:

> ... you must shape in your mind some people, people well-known to you, to represent for you the people in the Passion ... When you have done this, putting all your imagination into it, then go into your chamber. Alone and solitary, excluding every external thought from your mind ... moving slowly from episode to episode, meditate on each one, dwelling on each single stage and step of the story.

With this epigram, Glück contextualizes the historical Margery Kempe's autobiography—*The Book of Margery Kempe*—in a tradition of religious practice that advocates using people one knows to represent the characters of Christ's passion (Passion, from the Latin *passionem* "suffering and enduring"). Who will play Mary? Mary Magdalene? The Apostles? Jesus himself? Practically vibrating with its own strange sexual energy, *The Garden of Prayer* advises "putting all your imagination into it," pursuing this practice when "alone and solitary." Given low medieval literacy rates[6] and the fact that the audience for this fifteenth-century text is young girls, the prayer book's authors must have imagined at least one other person reading this text to its addressees. Despite, then, its emphasis on the individual, the exercise requires a community—the church, the prayer book, a literate reader, and the young girls endeavoring to put themselves into and *feel* the story of Christ's passion.[7] With this fitting epigram, Glück frames and contextualizes the historical life of Kempe, fifteenth-century mystic and pilgrim, failed saint, and author of what is frequently referred to as the first autobiography in English, and he thematizes in this *mise-en-abîme* the formal construction of his New Narrative novel, one that is predicated on affect and emerges from and is dependent on community.

Kempe's book also begins with a paratextual feature—in her case, a proem. Her proem addresses her text's form, explaining the book's belatedness, genesis, organization, collaborative composition (with two scribes: one an Englishman and the other a priest), and purpose:

---

6 See Franz H. Bäuml, "Varieties and Consequences of Medieval Literacy and Illiteracy," *Speculum* 55, no. 2 (1980). Bäuml reminds us: "At all levels of society, the majority of the population of Europe between the fourth and the fifteenth centuries was, in some sense, illiterate" (237). See Bale, "Introduction," in *The Book of Margery Kempe*. Bale states: "In the medieval era, those who *could* read and write often chose to be read to and to use a scribe, and reading was frequently a social, group activity" (xv).

7 See Bale, "Introduction." Bale locates this practice of "imagining oneself at scenes of Christ's life and death, not just as a spectator but as an emotional participant" in the fourteenth-century's "key work of popular mysticism, the *Meditationes vitae Christi*" (xxiii).

> Here begins a short and comforting treatise for sinful wretches ... by leave of our merciful Lord Christ Jesus, to the magnifying of His holy name, Jesus, this little treatise shall deal somewhat with parts of His wonderful works ...
>
> when it pleased our Lord, He commanded her and tasked her to have her feelings and revelations and her manner of living written down ...
>
> This book was not written in order ... but just as the story came to the creature in her mind, when it was to be written down ... therefore she wrote nothing other than that which she knew full well to be the whole truth.[8]

Kempe's *Book*'s proem embodies the contradictory push and pull, the collaborative and complex nature of her book's coming into being, including her own interventions; for example, she actively encourages her second collaborator, the priest struggling with poor eyesight and the difficult script of his predecessor: "she urged him to do as well as God would give him grace and to not leave off."[9] Anthony Bale asserts that it is important to understand the book in the context of "historically accurate categories of subject, amanuensis (or recorder), and scribe";[10] by drawing our attention to the fact that Kempe's *Book* "displays an abiding cultural literacy, an ability to engage with a world of signs, ideas, and other people's words," Bale informs us Kempe was educated aurally and had memorized texts.[11] He advocates that rather than "looking for a single author for *The Book of Margery Kempe*, we would do better to acknowledge the collaborative, and sometimes haphazard, way in which medieval writing was produced."[12]

Glück's book is also a collaborative endeavor, one that it announces. The book's title and epigram mark the intimacy of the collaboration as does the title for Part One: "The Rule of L: *I am thy loue & shall be thy loue wyth-owtyn ende.*" "L" belongs to the book's narrative of the troubled love affair between Bob and L, and the quote is from chapter five of Kempe's autobiography. Sutured together in one heading, the two stories, two temporalities, two worlds, two texts, are entangled. To tell the story of an obsessive love affair in which the gay lovers are attracted to and separated by their differences in geographic location, class, culture, religion, emotional accessibility, and personality, Glück's

8 Bale, *The Book of Margery Kempe*, 3–7. With regard to belatedness, the proem explains that while "some ... worthy and honourable clerics ... begged that she should have them write and make a book of her feelings and her revelations," Kempe refuses, waiting more than twenty years until God "commanded and tasked her" to do so (5).

9 Bale, *The Book of Margery Kempe*, 6.

10 Ibid., xviii.

11 Ibid., xiv–xv.

12 Ibid., xx.

book proclaims its unabashed appropriation of *The Book of Margery Kempe*. Much like Kempe's *Book*, Glück's will travel across centuries and class locations,[13] transgress gender norms and continents as it tells the stories of Margery Kempe and his narrator, his character Bob's sufferings and endurances, and the wagers each makes for a future different from the present. To do so, *Margery Kempe* appropriates and collages material from disparate sources, including Kempe's *Book* and Glück's life, language culled from medieval books of hours, lives of the saints, and Glück's friends and acquaintances.

The historical Margery Kempe lived during a time of religious upheaval in fifteenth-century Europe. Hers was a life of trespass as she countered the norms of her time. She traveled extensively, a fact that Terence N. Bowers asserts "is a violation of what 'women do'; her actions go against the very idea of what it means to be a woman ... self-initiated travel removes women from the space that has generally circumscribed their roles: the home."[14] Bowers notes that in "many of our paradigmatic stories, starting with the *Odyssey*," men are frequently associated with mobility, while women are characterized by "sessility;" that is, they are fixed in one place. Thus, a travelling woman is in fact, we might say, potentially not a woman at all.[15] On the other hand, Bale points out that while many "male writers were critical—or satirical—of the motives for women going on pilgrimage," it was not however unusual for women to do so. For example, "The records show groups of women travelling together in pairs or larger groups and women travelling with their husbands. However, many pilgrims seem to have travelled alone, as single women."[16] Nevertheless, importantly, "Kempe's movements ... form an attempt to assume the status of a free, autonomous person—something women could not be, regardless of class."[17]

Kempe did, in fact, achieve some autonomy. She left her husband to go on pilgrimage and was accused of being a Lollard (a sect which criticized "clerical privilege and hypocrisy")[18] and a heretic.[19] Despite having some 14 children, she

13 Kempe's *Book* leaps centuries in several ways: in the content of her narrative, as Kempe details how she is present at Christ's birth (chapter 6) and his crucifixion (which are of course, literally centuries before her own lifetime), and as a material text in that it is lost in the fifteenth century and then rediscovered in the twentieth century.

14 Terence N. Bowers, "Margery Kempe as Traveler," *Studies in Philology* 97, no. 1 (2000): 3.

15 Bowers, "Margery Kempe as Traveler," 4.

16 Bale, *The Book of Margery Kempe*, xxvii.

17 Bowers, "Margery Kempe as Traveler," 8.

18 Carolyn Dinshaw, *Getting Medieval: Sexualities and Communities, Pre- and Postmodern* (Durham: Duke University Press, 1999), 57.

19 See Bale, *The Book of Margery Kempe*, 103. In chapter 13 of her book, Kempe recounts her visit to Canterbury where she was "in the church amongst the monks, ... [and] she was deeply

refused the definitive role of motherhood and wore white (the color associated with virginity). She undid linear time (what we might think of as "straight time" á la José Esteban Muñoz)[20] as she found herself at Christ's birth and at his crucifixion. Her body writhed in pain—the pain Mary experienced at his birth and the suffering of Jesus himself on the cross. Kempe also spoke back to power, in the form of "preaching under cover." That is, while women could not preach, in her biblically astute and knowledgeable responses to questions from a variety of clergy, including various Bishops, about her white clothing, excessive weeping, and vows of chastity, Kempe managed to engage in theological conversation and explanation, and even offered advice—all at the behest, so she said, of God himself. For example, when the Mayor of Leicester questioned Kempe, she informed her readers (using the third person as the text often does): "So then he asked many questions, which she answered eagerly and intelligently, so that he could not make a cause against her."[21] When Kempe was in Rome, she encountered an Italian-speaking priest in the Church of St. John Lateran who "had one of the greatest offices of any priest in Rome."[22] With a translator, she spoke to him, advising him how to pray; and he, "desiring to please God ... followed her advice."[23] For all these reasons, medieval scholar and queer theorist Carolyn Dinshaw writes that Kempe's "Book ... records a life at odds with most every everyday thing in the late-medieval East Anglia."[24] She "enact[ed] her unnamable combination of orthodoxy and heterodoxy."[25] This is a combination that Glück's book also relishes.

Delineating in broad strokes the overlap in Kempe's time and his twentieth century in an essay about his book, Glück explains some structural similarities.

---

despised and reproached, both by monks and priests, and by the secular people ... Then she went out of the monastery, with them following her and shrieking after her, 'You shall be burned false Lollard' ... then, after she had made her prayers in her heart to our Lord two handsome young men came and said to her, 'Young lady, are you neither a heretic nor a Lollard?' And she said, 'No, sirs, I am neither heretic nor Lollard'" (29–30).

20 See José Esteban Muñoz, *Cruising Utopia: The Then and There of Queer Futurity* (New York: W.W. Norton & Co., 2016). Muñoz defines straight time this way: "Straight time tells us that there is no future but the here and now of our everyday life" (20).

21 Bale, *The Book of Margery Kempe*, 103. After a period of thirteen days, Margery and this priest are able to converse with one another, despite the fact that neither is fluent in the other's language.

22 Bale, *The Book of Margery Kempe*, 76.

23 Ibid.

24 Dinshaw, *Getting Medieval*, 144.

25 Ibid., 146. See Dinshaw's "Margery Kempe Answers Back," in *Getting Medieval* for her reading of Glück's *Margery*.

For example, "the emergence of the modern self and the end of the modern self, the decaying society in which Kempe lived, the decaying society in which I live, and our respective plagues. L's ruling-class status equals the divinity of Jesus. (In the fifteenth century, gods were closer to mortals—about as close as a Rockefeller.)"[26]

In the late twentieth century, the San Francisco Bay Area, where Glück lives, was home to many different writing communities, including groups organizing themselves as "Third World Writers" (to use the parlance of the late 1970s and 1980s, the period during which Glück's writing emerges), feminist, lesbian and gay writers, Beat and Bay Area surrealists, Asian writers, working-class writers. In one particular part of the scene, the Language writers—Ron Silliman, Barrett Watten, Carla Harryman, Lyn Hejinian, Bob Perelman, Steve Benson, and others —churned the waters, contesting and often refusing the individual "I," the lyric, and narrative, inciting what would be called the "poetry wars," what we might imagine is for one community, in miniature, to be sure, analogous to the religious wars of the Middle Ages.[27]

---

26 Glück, "My Margery, Margery's Bob," in *Communal Nude*, 78.

27 This is polemical, but given the rhetoric of war, there is some small truth here. The "poetry wars" began in the late 1970s, flaring up again in the mid-1980s when a provocative debate occurred in the pages of the Bay Area's publication *Poetry Flash*. In a 1984 article by the editor of the journal *ACTS*, David Levi Strauss discussed the out-takes for the KQED-TV PBS 1965 and 1966 films of poets Robert Duncan and Louis Zukofsky. The Zukofsky out-takes were about to be re-screened in June of 1984. Levi Strauss's article was incendiary in its discussion of the events that had occurred six years previously on the occasion of the December 8, 1978, screening of the Zukofsky out-takes just months after his death in May. The screening was introduced by Robert Duncan and followed by Language writer Barrett Watten performing a close reading of parts of Zukofsky's long work "A." At the beginning of the event Duncan announced the outline of the program: an introduction by Duncan, the screening of the out-takes, Watten's talk, and a planned follow-up discussion by Duncan of a selection from Zukofsky's *80 Flowers*. According to accounts in *Poetry Flash*, Watten was interrupted in his talk by Duncan, who disagreed with Watten's reading. Levi Strauss's presentation of this event clearly sides with Duncan—"Duncan's reading was truly exploratory" (10)—over Watten: "In retrospect, Watten's talk was perhaps well-meaning, but so tediously tendentious and closed that it did real violence to the work at hand." A flurry of letters followed the *Flash*'s (then edited by Steve Abbott) invitation for reader response, including one from Ron Silliman which contains the following statement: "I have been disturbed for the past year or so at a game which is rapidly becoming the pastime of the poetry scene. It's called Bash the Language Poets, and Levi Strauss's swipe at Watten is only the most recent example" (July 7, 1984). The Silliman letter was followed by those from a variety of others—Andrei Codrescu, Carl Grundberg, Dawn Kolokithas, Darrell Gray, Duncan McNaughton, Alastair Johnson, and others. Having listened to the audiotape, I would say that much of the contention around this event seems to have happened after the fact and this is reflected in the changing availability of the audio tape itself. Duncan's introduction is entertaining

Working to foster collaboration among writers whose aesthetics and poetics were diverse, but who shared an engagement in leftist politics, Glück, Bruce Boone, and Steve Abbott organized and hosted the Left/Write Conference in 1981. That conference was complex and pivotal.[28] Over the years, Glück, Boone, and Abbott wrestled most intimately with the center-stage contributions and provocations of the Language writers, though as Glück has written, his and Boone's urgent questions and lived experience led them in other directions:

> I experienced the poetry of disjunction as a luxurious idealism in which the speaking subject rejects the confines of representation and disappears in the largest freedom, that of language itself. My attraction to this freedom, and to the professionalism that purveyed it, made for a kind of class struggle within myself. Whole areas of my experience, especially gay experience, were not admitted to this utopia. The mainstream reflected a resoundingly coherent image of myself back to me—an image so unjust that it amounted to a tyranny that I could not turn my back on. We had been disastrously described by the mainstream—a naming whose most extreme (though not uncommon) expression was physical violence. Combating this injustice required at least a provisionally stable identity.[29]

---

and informative, though also peppered by a certain number of playful but nevertheless self-aggrandizing comments about Duncan's own role in the film and as an advisor to KQED. Watten's talk is not as organized or as confident as Duncan's. It is focused less on the personal details of Zukofsky's life and the substance of the film out-takes, and more on a close formal reading of the text. There is a great deal of discussion among Watten, Duncan, and various audience members, including Larry Eigner, in the midst of Watten's exegesis. While questioning some of Watten's reading of Zukofsky's poem, Duncan seeks to ground it in details from Zukofsky's personal and family life as well as Zukofsky's reading. The audio version of the event hardly suggests that things came to fisticuffs. However, these struggles at the time are experienced as a kind of war, the period of the late 1970s and 1980s coming to be known in the Bay Area as the "language wars" or the "poetry wars." The stakes here include a struggle over literary paternity, lineage, and power. In *The Grand Piano Part 4*, Tom Mandel contends that "Duncan used his powers to win a battle that night, and he helped roust me out of the Poetry Center [Mandel was the director] some months later. So began the 'language wars.' Poetry as agon not conversation" (61). See Rob Halpern's critique of Silliman's reference to "bashing." Halpern pointed out that "language doesn't get bashed, people do," making legible the problematic appropriation of a term describing the physical violence experienced by people, specifically gays and lesbians ("Restoration") and his analysis of the poetry wars, Language writing and New Narrative. See Rob Halpern, "Realism and Utopia: Sex, Writing, and Activism in New Narrative," *Journal of Narrative Theory* 41, no. 1 (2011): 82–124. For more on the poetry wars, see also Lisa Jarnot, *Robert Duncan, The Ambassador from Venus: A Biography* (Berkeley: University of California Press, 2012) and Mark Scroggins, *The Poem of A Life: A Biography of Louis Zukofsky* (Berkeley: Shoemaker & Hoard, 2007).

28 See Kaplan Page Harris, "New Narrative and the Making of Language Poetry," *American Literature* 81, no. 4, (2009): 805–832.

29 Glück, "Long Note on New Narrative," in *Communal Nude*, 14–15.

As Glück alludes to above, the subject and self were contested sites for writing at this time. In 1988 an article entitled, "Aesthetic Tendency and the Politics of Poetry: A Manifesto" co-authored by Language writers Ron Silliman, Carla Harryman, Lyn Hejinian, Steve Benson, Bob Perelman, and Barrett Watten appeared in the journal *Social Text*.[30] In it the authors assert: "we are arguing for the significance of a group against the canonical individual of the 'expressivist' tendency, itself a social movement," one that is naturalized so to appear to "provide an ideology of no ideology."[31] The authors provide examples of the problematic construction of a transcendent, isolated individual proffering personal experience in a variety of poems and assert that in such cases, "authorial 'voice' lapses into melodrama in a social allegory where the author is precluded from effective action by his or her very emotions."[32] It is "this kind of worked-over accounting of 'experience,' we think, [that] is primarily responsible for the widespread contemporary reception of poetry as nice but irrelevant."[33] Wanting their writing to engage with the social and political issues of the day, and advocating for a more complex conception of the "I" as a critical project (by way of Coleridge, Rimbaud, and others),[34] they point out that: "The individual is seen as under attack," and acknowledge that "this is largely true: the self as the central and final term of creative practice is being challenged and exploded in our writing in a number of ways."[35] Although New Narrative writers, whose work emerges within the context of the experimental poetry community, are not mentioned directly in this article, some of the claims in it appear to address criticisms articulated by these writers, including, for example, in Glück's quote above.[36]

---

30 Ron Silliman, Carla Harryman, Lyn Hejinian, Steve Benson, Bob Perelman, and Barrett Watten, "Aesthetic Tendency and the Politics of Poetry: A Manifesto," *Social Text*, no. 19/20 (1988): 261–75.

31 Silliman et al., "Aesthetic Tendency," 273, 264.

32 Ibid., 265.

33 Ibid., 264.

34 Ibid., 266: "Coleridge, writing in the *Biographia Literaria*, similarly argues for a dissociation of what he calls the *ego contemplans* the I that thinks—from the *ego contemplatus*—the I that is the object of thought ... Coleridge attempts to describe a poetic intentionality that opposes itself to the elision of consciousness that occurs in habitual constructions of belief. It's not difficult to arrive, from this understanding of the self as a critically necessary project, at the possibility of a dissociated self as a critique."

35 Ibid., 263.

36 While this article does speak to some of New Narrative writers' criticisms of Language Poetry, it also engages primarily with criticisms from more mainstream poetry communities (for example, poems published in *Poetry* magazine at this time) and also from the right, in an article, for example, published in *The New Criterion*. See, for example, Silliman et al., "Aesthetic Tendency," 263.

People took social, aesthetic, and theoretical sides on the status of narrative in contemporary writing as well. Three years before the article on the individual self, two of these same writers, Lyn Hejinian and Barrett Watten, co-edited a special issue of *Poetics Journal* entitled NON/NARRATIVE on the topic.[37] The issue's polemical title marks the (for some) heretical divide, highlighting the tension between negativity ("non") and narrative, narrative and that which is not narrative or working against narrative. The issue's centerpiece is entitled more benignly: "Symposium on Narrative: What is the Status of Narrative in Your Work?" Contributions include pieces asserting divergent viewpoints. For example, video artist Doug Hall claims, "I would say right from the start that I don't consider myself a narrative artist ... I think good art long ago abandoned narrative as the primary organizing element,"[38] while Alice Notley is more ambivalent: "I don't tell that many stories in my poetry ... On the other hand, part of my fascination with diary forms & with poems built from putting the writing down on paper on successive days, comes from the fact that a story always unfolds."[39] Carla Harryman writes, "I prefer to distribute narrative rather than deny it."[40] Michael Davidson's contribution is a summary overview of structuralist narrative theory that then advocates for Mikhail Bakhtin's "useful corrective to this tendency toward the taxonomic and descriptive by speaking of the socially contextualized frames through which stories as it were 'speak the speaker.'"[41] In her "Error Message," Tina Darragh asserts, "I need a narrative structure to be part of my writing, but I have to identify that need as 'embarrassing' (i.e.: 'something wrong,' an 'error condition') to even begin discussing it."[42] Salvaging narrative and self, Glück's contribution uses his own version of the form under contestation—narrative—to respond, retelling multiple stories—Baucis and Philemon, and Elijah's search for shelter and food—in order to take apart how narrative works, explaining: "I write about these forms—that are myself—to acknowledge and then dis-

37 Lyn Hejinian and Barrett Watten, eds., "Non/Narrative," *Poetics Journal* 5 (1985).
38 Doug Hall, "Forgotten Tyrant," in Lyn Hejinian and Barrett Watten, eds., "Non/Narrative," *Poetics Journal* 5 (1985): 96.
39 Alice Notley, "Narrative," in Lyn Hejinian and Barrett Watten, eds., "Non/Narrative," *Poetics Journal* 5 (1985): 96.
40 Carla Harryman, "Toy Boats," in Lyn Hejinian and Barrett Watten, eds., "Non/Narrative," *Poetics Journal* 5 (1985): 104.
41 Michael Davidson, "Framed by Story," in Lyn Hejinian and Barrett Watten, eds., "Non/Narrative," *Poetics Journal* 5 (1985): 78.
42 Tina Darragh, "Error Message," in Lyn Hejinian and Barrett Watten, eds., "Non/Narrative," *Poetics Journal* 5 (1985): 120.

pense with them, to demonstrate their arbitrariness, how they disintegrate before a secret (the world, the sublime)."[43]

When the self and narrative were considered debased, even heretical literary tools for innovative writing, Glück, Boone, and Abbott advocated for their critical and imaginative value as a socially activist and experimental queer writing, coining the term "New Narrative" to describe their work. Soon they were joined by Dodie Bellamy, Kevin Killian (whom we lost in 2019), Camille Roy, Sam D'Allesandro (who died from AIDS in 1988), Mike Amnasan, and others. Many of these people were part of Glück's original writing workshop hosted at Small Press Traffic (SPT) where he wore a variety of hats as volunteer, its co-director, and reading series curator (1976–1985).

One of New Narrative's most prominent and frequently discussed formal features is what Boone called text/metatext; Glück describes this as Boone's "abstraction," explaining he elaborated it from the practices of the "poems and stories" he and Glück were writing:

> a story keeps a running commentary on itself from the present. The commentary, taking the form of a meditation or a second story, supplies a succession of frames. That is, the more you fragment a story, the more it becomes an example of narration itself—narration displaying its devices—while at the same time (as I wrote in 1981) the metatext asks questions, asks for critical response, makes claims on the reader, elicits comments.[44]

Text/metatext is one strategy for navigating narrative as an ideologically and politically polluted form. Rather than avoid or reject narrative outright, New Narrative writers opt to fragment and multiply story, *uncloseting* the fabrications, desires, complicities, and constructions of narrative and self. It is not an accident that New Narrative, writing that knows itself as construction, arises from a community of gay writers, for as Glück has pointed out, gay identity in the 1970s and 1980s was "new enough to know its own constructedness."[45] What a relief it must have been for Glück to have a community, a language, and others with whom to shape self and story to interrupt the mainstream's homophobic and often violent, "resoundingly coherent image."[46] Story might be sullied for some because it is too easily associated with political double-speak and a consumable good. Glück and Boone take these as givens, reversing narrative's double-bind, turning it inside out. Likewise, self as social construction need not be

43 Robert Glück, "Baucis and Philemon," in Lyn Hejinian and Barrett Watten, eds., "Non/Narrative," *Poetics Journal* 5 (1985): 113.
44 Glück, "Long Note," 17.
45 Ibid., 14–15.
46 Ibid., 15.

emptying or extinguishing or merely theoretical, but instead might offer possibilities for living and a world that is not predicated on the "state of captivity (the dishonest fiction) which the present is for everyone."[47]

The present as a state of captivity, a dishonest fiction: in *Narrative Theory Unbound: Queer and Feminist Interventions*, Susan S. Lanser cites D. A. Miller's assertion that for Roland Barthes "gay narrative is simply not feasible."[48] In 1966 this was certainly true for Robert Glück's 19-year-old self, as he sat down to "a battery of psychological exams, which included a long written text" to win entrance to a study abroad program in Scotland while a student at UCLA.[49] The exam required him to describe a male and a female friend. Elsewhere I have written about Glück's recounting this incident in his essay "My Community."[50] I am fascinated with how Glück improvised in "a scene of constraint"[51] as he realized that in order to provide descriptions of a male and female friend (who can say why the exam asked him to? though it is easy to postulate an implicit homophobia), he needed to provide answers that were as normative as possible. To do so, he lit upon the strategy of appropriating the voice of an eighteenth-century American exemplar, Benjamin Franklin: "I had just finished Benjamin Franklin's *Autobiography*. In the tidy little testing room I'd had a stroke of inspiration, I realized that if I answered the questions as Franklin, I might create the effect of a normal man."[52] Glück explains that as a young gay man in the 1960s:

> Most of the things I felt were literally nameless to me because of my age and the age of the decade ... I was able, had the writing skill and observation, to delineate most of Andrea's body more accurately and her character too, a mix of starts and stops, bravery and affection. I had the skill to describe Larry's tapering fingers, cornflower eyes, convulsed laughter. The writerly ability to skew these descriptions was bound up with a homosexual's sickening, unwanted knowledge of *the fiction of gender roles*, which led to knowledge of the difference between a dishonest fiction and an honest one.[53]

---

47 Glück, "My Community," in *Communal Nude*, 35. Once again, Glück's framing of the present underscores—though it preceded—Muñoz's conception of straight time cited earlier.
48 Robyn Warhol and Susan S. Lanser, eds., *Narrative Theory Unbound: Queer and Feminist Interventions* (Columbus: Ohio University Press, 2015), 31.
49 Glück, "My Community," 35.
50 See Robin Tremblay-McGaw, "New Narrative Remix: 'Not Resembling the Face in the Mirror,'" in *From Our Hearts to Yours: New Narrative as Contemporary Practice*, ed. Rob Halpern and Robin Tremblay-McGaw (Oakland, CA: On Contemporary Practice, 2017).
51 Judith Butler, *Undoing Gender* (Abington, UK: Routledge, 2004), 1.
52 Glück, "My Community," 30.
53 Glück, "My Community," 31, my emphasis.

It is worth recalling that Glück took his test before Stonewall, right before gay liberation, when "homosexual acts" were still illegal, and perhaps to remember that across the ocean, E. M. Forster's gay novel *Maurice*, written in 1919, remained unpublished until 1971.[54] 1966 is also the year Robert Duncan's *The Years as Catches* was published—a book I will return to later in this essay.

Glück's appropriation serves its purpose: he gets the opportunity to go abroad; however, he is left with the uncomfortable knowledge that this fiction is a lie, not because he appropriated and impersonated a self, but because the impersonation covers over truths, or rather, social fictions passing as fact. Because there was much he could not tell, Glück created a version of himself that complied with heteronormative patriarchy, though the language for that would not come until later. I keep returning to this moment in Glück's writing because there is something primal about the scene. It does not tell a moralizing tale about what some might take for a form of plagiarism; it is not a valorization of American self-invention or Emerson's self-reliance, or the fantasy of an authentic and resolutely solid New England self with which I was brought up. Rather, because of a sense of his otherness in a heteronormative world and before he has a language or narratives with which to speak it, Glück's "unwanted knowledge of the fiction of gender roles ... [fuels] his awareness of the difference between a dishonest fiction and an honest one."[55] Glück learns to appropriate a voice, as if in a rhetorical exercise of ancient and early modern *imitatio*, but, to be sure, undergirded in 1966 by his position *in extremis*, in the necessity of passing as a "normal" man, of telling only a certain kind of story or description.

This same essay recounts other literary appropriations and acts of imitation. When Glück is 16, he memorizes, and then writes out the poems of John Keats "just to see what it felt like to be Keats writing incontestably great literature";[56] in 1968, he discovers Frank O'Hara:

> The freedom of O'Hara's community was represented in his poems by formal innovation, by language choice, flighty, engaged, romantic. He was excited—didn't I want to be excited—to throw off all my loathsome boredom and anxiety? With the zealousness of a convert I be-

54 See William N. Eskridge, *Dishonorable Passions: Sodomy Laws in America, 1861–2003* (New York: Viking, 2008). Sodomy and "buggery" were illegal in the U.S. from Colonial days until the nineteenth century when sodomy laws also shifted to include fellatio. In 1986, *Bowers v. Hardwick* reaffirmed Georgia's sodomy laws and it was not until 2003 with *Lawrence v. Texas* that all state sodomy laws were abolished.

55 Glück, "My Community," 31.

56 Ibid., 33.

> came O'Hara. The mess and quick breath of his poems corresponded to my life. His longing and friendships and way of being became mine.[57]

The young Glück turns to writing and writers to try out a variety of languages, forms, selves, ways of being in the world; coming out, reading, and writing overlap, are all strands in the weaving of texts and the discovery of possibilities for self, writing, and a future. Some selves fit better—say O'Hara's complex messiness over Franklin as "gruesomely soulless, a caricature in his bland unconscious egotism, his endless energy to dominate ... fate or at least circumstance."[58] Glück's mature writing resists a linear teleological narrative of self-discovery and transparent freedom (e.g., as in the coming out novel); instead, his writing will speak into being the dilemma and possibility of its own arrival.

The historical Margery Kempe, too, looked to other texts for models. Dinshaw calls what she does "role-playing:" "she [Kempe] replays Christ's life in hers; she replays the Virgin Mary's, too, and Mary Magdalene's, and Saint Bridget's."[59] Through quotation and allusion, a requirement for books in the Middle Ages considered authoritative, Kempe turned to previous exemplars and texts—the Bible, the *Revelations* of St. Bridget of Sweden, texts by the mystic Walter Hilton, Richard Rolle's *Incendium Amoris*, and *Stimulus Amoris* (misattributed to St. Bonaventura)—as sources for fashioning her spiritual life and autobiography.[60] Additionally, Kempe's *Book*, like other mystical works of her period, foregrounds the difficulty of writing about, putting into language, her experience of God.[61] A difficulty compounded, perhaps, since medieval women, as Bale reminds us, must rely on "educated or ordained men" to write their texts.[62]

Kempe's difficulty in expressing her experience is linked to her access to God through suffering. The proem explains that "the Lord Christ Jesus ... benignly ... charitably ... having pity and compassion for His handiwork and His creature, turned health into sickness, prosperity into adversity, esteem into disgrace, and love into hatred," all of which, paradoxically, "stir[s] [her] to enter upon the way of perfection," though she suffers "great bodily sickness through which she lost her reason and her wits for a long time."[63] Acknowledging her ex-

---

57 Ibid.
58 Ibid., 31.
59 Dinshaw, *Getting Medieval*, 157–58.
60 See Barry Windeatt, "Introduction," in *The Book of Margery Kempe* (London and New York: Longman, 2000) and Bale, "Introduction," in *The Book of Margery Kempe*.
61 Bale, *The Book of Margery Kempe*, xx.
62 Ibid., xix.
63 Ibid., 3.

cessive weeping and sobbing and the amazement and sometimes consternation it provoked among people, Kempe writes "she herself could never tell of the grace that she felt, it was so heavenly, so high above her reason and her bodily wits, and her body was so feeble in times of the presence of grace that she could never express it with words as she felt it in her soul."[64]

While Glück garners a lot by turning to *The Book of Margery Kempe* as a source for, among other things, expressing Bob's love-sick suffering, recently I have been struck by the centrality of another writer in Glück's body of work—the poet Robert Duncan. Although Glück acknowledges in his "Long Note on New Narrative," that he and Bruce Boone "were aspiring to an ideal of learning derived as much from Spicer and Duncan as from our contemporaries," in the list of influential writers that follows, including among others—Althusser, Bataille, Lukács, Benjamin, Foucault, Barthes, Dennis Cooper, and Kathy Acker, Robert Duncan is absent.

Glück met Duncan in the late 1970s and interviewed him for the *Advocate* in 1984, eventually becoming "an intimate of Robert and Jess's house."[65] Glück's writing isn't much like Duncan's, except in its exquisite attention to language, to the domestic, and in its commitment to a capacious understanding of the possibilities of a constructed self and poetics. In the Introduction to *The Years as Catches: First Poems (1939–1946)*, Robert Duncan describes his sense of self as poet "as an ever-shifting possibility of the poet I am—at once a made up thing and at the same time a depth in which my being is."[66] Coincidentally published in 1966, the year of Glück's study abroad test and his Franklin appropriation, in *The Years as Catches*, Duncan acknowledges the fiction of self and writer —"the poet I am"—as a source of "depth" rather than a sign of the superficial or vacuous. Upon re-reading Glück's collected essays *Communal Nude*, I have been surprised by the recurring and frequent citation and collaging of this quote across Glück's body of work.[67]

Duncan's quote appears in Glück's essay "The Mouse's Tale," first published in *Artforum*, about Duncan's life partner, the artist Jess (Collins), and his paste-up, "The Mouse's Tale," an image of a crouching man largely comprised of numerous collaged black and white photos of naked men from physique magazines

---

64 Ibid., 4.

65 Glück, "Robert Duncan: Tribute," in *Communal Nude*, 253.

66 Duncan, *The Years as Catches*, x.

67 For a fuller discussion of Duncan's introduction and Glück's use of this phrase, see Robin Tremblay-McGaw, "'A Made Up Thing' Full of Depth: The Queer Belonging of Robert Duncan and New Narrative," *Sillages Critiques* 29 (2020): https://doi.org/10.4000/sillagescritiques.10711.

(with two glimpses of Jess!).[68] This image, in fact, adorns Glück's *Communal Nude: Collected Essays*, the first section of which, again, recalling Duncan, is entitled "A Real Fictional Depth:"

> I am a writer who learned from visual art, and Jess is an artist who learned from literature. In the fifties, he solved the exact puzzle I was working on in the late seventies: how to tell a story that also knows itself as writing—"a made up thing and at the same time a depth in which my being is," as Duncan said of his poet self.[69]

Duncan's line turns up elsewhere in Glück's essays, for example, in "Allegory" on Kathleen Fraser's, Beverly Dahlen's, and Dennis Cooper's work. Rob Halpern also pointed out that it appears, unattributed but italicized, near the conclusion of *Jack the Modernist* (1985) when the narrator, Bob, discusses George Méliès's film, *A Trip to the Moon:* "They seem affronted and reproachful but their grievance takes a collective form charting out a crude melody—call it 'Meaning'—with heads as notes and the song increasingly legible rather than audible, *at once a made up thing and depth in which my being is.*"[70] What is salient here is the way the fragmented quote travels across Glück's oeuvre, becoming attached to more than self, referencing narrative, story, meaning, and underscoring what is manifestly clear in Jess's "The Mouse's Tale" and all of Glück's work: story, self, images, the world have been made up. And they can be torn down and rebuilt, exposed in their fictions and fragmented, and made anew, offering representations of the world as it is experienced, felt, forged, and—as it might be—at once artifice and deeply felt, a strategy particularly salient, perhaps, for queer writers and artists battling the homophobic images produced by mainstream culture and reveling in the pleasures of producing their own representations from a variety of sources, high and low. At the close of Glück's essay "Truth's Mirror is No Mirror," he asks: "I wonder if it's possible to be aware of the artifacted nature of the self and not be contemptuous of it—to understand it as a construct and be moved by its depth."[71] It is as if Glück wants us to acknowledge all the "words related" to

68 Glück, "The Mouse's Tail," in *Communal Nude:* 139–43.
69 Glück, "The Mouse's Tail," 142.
70 Robert Glück, *Jack the Modernist* (New York: A SeaHorse Book/Gay Presses of New York, 1985), 165. Interestingly, on the verso of the title page, Glück calls his art collage and includes an "incomplete list of writers and works present one way or another" in his book. While Bataille, Denis Diderot, Baudelaire, Lafcadio Hearn, and others are listed, Duncan, again, does not appear.
71 Glück, "Truth's Mirror," in *Communal Nude*, 51.

artifice—gimmick, contrivance, duplicity, inventiveness, dodge, maneuver, ploy, scam, savvy, stratagem, subterfuge, ruse, racket, tactic, device, wile, gambit—but also, to recall its Latin and Anglo-French roots, tying artifice to craftsmanship, art, making. We are invited to experience the awe in the presence of the thing made.[72] In his essay "Allegory," Glück proposes that this "'made up thing ... at the same time a depth in which ... being is' might signal a new relation to audience—not vanguardist or utopian, *but inviting, shared*."[73] *Margery Kempe* is an exemplary experiment in these propositions.

Many years after Glück's impersonation of Benjamin Franklin in 1966, in *Margery Kempe* he appropriates the voice and autobiography of another historical figure; this time, not an exemplary American citizen, but an unruly, middle-class woman who, because of her gender, is a marginal subject. Some of the myriad ways in which Glück's *Margery* marks or reveals narrative as "made up" are illustrated in these quotes: "my book depends on the tension between maintaining an impersonation and breaking it";[74] "the book is a triptych: I follow L. on the left, Margery follows Jesus on the right, and in the center my fear hollows out 'an empty space that I can't fill'";[75] "This novel records my breakdown; conventional narrative is preserved but the interest lies elsewhere. Like L., Jesus must be real but must also represent a crisis."[76] *Margery* does what the prayer book advises its young female readers do: "shape in your mind some people, people well-known to you, to represent for you the people in the Passion." Making this explicit and soliciting opinion, inviting us in, or maybe daring us to protest, Glück writes: "Jesus and Margery act out my love. Is that a problem?"[77] These quotes are recognizable as instances of New Narrative's metatext; that is, they step outside of plot, and comment on, fragment, and reframe the narrative, drawing our attention as readers to the content of the form; its assemblage, constructed fabrication.[78]

While the narrator asserts Jesus and Margery "act out my love," many of Glück's characters borrow some of their liveness from his friends and acquain-

---

72 See *Oxford English Dictionary*, s.v. "artifice (*n.*)," accessed August 24, 2020, https://www.oed.com/view/Entry/11206?rskey=lixq15&result=1&isAdvanced=false#eid and *Merriam-Webster*, s.v. "artifice, (*n.*)," accessed August 24, 2020, https://www.merriam-webster.com/dictionary/artifice.
73 Glück, "Allegory," in *Communal Nude*, 68, my emphasis.
74 Glück, *Margery*, 20.
75 Ibid., 41.
76 Ibid., 78.
77 Ibid., 81.
78 See Warhol and Lanser, *Narrative Theory Unbound*. Another way to consider this is that via metatext, New Narrative carries the narratological—the "study of how narrative forms make meaning" into narrative (2).

tances. Glück explains this in the book’s “Acknowledgments,” and metatextually in chapter 30:

> I asked my friends for notes about their bodies to dress these fifteenth-century paper dolls. I clothe the maid, Willyam Wever, the Archbishop of Lincoln in Camille’s eruption of physicality, Ed’s weekend of tears, Dodie’s tangled nerve endings, Steve’s afternoon nap. My story proceeds by interaction. My friends become the author of my misfortune and the ground of authority in this book. We are a village common producing images.”[79]

In *Writers Who Love Too Much*, Dodie Bellamy and Kevin Killian describe this as “crowd sourcing” *avant la lettre* or “mass collaboration,” contextualizing it as “drawn from surrealist games like the exquisite corpse,” pointing out how it “made for a certain camaraderie.”[80] I remember the frisson of getting my copy of Glück’s book and finding in it one of the details I had given him: “Margery liked her rosy curves and caverns and strength: she outdistanced John going uphill.”[81] The love of her strength and her ability to outpace John are descriptions I recognize as my own—at least I think I do—though I suspect the “rosy curves” might belong to someone else. I don’t remember. It is hard to know an earlier version of oneself, isn’t it? Glück asked for these details decades ago. And isn’t that the point? That in their potential specificity and generalizability, they belong to the characters and all of us, Glück’s readers, the world: “the village common producing images”?

Glück seems to say as much after telling us that Flaubert’s “The Legend of St. Julian Hospitaler” was his “model.” However, unlike Flaubert, he finds:

> I am drawn to modernism but my faith is impure. I am no more the solitary author of this book than I alone invent the fiction of my life. As I write, I read my experience as well as Margery’s. Is that appropriation?—that I am also the reader, oscillating in a nowhere between what I invent and what changes me?[82]

Perhaps Modernism’s solitary genius, “the individual talent,” and to some extent the avant-garde in general, is linked with what today we would name toxic (often, though not only, heterosexual) masculinity. Perhaps despite a rhetoric that might suggest otherwise, Modernism’s “individual talent,” expresses the de-

---

79 Glück, *Margery*, 90.
80 Dodie Bellamy and Kevin Killian, “Introduction,” in *Writers Who Love Too Much: New Narrative 1977–1997*, ed. Dodie Bellamy and Kevin Killian (New York: Nightboat Books, 2017), xii.
81 Glück, *Margery*, 7. In the mid-1980s I was a graduate student at San Francisco State University, and in the later 1980s, began attending Bob’s Saturday writing workshop held in his home. I was one of those 40 or so people who gave Glück descriptions of physical life.
82 Glück, *Margery*, 80–81.

sire, even the necessity, of keeping things—including people—in their places (the avant-garde writer is always "before" or out in front of others), while it also preserves the lie that a writer, any writer, is "the solitary author" of his or her book.[83] "Appropriation," Glück writes, "puts in question the place of the writer"[84] and "challenge[s] the distinction between public and private."[85] While "fictional depth" might signal a new relation with audience, one that is "shared and inviting," appropriation puts the "place" or presumed sovereignty of the writer and "the distinction between public and private" in question, and thus makes writing risky.

Glück's *Margery Kempe* is predicated on risk. Let's return to the epigram for a moment. While the prayer book and church give people permission to imagine themselves, at least temporarily, as travelling through or across time and also to mix the public (story of the Passion) and the private as they meditate on Christ's Passion, I think we can infer that there is an unstated but implied rule that these transformations—the practice of bringing people the reader knows into the story —should not cross genders or sexes. Glück's book refuses this normative orthodoxy. Early in the book, Bob *becomes* Margery: "I'm Margery following a god through a rainy city";[86] "As Margery, I wake up and enter the dark street hoping to catch a glimpse of Jesus and trying to avoid him ... I didn't know I had a cunt till he wriggled his fingers inside me";[87] and Jesus looks like L—"Jesus had L's Scottish face—high narrow brow with smooth features crowded beneath, eyebrows defined more by delicate bones than hair."[88] In these sentences, lovers, subjects, and indeed bodies shift and blur.[89]

Arguing that the historical Margery Kempe performs a transgressive critique of medieval Christianity, Dinshaw explains this is most visibly signaled by Kempe, who is both wife and mother, when she attires herself all in white, the clothing of chastity:

---

83 Of course, there is a built-in contradiction here given, for example, T. S. Eliot's own use of quotation and appropriation in "The Waste Land," to name one example.

84 Glück, "Long Note," in *Communal Nude*, 21.

85 Glück, "Fame," in *Communal Nude*, 39.

86 Glück, *Margery*, 13.

87 Ibid., 87.

88 Ibid., 14.

89 See Earl Jackson, *Strategies of Deviance: Studies in Gay Male Representation* (Bloomington, IN: Indiana University Press, 1995). About the New Narrative subject, Jackson writes, "the subject in New Narrative writing is a psychosomatic materiality that is historically realized but not reified, a multiply articulated and articulate intertext whose own signifying practices shift the terms of its identities" (180).

> When we look at, not through, the mother wearing the clothes of a virgin, and when we listen to her own words about her experience as well, we perceive a creature that itself is not clearly categorizable in her community's bourgeois heteronormative terms, terms that would ease the contradictions of Christian dogma by leaving perfection to others and adjusting desires accordingly ... Margery's white clothes point to the disjunction in an orthodox Christianity which establishes marriage as a sacrament yet always maintains its taint, maintains that it is a perversion from the ultimately perfect perfection.[90]

Kempe's text and speech also contested gender norms under clerical patriarchal power structures, as scholar and editor Barry Windeatt points out: "her constant talking of pious subjects was readily construed by some who heard it as a woman's presuming to preach, a usurpation of the literate and licensed male clergy's authority."[91] As I have discussed above, Kempe did in fact expound on the Bible and even advised lay people and men of the cloth. Additionally, she also wrote with frankness about her own sexual desire, including describing a moment when she "had no wish to have sexual contact with her husband," but when propositioned by another man, "was so troubled and vexed all night," she finally accepted his offer.[92]

Tracing desire's capacity to trouble and make legible the social construction of gender and sex, Glück's book probes the play and plasticity of gender's fiction writ large. In *Margery*, he writes: "Jesus got dressed as a knight. His purple doublet was padded over the chest; he fastened the four-petaled buttons and set a heavy gold belt around his hips," naming the "tension between masculine-feminine and inside-outside" that "pervades all levels of my community."[93] In varying pitches—both directly and subtly—Glück's book recognizes and works this gendered tension, locating it in and extending it beyond the gay community: "She was moved but also disturbed by his torso, a face without features. Jesus lowered his lids and tipped his head back, basking and effeminate. Two tiny points of hair on his chin were his beard. She questioned her attraction and answered yes, it was strong."[94] That is, there are a variety of possibilities in this passage: if the "she" is Margery assessing her attraction to the effeminate Jesus, the text calls attention to gender norms within heterosexuality; but if

---

90 Dinshaw, *Getting Medieval*, 148–49.

91 Windeatt, "Introduction," in *The Book of Margery Kempe*, 24.

92 Bale, *The Book of Margery Kempe*, 18. However, after she offered herself to this man, he brutally refused her: "he said he would not for all the wealth in this world; he would rather be hacked as small meat for the pot!" (18).

93 Glück, *Margery*, 48.

94 Ibid., 115.

we read Margery here as a stand-in for Bob, then Jesus's effeminacy is surveyed within the context of gay life as well.

This tension, as Glück's text reminds us, has permeated most cultures organized around norms tied to gender and sex binaries—an organization always tenuous and vulnerable to implosion. One of my favorite passages from this novel provides an excellent example:

> Farmers tilled their small fields to the limit. Women carded and combed, clouted and washed, and peeled rushes as in Lynn. One woman became a man when he jumped over an irrigation ditch and his cunt dropped inside out: gender is the extent we go to in order to be loved. [95]

With their alliteration and lyric pleasures, these sentences illustrate the gendered division of medieval labor, while simultaneously exposing the *distance* a person will go to be loved, and the always immanent/imminent collapse of gender and sex binaries. Glück's narrative of sexual transformation, mid-leap, closely echoes one recounted in Ambroise Paré's sixteenth-century *Des Monstres et prodiges*, a text that catalogs and illustrates a number of such transformations of women or girls into men; importantly, however, it claims that "we ... never find in any true story that any man ever became a woman, because Nature tends always toward what is most perfect and not, on the contrary, to perform in such a way that what is perfect should become imperfect."[96]

As the quote from Paré illustrates, communities erect ideological limits to transformative possibilities, particularly when it comes to gender, sex, sexuality. In "My Community," by way of elaborating some of his sexual fantasies, taken "from life" and shaped by community "strands of identification, desire, and racism,"[97] Glück identifies some limits in his community. While I have written else-

---

95 Ibid., 57.

96 See Ambroise Paré, *On Monsters and Marvels*, trans. Janis L. Pallister (Chicago: University of Chicago Press, 1982), 33. It is interesting to note, given the appropriation and collage in Glück's work, that Paré experienced "repeated accusations of frequent 'borrowings' from other writers" (xvi). It is also true that there are questions surrounding the authorship of Kempe's book, since she had two copyists. Windeatt asserts: "Whether the priest is to be thought of as the amanuensis of *The Book of Margery Kempe*, or as its author, or as something between the two, remains a matter of inference, as does the possibility that all reference to the male writer is a protective and enabling fiction deployed by Kempe, along with her deployment of the figure of 'Margery'" (6).

97 Glück, "My Community," in *Communal Nude*, 36.

where about Glück's discussion of race and racism in this context,[98] what I want to notice here are the ways in which, at various times, communities—including queer and other liberatory communities—have controlled, policed even, representations and transformative possibilities:

> I haven't allowed myself to be woman since early teenhood, so now I am in the position to wonder: Have I repressed that image for thirty years out of shame for not resembling the face in the mirror my community holds up, first of a normal man, later of a feminist woman, and finally of a normal homosexual?[99]

In *Margery*, published just three years after this essay, Margery and Bob and the writing itself refuse the tyranny of normative categories, the reflections community and story hold up: gender and sex are not fixed, but rather constantly "done" and "undone" and propelled by desire.[100] In chapter 7, Jesus says to Margery, "'Like a mother I give you my breast to suck'" and then asks Margery "to help nurse him" at which point, the prose shifts, remaking, re-gendering two central twentieth-century figures in art and critical theory. In Glück's book, Margery becomes Paul Klee's "Angelus Novus," and Walter Benjamin's "angel of history":[101] "She moved through the resistance of time—her mantle billows backwards into the future as her forehead met the past."[102] These allusions are easily recognizable to the experimental poetry community in which New Narrative percolates, and along with Glück's other strategies exposing the constructed nature of his text, they underscore "the made-up thing" that are the selves that are Margery and Bob.

---

98 See Tremblay-McGaw, "New Narrative Remix: 'Not Resembling the Face in the Mirror,'" in *From Our Hearts to Yours: New Narrative as Contemporary Practice*, ed. Rob Halpern and Robin Tremblay-McGaw (Oakland, CA: On Contemporary Practice, 2017): 111–35.

99 Glück, "My Community," 36.

100 See Judith Butler, "Introduction: Acting in Concert," in *Undoing Gender* (Abingdon: Routledge, 2004). As Butler writes: "One does not 'do' one's gender alone. One is always 'doing' with or for another, even if the other is only imaginary" and "it is only through the experience of recognition that any of us becomes constituted as socially viable beings" (1).

101 See Walter Benjamin, "Theses on the Philosophy of History," in *Illuminations*, ed. Hannah Arendt (New York: Schocken Books, 1968), 253–64. "A Klee painting named 'Angelus Novus' shows an angel looking as though he is about to move away from something he is fixedly contemplating. His eyes are staring, his mouth is open, his wings are spread. This is how one pictures the angel of history. His face is turned toward the past. Where we perceive a chain of events, he sees one single catastrophe which keeps piling wreckage upon wreckage and hurls it in front of his feet."

102 Glück, "My Community," 22.

Immediately after the section just discussed, the prose in the body of the novel migrates from the for-the-most-part quarantined third-person narrations of Margery's passion for Jesus, and first-person stories of Bob's desire for L, to a section written in the first person but addressed to Jesus: "Jesus, when I feel the difference between my stale life and the ecstasy of life with you, I revive the desolation I felt before meeting you in order to coax your appearance. I begin crying so intently my voice sounds hoarse and strange."[103] Who is this "I"? Margery? Bob? Both? Glück's prose has scandalously united Margery and Bob, two impassioned subjects propelled by their desire to go to any lengths, leap whatever chasms necessary, in pursuit of the beloved. Bob has inserted himself, as did Margery Kempe before him, in the story of Christ's Passion, though *not* merely as one of the figures *in* it, but *as* the controversial creation of her own narrative, trespasser of time, heretical interloper, everywhere-at-once, the author of the first English autobiography, Margery Kempe. Formally, Glück's text reflects and refracts the content—her "manner of living"—described in the historical Kempe's narrative while it also draws attention to Bob's everyday life and the text's self-reflexive coming-into-being, marking, elaborating, and exposing the productivity and problematics of self, narrative, gender, and desire that are the very stuff with which the character Bob, Glück the writer, and Glück's text wrestle.

Merely a few pages prior to this address to Jesus by the first-person "I" but nevertheless plural (Margery and Bob), the narrator has told us "my book depends on the tension between maintaining an impersonation and breaking it."[104] *Telling*, that is, exposing via metatext its narrative transtextual entanglements, Glück's prose synchs and frays, tells and worries the implications of his narration:

> I perform my story by lip-synching Margery's loud longing but I wonder if that visible self-erasure is just a failure to face L. I want to be a woman and a man penetrating him, his inner walls rolling around me like satin drenched in hot oil, and I want to be the woman and man he continually fucks. I want to be where total freedom is. I push myself under the surface of Margery's story, holding my breath for a happy ending to my own.[105]

The narrator's reflective narration as a character whose author shares his name—"Bob"—puts the author and his narrative at risk.[106] "Bob" reveals the distance

103 Ibid., 27.
104 Ibid., 20.
105 Ibid., 49.
106 This strategy signals risk and marks the self as "made-up" and as such is one way to undo the "transparent self" under critique by Language writers.

his desire travels; his desire to be both a man and a woman suggests that Paré was wrong about a man never becoming a woman. The reader might protest that Paré belongs to the sixteenth century, that the intervening centuries have shifted our ideas, possibilities. Yet, echoing his excavation of community norms and desire in "My Community," in his discussion of a story called "Night Flight," written before *Margery*, Glück illustrates the ongoing effort required to leap the gender gap. For this story, he appropriated a plot from the Marquis de Sade and turned the "unfortunate heroine" into a man. Glück explains:

> I turned her into a man named Felix, the object of my obsession, and I was writing along till I got to my hero's pregnancy and motherhood. For a few days I was stumped. Perhaps I was curtailed by the assumptions that belonged to the audience in my imagination? ... In an elated trans moment I realized that I would simply make Felix pregnant and then a mother. A mother with a masculine pronoun. Even now I wonder what gap was crossed.[107]

So, even in San Francisco, Margery Kempe and the Middle Ages are perhaps unorthodox "faces in the mirror" for a Jewish gay leftist experimental writer living in the wake of AIDS in the late twentieth century. That is, there are risks for "not resembling the face in the mirror" a particular community holds up. A deep history of patriarchy's implicit misogyny and femme-phobia, beginning long before but marked by Paré's quote above, signaled by Glück's comments at the close of "My Community," and revealed in contemporary reviews of *Margery*, travels into the present.

If the experimental writing community might be troubled by Glück's use of self and narration, elements of autobiography, etc., clearly, mainstream culture was bothered by the many and complex dismantlings and reimaginings of gender, sex, and sexuality in Glück's book. Take, for example, a review of *Margery* appearing in *Publishers Weekly*.[108] The anonymous reviewer's vitriol and dehumanizing language is on full display: "Glück's character is rendered as an offensive creature who seeks sainthood through a sexual alliance with Jesus ... Glück's Margery is so ugly and coarse she doesn't come across as a woman at all—just a man's skewed rendering of one."[109] Transgressing the gender/sex binary, Margery is a "creature" and "not a woman at all."[110] Whitney Scott's review in *Booklist* finds the book "steamy," apparently appreciating Margery's "lust" and "sex-

---

107 Glück, "Writing Sex Body," in *Communal Nude*, 107.
108 "Margery Kempe," *Publishers Weekly* 241, no. 39 (1994): 61.
109 "Margery Kempe," 61.
110 It is true that Kempe's *Book* uses the third person and frequently refers to Kempe as a "creature." Glück's reviewer, from what I can tell, is unaware of Kempe's use of this word, employing it as gendered criticism.

ual bliss with a well-endowed Jesus."[111] This reviewer, too, however, has reservations, though the writer grants the book a "niche audience." For Scott, it is the scandal of a heretical vision of a horny Jesus co-mingling with gay eroticism that is the problem: "Although many may find a Jesus who tongue-kisses and says, 'I'm horny,' dismaying, and Glück's intercutting of fifteenth-century visions and twentieth-century gay eroticism disorienting, the book's sheer audacity may help it find an avid niche audience."[112] A *Lambda Book Report* review at least recognizes the novel as "a dense, swooning, fire-breathing love poem" valorizing the book's capacity to "evoke everything from the Bosch-like beauty of a medieval world still rang by miracles to the blind heat of lust," it too seems to miss some of the work Glück's book does as Raphael Kadushin claims "the fact is, Glück doesn't need to update" Kempe's "cracked passion" and "ecstasy."[113]

Perhaps these reviews, particularly the *Publishers Weekly* review, expose *exactly* the power and scandal of Glück's fiction. For as he has asserted:

> any art wants to take the place of your reflection in the mirror and calls for your recognition. *It makes you become it like a magic spell—with words, images, representations.* That is why a new self, like a new aesthetic form, like any new approach to art, is something of a scandal. *That's why readers experience shock and outrage, or relief and urgency.*[114]

Interestingly, upon its twentieth-century rediscovery and publication in December 1934, Kempe's *Book* too garnered mixed reviews. Bale explains:

> Mostly, these reviews valued Kempe's *Book* highly but also passed judgement on the protagonist of the *Book:* Kempe herself. *The Evening Standard* found Kempe "certainly queer, even in a queer age" whilst the *Daily Telegraph* described Kempe as a "wet blanket in any company which was innocently enjoying itself" ... R. W. Chambers, in his introduction to the first Modern English translation, said rather patronizingly, "[t]he reader should therefore be warned at the outset that poor Margery is to be classed with those hotels which Baedeker describes as 'variously judged.'"[115]

Perhaps the risk and scandal of a new self, even for the writer, is best illustrated by another New Narrative text, one that was probably written in the 1980s or 1990s and left unfinished.[116] Bruce Boone's selected works, *Bruce Boone Dis-*

---

111 Whitney Scott, "Margery Kempe," *Booklist* 91, no. 5 (1994): 477.

112 Scott, "Margery Kempe," 447.

113 Raphael Kadushin, "Margery Kempe," *Lambda Book Report* 4, no. 7 (1994): 21.

114 Glück, "My Community," in *Communal Nude*, 34, my emphasis.

115 Bale, *The Book of Margery Kempe*, x.

116 The date of composition for this text is a best guess based on the material fact that it was printed on a dot-matrix printer and Boone had not dated it.

membered (2020), includes "Note on *Carmen*," a brief piece recently composed as a preface for the selections from *Carmen* that follow it.[117] It reads:

> What about *Carmen* then? In this failed literary project, I tried to take the work of *Century of Clouds* to a "higher level," following up on community lessons by way of a drag-queen narrator named Orlando (thank you Virginia Woolf). Orlando was very gender fluid, emotive, gushy, and paranoid, to boot. But out of cowardly fear, I abandoned it. I just caved, thinking—ohmigosh, this is way too far out!, and out of cowardice, I dumped this work into the garbage can of history. Dear Orlando, Dear Carmen, so sorry! Would that I had been more courageous![118]

Why did Boone abandon this project? Was his "drag-queen narrator" too femme? "Too far out"? Too much "not the face in the mirror" his community held up? Looking back at Boone's essay on "Robert Duncan and Gay Community" (1983), I see Boone registering the challenges of being a femme gay man in Duncan's time and in his own.[119]

> Butch/femme.What's interesting here is how early Duncan was to give a positive valuation to the femme part of that opposition, to insist on it as a matter of fact. To judge from Duncan's accounts, he accepted an identification at the femme end of the spectrum—surely even more difficult then than it is now ... It's noticeable in patriarchal society that femme gays are treated more harshly than their butch brothers.[120]

What are these categories that so fix us publicly, privately, in and outside of our communities?

In her loquacious bid for a different life, on the cusp of modernity, the historical Margery Kempe had the audacity to name and challenge the religious and social orthodoxies of her time, and produced a collaborative text, a self, *avant la lettre*, and a new form—in her case, the autobiography—to go with it. Similarly, Glück's *Margery Kempe* makes legible a whole host of orthodoxies—within diverse mainstream, gay, and experimental writing communities, while marking out a space for crossings, transformations, leaps that call for our recognition, not necessarily via identity or sameness, but with the acknowledgment of their fiction and depth. In his essay "Truth's Mirror is No Mirror," Glück elaborates: "The self is a depth *and* a boundary ... I am describing a nonironic dou-

---

117 Bruce Boone, "Note on Carmen," in *Bruce Boone Dismembered: Poems, Stories, and Essays*, ed. Rob Halpern (New York: Nightboat Books, 2020), 208.
118 Boone, "Note on Carmen," 208.
119 Bruce Boone, "Robert Duncan and Gay Community," in *Ironwood: Robert Duncan Special Issue* (Tucson, AZ: Ironwood Press, 1983), 66–93.
120 Boone, "Robert Duncan and Gay Community," 75.

bling, holding two points of view at once, rather than irony's doubling that operates on (and doubts) the single plane of the author's voice."[121]

Glück's Bob/Margery perform(s) a kind of gendered and "genred" doing and undoing at every turn. Even Margery, a bottom with a strong force of will, learns to imitate Jesus's aristocratic top's effeminate masculine ease:

> When she journeyed towards the old clock, she was Jesus walking down the corridor and the emptiness stopped assaulting her. She said hello, copied his voice like a birdcall: two notes rising, one sinking halfway. She rehearsed the tension in his jaw. His elegant features jumped expressions under the clear sky of his brow.[122]

She discovers:

> *when information circulates it transforms*; she looked from a gold face through strong blue eyes; she walked on long legs with an athlete's pleasure and became the forward stiff-legged gait, the awareness of ass in the short tunic. She abandoned her breasts and belly for a flat expanse of skin.[123]

Like Kempe's *Book*, written in the fifteenth century but newly discovered in the twentieth century, it is in mobility and transformation that Glück's *Margery* finds hope and a possible future, where the writer risks their own sovereignty and *shock and outrage, or relief and urgency*, where "travel [that is, mobility] itself [is] an authentic place to speak from—where events unfold, the crest of duration."[124] At the close of Glück's book, in the fourth section titled "Margery's Passion": "*a-non aperyd verily to hir syght an awngel al clothyd in white beryng an owge boke be-forn hym*," both Margery and Bob, having lost Jesus and L, find that their "huge books," their radical stories are borne by an angel all clothed in white. They have travelled; there is mystery, mobility. Glück writes "I feel I am a contributor to Margery's life, an event in her posthumous life, and she has certainly contributed to my own sense of self."[125] "Without Jesus, Margery's story was open-ended";[126] and for Bob, as a result of Margery's book and his own, he informs us—"at last my position is not so fixed."[127] Maybe heaven is a kind of lived, textual, and trans/textual plenitude, where feeling—passion—coex-

121 Glück, "Truth's Mirror," in *Communal Nude*, 46.
122 Glück, *Margery*, 147.
123 Ibid., my emphasis.
124 Ibid., 106.
125 Glück, "My Margery, Margery's Bob," in *Communal Nude*, 147.
126 Glück, *Margery*, 159.
127 Ibid., 162.

ists with the capacity to "maintain a critical and transformative relation" to the various norms and demands, the mirrors held up by the social world and the communities in which we live;[128] appropriation, collage, and the made-up constitute an "infinite field"[129] for self, story, community, feeling. In short, a future. Reader, I am attracted. Are you?

---

128 Butler, *Undoing Gender*, 3.
129 Glück, "Long Note," in *Communal Nude*, 23.

Christopher Roman

A Basket of Fire and the Laughter of God: Anne Sexton's Queer Theopoetics

I am no more a woman
Than Christ was a man.
– Anne Sexton
"Consorting with Angels" (1962)

Anne Sexton explores a queer relationship with God via her posthumously published collection *The Awful Rowing Toward God*, positing queer ways to approach God and eschewing the traditional triad of omniscience, omnipotence, and omnipresence usually associated with the divine in order to discover God baked into the material, the animal, and the body. As Sexton said in a *Paris Review* interview in 1971, "I have visions—sometimes ritualized visions—that come to me of God, or of Christ, or of the Saints, and I feel that I can touch them almost."[1] As this quote attests, Sexton's approach to God is sensual and harkens back to the ritualism indebted to medieval mystics. Her poems in *The Awful Rowing Toward God* address a queer, theophanic materiality. Theophany explores and looks to the material world and the body as sites of divine presence in which God can be found; for Sexton, that body is queer: hybrid, open, fluid, and messy. In this essay, I utilize tools from queer theology as a way to unpack Sexton's representation of God and the complicated representation of the human-divine relationship found in this posthumous collection of poems. I will address Sexton's queer theopoetics through her language use (the breakdown of the binary between apophatic and cataphatic mystical language), the hybrid body of the narrator and God, and, ultimately, Sexton's representation of queering death. Each of these elements of her poetry builds toward a queer theology that, while resisting constraining systematization, reveals a poetics that dismisses masculinist, systematic theology in order to approach God in a variety of shapes and sizes and bodies. Christ is no man.

Anne Sexton is considered a twentieth-century confessional poet. Born in 1928 in Newton, Massachusetts, Anne Gray Harvey (Sexton's birth name) began writing poetry when she attended a poetry workshop led by John Holmes (a poetry professor at Tufts) at the Boston Center for Adult Education. During her early years of psychotherapy, which she underwent because of suicide attempts,

---

1 William H. Shurr, "Mysticism and Suicide: Anne Sexton's Last Poetry," in *Critical Essays on Anne Sexton*, ed. Linda Wagner-Martin (Boston: G. K. Hall, 1989), 203.

https://doi.org/10.1515/9781501511189-004

she was encouraged to write by her doctor. Therapy plus the workshop honed Sexton's poetic approach. Sexton began to forge a confessional style marked by her early poems "The Suicide Note" and "One Life Asks the Questions."[2] This confessional poesis intersects with a search for God in *The Awful Rowing Toward God* (1975), published after her death by suicide on Friday, October 4, 1974.

The initial draft of *The Awful Rowing Toward God* was written during a flourishing bout of writing during the months of January and February in 1973. As Diane Wood Middlebrook recounts, "every day at 5 P.M. she would phone Maxine Kumin, who was writer-in-residence at Centre College in Kentucky for six weeks that winter, and go over the day's work."[3] Kumin, writing the foreword to Anne Sexton's *The Complete Poems*, comments that "the pace terrified me"; Sexton was "a ravaged, obsessed poet fighting to put jigsaw pieces of the puzzle together into a coherence that would save her—into a 'whole nation of God.'"[4] Sexton dedicated this collection to James Wright, who reportedly edited the text mercilessly when he received a draft (Kumin defended the poems against his slashing pen),[5] and Brother Dennis Farrell, "perhaps because they had been sources of religious insights."[6] Farrell was an early fan who had written her a letter after reading Sexton's early collection, *Bedlam*. They corresponded throughout Sexton's life, often wrestling with theological and personal problems. The themes of God and death are peppered throughout her work (see *The Jesus Papers* in her 1972 book *The Book of Folly)*, but it is in *The Awful Rowing Toward God* that Sexton's poems are the most theologically bent, offering up God, not as a comfort; rather, Sexton presents us with a God full of flesh and death, resisting the boundaries of finitude at the same time as poking His finger in the vital materiality of life.

Anne Sexton engages with medieval mysticism throughout her oeuvre. Part of the problem set out by medieval mysticism is how to relate the experience of a sensory experience with God in writing—the mystic must relate something beyond the human. We can take, for example, the work of the medieval anchorite, Julian of Norwich, to think about the process of mystical creation: sickness, visions, anchorhold, parchment, pen, and within that assemblage, the problem

2 The standard biography of Anne Sexton is Diane Wood Middlebrook's *Anne Sexton: A Biography* (Boston: Houghton Mifflin, 1991).

3 Middlebrook, *Anne Sexton: A Biography*, 367.

4 Maxine Kumin, "Foreword," *Anne Sexton: The Complete Poems* (Boston: Houghton Mifflin, 1981), xxxi. In this essay, all references to Sexton's poems derive from this edition of her work. I cite the poems parenthetically by title and page number.

5 Middlebrook, *Anne Sexton: A Biography*, 368.

6 Ibid., 367.

of Christ's bleeding like fish scales, a mother-Jesus, a womb we will die into and not be released from. In Julian's work, queer poetics orients the body differently to sensory experience (for example, wombs are traditionally something to be released from, not necessarily something to be born into without being born out of) and thinks about language differently—as critics have commented, the mother-Jesus blurs the gendered lines of both Christ and his worshipper.[7] This mystical moment where sensory, bodily, and linguistic practices are re-envisioned is a persistent challenge, and one found in contemporary literature, as well. Anne Sexton's *The Awful Rowing Toward God* offers up a theological journey in which God is multiplicitous and fleshy, an unreachable island, as well as pieces inside of the body. Sexton, in a Whitmanesque mode, presents herself as containing pieces of God that are everyone.

I am reading Sexton's work as touching the medieval mystic queerly. Sexton reveals her medieval *bona fides* in *The Awful Rowing Toward God* in the poem "The Saints Come Marching In." In that poem, Sexton refers to saints Catherine of Siena, Augustine, and Teresa of Ávila, the prophet Elisha, as well as Nicholas the Pilgrim,[8] Bertilla Boscardin,[9] Vincent Pallotti,[10] and St. Dominic. The confluence of prophets, medieval saints, mystics and theologians, and modern saints, lays the groundwork for Sexton's thinking about God as palpable and fleshly, as well as borrowing these mystics' and theologians' sense of God as she touches them in a myriad of ways—both sensually and spiritually—as a way to reconsider a relationship with God through a queer body. Although it is beyond the scope of this essay to explore the ways in which all of the above religious figures have left their fingerprints on this collection of poems, Sexton opens this poem by writing,

---

7 See Julian of Norwich, *The Shewings of Julian of Norwich*, ed. Georgia Ronan Crampton (Kalamazoo, MI: Medieval Institute Publications, 1994). For a discussion of Julian of Norwich's cataphatic language, see Arabella Milibank, "Medieval Corporeality and the Eucharistic Body in Julian of Norwich's *A Revelation of Love*," *Journal of Medieval and Early Modern Studies* 46, no. 3 (2016): 629–51; Jon Shickler, "The Cross and the Citadel: Reconciling Apophatic and Cataphatic Traditions in the Showings of Julian of Norwich," *Studia Mystica* 21 (2000): 95–125; Christopher Roman, *Domestic Mysticism in Dame Julian of Norwich and Margery Kempe: The Transformation of Christian Spirituality in the Late Middle Ages* (Lewiston, NY: Edwin Mellen, 2005).

8 Nicholas the Pilgrim or Nicholas of Trani (1075–1094) was a Greek shepherd who was known for his repetition of the *Kyrie Eleison*. He died while on pilgrimage to Apulia. He was canonized by Pope Urban II in 1098.

9 Maria Bertilla Boscardin (1888–1922) was an Italian nun who worked with children and the sick during the air raids of World War I. She was canonized by the Catholic Church in 1961 by Pope John XXIII.

10 Vincent Pallotti (1795–1850) was an Italian ecclesiastic who was the founder of the Pious Society of Missions, the Pallottines. He was canonized by Pope John XXIII in 1963.

"The Saints come/ as human as a mouth,/ with a bag of God in their backs."[11] Thus, Sexton models her sensual approach to God on this opening image; her poems are saintly mouthfuls of God needing to be unpacked.

I'm utilizing queer theology in this essay as it is a form of theology that resists traditional forms of oppressive theology, allowing for an analysis of embodied, lived experience, a critique of the Church for ignoring the poor and oppressed while creating a space for those very poor and oppressed, as well as those formally marginalized, such as queer people, or welcoming women's voices in the creation of a living, changing, and fluid theology. Queer theology also holds space for a positive valuation of all genders and sexualities, as well as sex itself, and an approach to Christianity that allows for Christianity's metaphorical and poetic powers to be in play. The task of this theology, as Marcella Althaus-Reid writes, is to "deconstruct a moral order which is based on a heterosexual construction of reality, which organizes not only categories of approved social and divine interactions but of economic ones, too."[12] Sexton's voice is a mystical, theological voice, that undoes oppression, valuing the poor, the old, the (formerly) voiceless, as she finds pieces of them as God within her body.

In this collection of poems, Sexton speaks in the voice of a prophet, in the voice of one broken, in the voice of the old, the voice of the omniscient as a way to connect with God's multiplicity—the voices are never standing still. Sexton suggests that perhaps rather than considering the mystical experience from the standpoint of a single, stable identity—the abject mystic, the transcendent God—there is a fusion of above and below, there is a theological and mystical investigation of what separates the human from the non-human. Sexton's poems posit that rather than the mystery of the divine-human relationship as frustrated by the limitation of language, the relationship between mystic and God must be made multiple on both ends—must be made queer through poetic play, through language and the body themselves. In these poems, God appears in various guises. If the relationship between God and mystic is always kept from settling, from standing still, then we have a "basket of fire," as Sexton suggests, the wood of the basket feeding the fire that, in turn, never uses up the basket in its fire.

Before examining the poems, I want to also suggest that Sexton is addressing the issue of what *counts* as a relationship with God. At the end of her essay on Michel Foucault's "What is Critique?," Judith Butler writes that virtue is connected to the process of de-subjugation, which leads to asking "who will be a

11 Anne Sexton, *The Complete Poems* (Boston: Houghton Mifflin, 1981), 469.
12 Marcella Althaus-Reid, *Indecent Theology* (London: Routledge, 2000), 2.

subject here, and what will count as a life, a moment of ethical questioning which requires that we break the habits of judgment in favor of a riskier practice that seeks to yield artistry from constraint."[13] What Butler outlines, and what I hope to show in relation to the artistry of Sexton's poems, is the way the constraint of how one relates to God (say in standard prayers or in "approved" visions or by the shaping of the document by the proper amanuensis) is released in the theopoetic, the metaphoric. In this way, Sexton, too, explores a risky relationship with God.

Queering Language

The first way in which Sexton queers God is the play between apophaticism and cataphaticism. Simply put, apophaticism and cataphaticism are complementary ways to speak about God that stretch back to the work of the fifth-century theologian Pseudo-Dionysius the Areopagite. Pseudo-Dionysius was originally thought to be one of the early converts of St. Paul, but in the 1400s this identity was questioned; later theologians and scholars placed him between 485–518 C.E. as a student of Proclus, thus providing context for Pseudo-Dionysius's blending of Christianity and Platonism. The Pseudo-Dionysian (and Neo-Platonic) tradition is far-reaching and influential, finding its way into medieval and early modern mystical and theological works. Pseudo-Dionysian apophaticism states that we cannot know God, language cannot capture God, and so, a way to approach God is through negation, to say what God is not. For example, Pseudo-Dionysius writes that "the theologians praise it by every name—and as the Nameless One. For they call it nameless when they speak of how the supreme Deity, during a mysterious revelation of the symbolical appearance of God, rebuked the man who asked, 'What is your name?'"[14] God has no name because the name that God has is above and beyond every name.

As Andrew Louth writes, Pseudo-Dionysius uses the language of apophaticism and cataphaticism as a journey: "the cataphatic theologies (in the sense of ways of talking about God) descend from affirmations about the being of God, who is both one and three, through the Incarnation, to the concepts we

---

13 Judith Butler, "What Is Critique? An Essay on Foucault's Virtue," in *The Political*, ed. David Ingram (Malden, MA: Blackwell, 2002), 226.
14 Pseudo-Dionysius, *The Divine Names. Pseudo-Dionysius: The Complete Works*, trans. Colm Luibheid (New York: Paulist Press, 1987), 54.

use of God and the images that scripture applies to him."[15] For some theologians, cataphaticism is affirmative theology, opposite to apophaticism. This strain of theology uses language positively, suggesting the divine is revealed in the superabundance of life. While apophaticism suggests that language and, therefore, life itself as humans frame it, cannot contain God, cataphatic mysticism affirms God in all things. As Eugene Thacker writes, "the long tradition of meditation on the divine names is often split: those who make positive claims for the divine (the divine can be named, but qualified in a way that places it transcendentally above all things), and those who make negative claims for the divine (the divine can only be named as not-this or not-that)."[16] For example, in the medieval theological work *The Dialogue* by Catherine of Siena, Catherine uses an array of sensual metaphors to capture her experience with Jesus and God. Her description of Jesus's take on gaining truth is rich in motherhood metaphors:

> Just as all truth is gained by the light of faith, so falsehood and delusion are won through infidelity. When I speak of infidelity I am referring to those who have received holy baptism. When they reach the age of discernment, if they had exercised themselves in virtue, they would have kept the light of faith. Then they would have given birth to living virtues, producing fruit for their neighbors. Just as a woman bears a living child and presents it living to her husband, so they would have presented me, the soul's spouse, with living virtues.[17]

In this passage, Catherine relates Jesus's voice as one of a spouse and the virtues as a baby presented to Him by the right-living soul. Similarly, and in a move that queerly touches Sexton's poems and theology, in "The Saints Come Marching In," Sexton writes "Catherine of Sienna, / the illiterate girl who lectured to Popes,/ each word a flower,/ yet hung out cold in its loneliness," becoming a figure for Sexton's narrator, speaking back to power in the hopes of recovering flowering connections.[18] The sexual-spiritual metaphors are rich in Catherine's and Sexton's work; in the above section, Jesus has copulated with the soul to produce these baby-virtues that are presented to him as proof that he has won the soul (no matter the sex of the body). Thus, Catherine's cataphatic language reveals a sensual God, one who is accessible through spousal and sexual metaphors. God *is* a spouse; Jesus *is* the voice speaking to Catherine; the virtues *are*

15 Andrew Louth, "Apophatic and Cataphatic Theology," in *The Cambridge Companion to Christian Mysticism*, ed. Amy Hollywood and Patricia Z. Beckman (Cambridge: Cambridge University Press, 2012), 140.

16 Eugene Thacker, *After Life* (Chicago: The University of Chicago Press, 2010), 38.

17 Catherine of Siena, *The Dialogue*, trans. Suzanne Noffke, OP (New York: Paulist Press, 1980), 94.

18 Sexton, *The Complete Poems*, 469.

children. This echoes Sexton's own materialist celebration of God: "There is hope./ There is hope everywhere./ Today God gives milk/ and I have a pail."[19]

Rather than eschew language for its unwieldiness as one gets closer to God, Sexton uses language's fluidity and indeterminacy to constitute God and God's relationship with the human. Sexton takes the apophatic and cataphatic traditions and queers them by never resting on one or the other. Sexton resists the apophatic/cataphatic binary in order to prevent a naming of God, as God appears in both the material and the immaterial. God is and is more than. And Sexton never rests, as God is always an imperfect process rather than a stable and locatable being. In the poem that leads off Sexton's book, "Rowing," she suggests that God is more than can be contained and yet something revealed in the rowing. "I am rowing, I am rowing," Sexton writes.[20] The inevitable goal is the island which is God: "I know that that island will not be perfect,/ it will have the flaws of life,/ the absurdities of the dinner table,/ but there will be a door."[21] This poem encapsulates the life story of the voice, tracing the journey from being "stamped out like a Plymouth fender" to "school,/ the little straight rows of chairs" to "life/ with its cruel houses."[22] In all of these phases of life, the narrator is stamped, shaped, formed like the plastic dolls and "the devotion to their plastic mouths" of their youth. Sexton creates a world in which the narrator is confined by normality. She could almost be singing Malvina Reynold's 1962 folk hit, "Little Boxes"; Sexton's narrator has had it up to here with this "ticky tacky."

The way to remove herself from the confinement of the normal is through the investment in a relationship with God. Incarnational theology is queered in Sexton's text in that the body is not a stable identity marker (it moves and is fluid), nor is it in binary opposition to divinity. As Linn Marie Tonstad argues, "there is not as such a 'boundary' between divine and human, and certainly divine and human are not a binary. It's because God is God—transcendent—that God can be united with creation, with humanity, in Christ without either violating creaturely existence or giving up God's divinity."[23] The body is not *only* a prison as Sexton states multiple times: "I have a body/ and I cannot escape from it."[24] The body is also the site of divinity. Sexton is arguing for a return to the body in order to find the divine. Sexton challenges us to invent a new language for

---

19 Sexton, "Snow," 468.
20 Ibid., 417.
21 Ibid., 418.
22 Ibid., 417.
23 Linn Marie Tonstad, *Queer Theology* (Eugene, OR: Cascade Books, 2018), 33.
24 Sexton, "The Poet of Ignorance," 434.

God, as binary-gendered language is too confining; gendered language is the prison of the body. Her theology is materialist in that God is often in the acts of matter rather than of spirit. Language is a prison *and* is also the key to unlock that imprisonment.

Despite Sexton's emphasis on process, there are difficulties with a pure process theology. For one, if everything is in process, nothing ever becomes. As a way around pure process theology, and with a move toward a queer mystical theology, Sexton presents a God who has desires and wants: an embodied God. As Sexton writes, God, too, wants a body: "God loafs around heaven,/ without a shape/ but He would like to smoke His cigar/ or bite His fingernails."[25] Sexton is not only practicing a queer theology of the body, but one that encompasses the divine body. As she progresses through this collection, it is a specific approach to the body—we can call it normative—that is confining. Sexton argues that it is the site of the body in which theology is practiced—both God's body and her own. As well, Sexton's theology is here to disturb the normative confines of bodies in order to find God buried within.

Sexton employs cataphatic language as she relates how she grows and "God was there like an island I had not rowed to,/ ignorant of Him."[26] And this is the queer promise of *The Awful Rowing Toward God:* that she will row to him, show us how to row, even if it ultimately means death. Sexton even refuses us an ending in the traditional sense in this first poem. As the poem begins, the narrator exclaims "A story, a story!" but ends with "the story ends with me still rowing."[27] For now. Ending this poem-story with indeterminacy rather than certainty reflects the unstable notion of God that Sexton puts forth throughout. God is and is not.

Queering the Body

Sexton searches for God throughout *The Awful Rowing.* Sexton puts before us an experiential theology that does not agree with T-Theology (as Marcella Althaus-Reid calls traditional, masculinist theology).[28] Sexton's narrator is in tension with Heaven, although she experiences God in the material, other powers resist her experience. For example, in "Not So. Not So," she writes,

---

25 Sexton, "The Earth," 431.
26 Sexton, "Rowing," 417.
27 Ibid., 417–18.
28 See Marcella Althaus-Reid, *Indecent Theology* (London: Routledge, 2000).

He is in the grave of the horses.
He is in the swarm, the frenzy of bees.
He is in the tailor mending my pantsuit.
He is in Boston, raised up by skyscrapers.
He is in the bird, that shameless flyer.
He is in the potter who makes clay into a kiss.
Heaven replies: Not so! Not so![29]

Sexton's God is in the becoming, the swarm, the raising, the making. But, Heaven, which we can read as the official, T-Theology, refuses the narrator's experience of God. Ultimately, there is no resolution between experiential, queer theology and T-Theology until the narrator discovers and recognizes the God within herself as the collection progresses.

Sexton further investigates the being of God through the power of touch in the architecture of the creation story. In the poem "Two Hands," Sexton revisits Genesis, but in this poem, the narrator embodies the voice of a prophet. She is there to see this creation: "From the sea came a hand," she announces, "and God reached out of his mouth/ and called it man./ Up came the other hand/ and God called it woman./ The hands applauded./ And this was no sin./ It was as it was meant to be."[30] Sexton's revisiting of the creation story hydromorphizes God—He is of water, material, and from the water of His mouth comes the creation of humanity. The applause is the celebration of the creation, but Sexton allows the language to slide in this poem. By resisting purely gendered language, she asks us to consider how man and woman are the hands of God. Further, she presents us with a creation that is sensual sound. God creates Himself in the applause, rising from the sea as two hands; He, in turn, creates the sound; that sound is the "human," but the human is also the divine. There is no difference between handclap and author of that sound—the applause of humanity is inextricable from the hands that are man and woman but are also God's hands: both/and.

Later in the poem, the prophet narrator commands the world to applaud: "unwind, hands,/ you angel webs,/ unwind like the coil of a jumping jack,/ cut together and let yourselves fill up with sun/ and applaud, world, applaud."[31] This movement from God's creation through applause to our own creation of ourselves and God through sound bring the poem full circle. This creation is the coming together of hands, as well—mind you, by making one hand male and

29 Sexton, *The Complete Poems*, 472.
30 Ibid., 421.
31 Ibid.

the other female, Sexton does invoke heterosexual commingling; however, it is a queer sex in that there are no bodies to speak of, no orifices, no penetration, only skin surfaces, only sound. It is the coming together of hands that is the sex, the sound that is the joy of orgasm. Sexton represents here a God of sound and water, and in the process, denaturalizes concepts of creation that are found in Genesis, so that we also create each time our hands come together. Subtly, Sexton suggests we are God in our handclaps. However, Sexton has yet to find God fully, to discover his whereabouts within.

As Tonstad comments, "theology, in short, is about sex, money, and God. Theology is about bodies meeting bodies."[32] In "Two Hands," Sexton speaks with the authority of a prophet: I was there, I saw the hands, now get up, now applaud. Her confirmation of her vision is authoritative. In other poems, the struggle with God is more tortured; she invokes a dark ecology, one in which there is insurmountable space between self and God. In Timothy Morton's terms, Sexton begins to acknowledge the "gap," that is, "acknowledging the gap is a paradoxical way of having greater fidelity to things."[33] Sexton tells us in the longest and central poem in the collection, "Is It True?," that "God lives in shit."[34] In this poem, God is base and unknown, and Sexton meditates on how God was removed from her. Sexton writes: "maybe my mother cut the God out of me/ when I was two in my playpen./ Is it too late, too late/ to open the incision and plant Him there again?"[35] This removal of God launches the narrator on a quest. Sexton tries on multiple metaphors:

> Whose God are you looking for? Asked the priest
> I replied: a starving man doesn't ask what the meal is
> I would eat a tomato, or a fire bird, or music
> I would eat a moth soaked in vinegar ...
> I wouldn't mind if God were wooden,
> I'd wear him like a house,
> praise His knot holes,
> shine him like a shoe."[36]

Sexton cannot decide: if God has been excised, how does one or *can* one get Him back? Is He eaten, harkening back to controversies over the nature of the Communion wafer, and if He is edible, what form does He take? The narrator begins

32 Tonstad, *Queer Theology*, 75.
33 Timothy Morton, *Ecology without Nature* (Cambridge: Harvard UP, 2007), 142.
34 Sexton, *The Complete Poems*, 453.
35 Ibid., 448.
36 Ibid., 448–49.

with a tomato, a commonplace image, but then moves further away from the traditionally edible: the firebird, the music, the moth in vinegar. How does one eat these objects? And how does one truly digest the sound? Further, what if God is outside? Sexton attempts to wear him, shine him. They become a God as relatable as wood. These queer touches make Sexton remark that she "would not let Him burn./ I would not burn myself/ for I would be wearing Him."[37] God has become wearable—house, shoe—but, similar to the hands, God is inseparable from the narrator. The wearing of God makes the narrator their own kind of divine being, and thus needing to be protected and nurtured. Sexton gives us a number of these hybrid constructions in order to indicate the inability of distinguishing between the divine and the human, the body and the not-bodied.

This connection between the wood of God and the narrator's place in that ecology reflects another subtle theme that runs through *The Awful Rowing.* Sexton approaches nature and theology as intertwined; in Martin Luther's terminology, creation is the mask of God. Jacob Erickson uses Martin Luther's theology in order to uncover his eco-theological roots: "Luther's human creatures converse with all creatures in odd ways, and those creatures are indwelt with divinity … The finite and the infinite wrap around each other, and the edges blur or transfigure."[38] God is not immaterial, but relishes the fleshly, no matter its form. For Sexton, God "craves the earth."[39] Yet, the earth is also a fraught place in Sexton's work. On the one hand, it contains the joyful: "as new and smooth as a grape,/ as pure as a pond in Alaska,/ as good as the stem of a green bean."[40] But it is also the human-made site of the horrors of Auschwitz and the injustice perpetrated on Native Americans ("visit an Indian reservation and see/ their plastic feathers/ the dead dream").[41] This is not a pure earth, rather one that is both beautiful and destroyed by human interventions, injustice, murder, and oppression. Sexton's narrator admits as much. Despite these tragedies, it is still worth seeking this queer relationship with God, as part of the human comedy and tragedy of life is discovering the divinity within the material and finite.

As Jacob Erickson points out, queer theology and ecology are places in which God and Nature face each other queerly: "my flirtation is that ecological theology is, or can be, a poetry and practice of irreverent criticism, of irreverence

37 Ibid., 449.

38 Jacob J. Erickson, "Irreverent Theology: On the Queer Ecology of Creation," in *Meaningful Flesh: Reflections on Religion and Nature for a Queer Planet*, ed. Whitney A. Bauman (Middletown, DE: punctum, 2019), 69.

39 Sexton, "The Earth," 431.

40 Sexton, "The Evil Seekers," 440.

41 Sexton, "After Auschwitz," 432–33; "The Evil Seekers," 444.

to conceptual realities overwhelmed by ecological crises."[42] Sexton further reorients herself in terms of the natural object: "I have/ for some time, called myself Ms. Dog. Why?/ Because I am almost animal/and yet the animal I lost most—/ that animal is near to God,/ but lost from Him."[43] Ms. Dog and God are linked in their mutual animality.

The poem moves again, to a contemplation of language: Sexton writes:

> No language is perfect.
> I only know English.
> English is not perfect.
> When I tell the priest I am full
> of bowel movement, right into the fingers,
> he shrugs. To him shit is good.
> To me, to my mother, it was poison
> and the poison was all of me ...
> That's why language fails.
> Because to one, shit is a feeder of plants,
> to another the evil that permeates them ...
> So much for language.
> So much for psychology.
> God lives in the shit—I have been told.[44]

Sexton's line of thought is intriguing in that, building backwards, if God is in the shit, he is truly unknowable through language, since language means something different to different people. But, her final verdict that "God is in the shit" attempts to both deny the reliability of language and confirm where He can be found (and *named* by language). He is in her; if she is full of it, then His presence is there, and by indicating His presence in fecal matter, then it only goes to follow that He is in her, as well. The proof of God's being and materiality is present each time we flush. This is not obscene; rather, it is the divine in the human. It is the admittance that bodies even at their most base are linked with Incarnation.

If in these two poems we have Sexton exploring God through the voice of the prophet and the voice of one in abjection, then I want to next turn to Sexton's use of the voice of the triumphant. Tonstad writes that "queer hermeneutics, queer ways of interpreting and knowing, search for the alternatives that are already there and need to be found. They search for the bodies in which God is

42 Erickson, "Irreverent Theology," 60.
43 Sexton, "Is it True?," 452.
44 Ibid., 453.

to be found."[45] Throughout the collection, Sexton has worked to queer her body so that God can be found. In "The Civil War," Sexton returns to contemplating the God within her. However, this time she, not her mother, will be the one doing the excising of God. She writes: "I will take scissors/ and cut out the beggar./ I will take a crowbar/ and pry out the broken/ pieces of God in me … / I will put him together again/ with the patience of a chess player."[46] This image of removing the broken-pieced God in order to put him together again, "united" as Sexton writes at the end of the poem, takes on a Whitmanesque sound when she writes that she will "build a new soul/ dress it with skin/ and then put on my shirt/ and sing an anthem,/ a song of myself."[47] These multitudinous pieces are made up of "God dressed up like a whore," "God dressed up like an old man," "God dressed up like a child," and "others, others, others."[48] This God is non-binary. This God is old and young. This God is a whore. Sexton will "conquer them all" and "build a whole nation of God."[49] This idea of conquering the multitude, to make it one, as a way to sing a song of herself is the project of *The Awful Rowing Toward God*. I choose to read this not as an erasure of God as whore, old man, child, but rather an assembling, an extension of the being of God into queer identities. God's hybridity is a never-ending chain of identities. God is no longer in pieces, but a queer body that encompasses all of these "others, others, others." Sexton is the queer body that contains them all. Sexton's narrator refuses a stable body, opting for a hybrid body that most expresses her animal-being that allows for God's extensive being to be realized.

Queering Death

Perhaps the hardest issue that Sexton wrestles with is death. As she promises early on, "there will be a door/ and I will open it/ and I will get rid of the rat inside of me … / God will take it with his two hands/ and embrace it."[50] The rat inside the narrator is the narrator's pain that God will embrace. God does not recoil from the rat of pain. As God was contained in the body in life, Sexton implies in death, when the rowing is over, God will also embrace the animal-soul. As Tonstad comments, "Queerness then *affirms finitude*; it recognizes the

45 Tonstad, *Queer Theology*, 87.
46 Sexton, *The Complete Poems*, 418.
47 Ibid., 419.
48 Ibid., 418–19.
49 Ibid., 419.
50 Sexton, "Rowing," 418.

inescapable tragedy of human existence."[51] It is important to affirm our finitude because the promise of Resurrection, in turn, queers death.

In queer theology, the resurrection of Christ "overwhelms death with life."[52] Elizabeth Stuart calls for an "*ars moriendi* for our time in which we queer cultural constructions of death to reveal the sacramental nature of dying."[53] In Sexton's final poem, "The Rowing Endeth," the narrator moors their boat "onto the flesh of the Island;" this is "the island called God."[54] There the narrator plays poker with God. God, however, is a crooked poker player, though His cheating results in laughter: "such laughter that He doubles right over me/ laughing a Rejoice-Chorus at our two triumphs./ Then I laugh, the fishy dock laughs,/ the sea laughs. The Island laughs./ The Absurd laughs."[55] This laughter, this sound, is the sound of the promise of the joy of resurrection. Like the handclap was the sound of creation, the laugh is the sound of resurrection and triumph. This universal laughter resonates historically with what Stuart describes as the *risus paschalis* (Easter laughter), which "involved preachers using earthly humor to the delight of their congregations. The humor encapsulated the joy at the resurrection and the end of death."[56] At the end of the rowing is not grief, even though the hands are inflicted with "blisters that broke and healed/ and broke and healed."[57] It is the laughter of God, who is also the Island itself, and the cheating poker player, and the fishy dock, and the Absurd that the narrator joins in laughter with; their polyphonous laughter is the sound of joy in the face of the defeat of death. The rowing may have ended, but the laughter is the note we go out on.

In considering Sexton's queer, materialist theophany, we can see the promise of reimagining our relationships with something that is both embedded in us and something that is completely not us. With Noreen Giffney and Myra Hird, who define queer theory's emphasis on "fluidity, uber-inclusivity, indeterminancy, indefinability, unknowability, the preposterous, impossibility, unthinkability, unintelligibility, meaninglessness and that which is unrepresentable in an at-

---

51 Tonstad, *Queer Theology*, 130.

52 Elizabeth Stuart, "Queering Death," in *The Sexual Theologian: Essays on Sex, God, and Politics*, ed. Marcella Althaus-Reid and Lisa Isherwood (London: T&T Clark International, 2004), 62. For a discussion of death in terms of queer grief, see Maia Kotrosits, "Queer Persistence: On Death, History, and Longing for Endings," *Sexual Disorientations: Queer Temporalities, Affects, Theologies*, ed. Kent L. Brintnall, Joseph A. Marchal, and Stephen D. Moore (New York: Fordham University Press, 2018), 133–44.

53 Stuart, "Queering Death," 63.

54 Sexton, *The Complete Poems*, 473.

55 Ibid., 474.

56 Stuart, "Queering Death," 65.

57 Sexton, "The Rowing Endeth," 473.

tempt to undo normative entanglements and fashion alternative imaginaries,"[58] Sexton queers herself and queers God by trying on God, being God, reducing God, turning God into a mouth and hands, which, in turn are man and woman, who make sound that is God, and that is good.

The basket of fire is a metaphor to end this paper: Sexton asks how does one hold fire? In the poem "The Witch's Life," Sexton makes of herself "a hermit/ opening the door for only/ a few special animals";[59] she is a hybrid spanning centuries, who waits "holding a basket of fire."[60] The image invokes the secluded hermit and the burning heart of Jesus. But it is also a queer image, one that resists cause and effect, in that the (wooden) basket is not eaten by the flames it holds. How do we keep the fire stoked if it does not eat that which is containing it? Along these same lines, we can imagine the body holding God: twisting, melting, merging, and in Butler's phrasing, de-subjugating. Sexton leaves us with the image of the narrator-rower, docked on the fleshy island that is God. They play the game of poker. God cheats; he has five aces, and the narrator has a royal flush. It is a surprising ending to a collection full of fraught searching. Much like the handclap that constitutes God and the human in the sound, in the end, laughter is the improbable reaction to death. Once the rowing-narrator realizes that God is the island itself, a geographical body of flesh, laughter results, immersing us in the joy of our finitude and materializing the queerness of God. As we read, as we journey, as we row through *The Awful Rowing Toward God*, God will also emerge from our mouths.

58 Noreen Giffney and Myra J. Hird, "Introduction: Queering the Non/Human," in *Queering the Non/Human*, ed. Noreen Giffney and Myra J. Hird (Aldershot: Ashgate, 2008), 4.
59 Sexton, *The Complete Poems*, 423.
60 Ibid., 424.

Candace Barrington

feeld Notes: Jos Charles's Chaucerian "anteseedynts"

Praedicat et subjicit, fit duplex terminus idem,
Grammaticae leges ampliat ille nimis.
– Alanus de Insulis, *Liber de Planctu Naturae*[1]

Well, we're taught—particularly, in elementary school—to learn a standardized language. And when you ask, why is it this way, why is this the standard, you arrive at a very arbitrary answer, and an answer which actually excludes, often, people of color. "Your English is wrong. This English is right." But, in fact, language is always changing. And I think it's the poets, the writers, and even the youth—they're using language to cast new meaning, in the same way Chaucer just winged English spelling. There was no standardized spelling.
– Ocean Vuong[2]

I'm always on the lookout for Chaucerian texts, so when I heard about a poetry collection written in Chaucerian English, I immediately ordered Jos Charles's *feeld* (2018).[3] With the rush of the semester, the slender volume sat on my desk for several months, but once I read it, I was immediately struck by how this use of Chaucerian English created a space where a non-trans reader could feel something akin to a trans experience. Because I came to Jos Charles's verse not as a member of the trans community or an LGBTQ scholar, but as a

1 "He is subject and predicate; one and the same term is given a double application," Alan of Lille, *The Plaint of Nature*, trans. James J. Sheridan (Toronto: Pontifical Institute of Mediaeval Studies, 1980), 68.

2 "Interview with Krista Tippett," April 30, 2020, in *On Being*, podcast and transcript, https://onbeing.org/programs/ocean-vuong-a-life-worthy-of-our-breath/.

3 I wrote this essay with the support of my colleagues, my university, and my friends. My departmental writers' group—Heidi Hartwig, Jaclyn Geller, and Katherine Sugg—read an early version and helped me articulate the insights medievalism can share with transgender studies. I presented early iterations of its argument at the ALSCW Conference at College of the Holy Cross, Worcester, MA, in October 2019. The seminar participants—Kathleen Kelly, Kathryn Lynch, Sarah Stanbury, and Anna Wilson—helped me articulate the insights transgender studies provides medievalism. And, as always, Mike Shea provided wise editorial advice.

https://doi.org/10.1515/9781501511189-005

Chaucerian and a trans ally, my initial reading was shaped by my familiarity and comfort with reading Middle English, my openness to appropriations, and my support for the trans community. This essay builds on that initial experience and subsequent study. My goal in this essay will be less to explain what *feeld* means and more to suggest some of the ways it makes that meaning. In doing so, I will not interrogate, unmask, expose, subvert, unveil, demystify, take issue, or take umbrage. As someone learned in Middle English, I see my task as guiding readers to see what is there—not what is hidden—and to suggest ways *feeld* can be a rewarding and moving experience for those unfamiliar with Middle English.

Both at the volume's publication and with its multiple honors—including its selection as the Winner of the 2017 National Poetry Series and its nomination as one of three finalists for the 2019 Pulitzer Prize in Poetry—much of the commentary and many reviews noted that Charles's incorporation of Chaucerian Middle English syntax, semantics, orthography, and reading conventions allows readers to explore—even experience—the emotional, physical, and social ramifications of a particular aspect of the trans(gender) experience: the medical alignment of an individual's gender through procedures that include pharmaceutical and surgical interventions.[4] Not unusual is R. L. Goldberg's praise in *Paris Review* for the collection's language that "itself transitions," "defamiliarize[s]" and in that process "opens to a poly-vocality where words contain hidden meanings."[5] As tempting as this assessment might be, I think it does not do justice to Charles's accomplishment. Rather than searching *feeld* for hidden meanings, I suggest that we return to its Middle and Chaucerian "anteseedynts" to find that Charles's poetics encourage us to see what has been there all along: readings we are not accustomed to seeing and meanings we've been trained to ignore or label as "wrong." In this way, we find that Charles has created a transpoetics more hopeful than might first seem possible.

Jos Charles's "anteseedynts" invoke a linguistic medievalism that defamiliarizes the familiar (our written language) and draws the reader into a most intimate process (the transition from one embodied gender to another). Across its 60 lyrics, we are taken from the room where "the grl beguines" and led to the point where she "a woake 1 mornynge / 2 see the hole whorld | off thynges befor me."[6] We

---

4 See "Finalist: *feeld*, by Jos Charles," The Pulitzer Prizes, https://www.pulitzer.org/finalists/jos-charles.

5 R. L. Goldberg, "Review: The Historical Future of Trans Literature," *Paris Review*, August 13, 2018, https://www.theparisreview.org/blog/2018/08/13/the-historical-future-of-trans-literature/.

6 Jos Charles, *feeld* (Minneapolis, Milkweed, 2018), 2, 61. In my text citations, the virgules [/] are from *feeld*; the vertical lines [|] indicate a line break at the right-hand margin and are my addition.

might be initially surprised by this invocation of fourteenth-century English for exploring "transitioning" because we erroneously limit our concept of "moving from one gender to another" with gender-confirming surgery, a medical procedure available only in the past 60 years.[7] Our misperceptions are corrected when we realize that *feeld* is concerned with a wide array of transitioning's social, physical, emotional, and medical aspects. In this light, Jos Charles's deft handling of Chaucerian English makes the juxtaposition seem inevitable. The resulting verse becomes, without pushing the analogy too hard, akin to medieval hocket (so brilliantly modernized by Meredith Monk in *Facing North*)—wherein two voices of different timbres share the melody line sequentially (not simultaneously).[8] Like hocket, *feeld* allows two timbres—Middle English and Present-Day English—to occupy the same line. Because it encourages us to engage playfully (and attentively) with language and meaning-making, the verse teaches Charles's readers to recognize and abandon engrained sensibilities that frequently govern literary interpretation. This defamiliarization and destabilization through playful readings also exposes the raw, uncertain realities of a trans experience to her readers, who are confronted with the uncomfortable question: "how manie | holes wuld blede / befor | u believ / imma grl."[9] Her use of Middle English recreates the felt experience of reading a text in a language simultaneously familiar and unfamiliar. At the same time she addresses the lack of linguistic options for describing a trans experience, she also challenges readers to explore new reading experiences. She explains in an interview that the "perceived difficulty" of the orthography reminds her of "trying to learn to read" and the "insecurity of not being sure how to pronounce things or what something means." This difficulty, she continues, lends itself to recreate that experience of "figuring out where one's place already is in language, where one fits —horribly, surprisingly, pleasantly—and doesn't fit."[10] The resulting transpoetics nudges readers away from a hermeneutic that defines either gender or semantics as predetermined, fixed, or hidden.

These "*feeld* notes" accept Jos Charles's invitation to engage with her transpoetics, which finds in the historical archives the language appropriate to repre-

---

7 Mary Collins and Donald Collins, *At the Broken Places: A Mother and Trans Son Pick Up the Pieces* (Boston: Beacon Press, 2017), 12.

8 Willi Apel, ed., *The Harvard Dictionary of Music*, 2nd ed. (1972), s.v. "hocket." Meredith Monk, "Hocket," on *Facing North*, ECM Records, 1992. Available online: https://www.youtube.com/watch?v=6q4puw29Xm4.

9 Charles, *feeld*, 55.

10 Jos Charles, "Bowl of Oranges: An Interview of Kaveh Akbar," *The American Poetry Review* 47, no. 5 (2018), https://aprweb.org/poems/bowl-of-oranges-an-interview-with-kaveh-akbar.

sent the transgender subject.[11] I will begin by describing some characteristics of Middle English that make it suitable for articulating a poetics that transgender literary theorists have described as a set of "techniques for communicating 'complex, unstable, contradictory relations between body and soul, social self and psyche,'" a series of goals not unique to transgender poets.[12] What distinguishes many transpoetic projects from others is the effort to trouble conventional boundaries defining not only gender identities but also any identities that would be managed and controlled by fixed systems and rigid binaries. Transpoetic techniques work to reveal the multifaceted possibilities of each utterance and of each individual. Thus, in the final line of Trace Peterson's "The Valleys Are So Lush and Steep," the narrator simultaneously rejects herself and turns back on that rejection: "How to end now wanting to be myself being not quite myself."[13] As do many other poetic efforts, transpoetics thrives where boundaries are blurred, relationships unstable, and meanings ambiguous, an environment resembling the one inhabited by Middle English texts and therefore making it a fertile landscape for Jos Charles's transpoetics.

By querying and queering Chaucer's experiments in poetic diction and speech registers, *feeld* also invites us to place it alongside a noted Chaucerian performance, the Wife of Bath. Like this Chaucerian gender performance, *feeld* builds upon and then upends the commonplace medieval analogy between grammar and gender as means for describing and regulating each. Ultimately, Charles' verse overturns Alanus de Insulis's critique that the rules of grammar and of nature are defied whenever an individual embodies the double position of both "subject and predicate." By embracing some central features of Middle English and Chaucerian poetics, *feeld* suggests that just as Chaucer created interpretive complexity in Middle English without needing a set of rigid grammatical rules to corral and limit the hermeneutical process, so can trans identity be articulated without recourse to the "currently dominant binary sex/gender ideology of Eurocentric modernity."[14]

---

11 Goldberg, "Review: The Historical Future of Trans Literature."

12 Rebekah Edwards, "Trans-poetics," *TSQ: Transgender Studies Quarterly* 1, no. 1–2 (2014): 252–53, with quotation from Joy Ladin, "Trans Poetics Manifesto," in *Troubling the Line: Trans and Genderqueer Poetry and Poetics*, ed. T. C. Tolbert and Trace Peterson (Callicoon, NY: Nightboat Books, 2013), 299–307 at 306.

13 Available online: https://poets.org/poem/valleys-are-so-lush-and-steep.

14 Susan Stryker, "(De)Subjugated Knowledges: An Introduction to Transgender Studies," in *The Transgender Studies Reader* (New York: Routledge, 2006), 3. In making this argument, I am aware that not all members of the transgender community see gender as non-binary. For them, gender is binary but misassigned. Jos Charles's verse (as well as published and private interviews and talks) suggest that for her gender is more fluid than binary dynamics would sug-

To see this process, I begin by describing four Middle English (ME) features that make it amenable to Charles's transpoetic project. First, it is the result of a diachronic accumulation of multiple linguistic ruptures. Second, ME thrived in a synchronic, multilingual milieu. Third, it was not subjected to a regime of correctness. And fourth, ME has been transmitted to us via a manuscript culture. Middle English's unfamiliarity to the general reader of Present-Day English (PDE) helps us see that differences we easily ignore or explain away as irregularities of PDE are actually integral to the formation of English as we know it. Next, by focusing on the first two lines of *feeld*'s first lyric, "thees wite skirtes," I trace how Middle English works as an integral element in Jos Charles's transpoetics. Finally, I consider the ways the collection reconceives the dramatic monologue of Chaucer's Wife of Bath.

One feature of Middle English that Charles's *feeld* exploits is the series of historical ruptures in the language's development, ruptures that might otherwise be invisible to modern readers. The historical roots of Chaucer's late-medieval English extend to Old English (OE), the language that evolved from the languages of Germanic tribes who displaced the indigenous Britons and dominated much of England after the sixth century. OE existed in multiple varieties, each shaped differently by the Anglo-Saxons' engagement with varieties of Norse, Celtic, and Latin. After the 1066 Norman Conquest, the English speakers absorbed, to varying degrees, the languages and dialects of the new Francophone ruling class. By the late fourteenth century, there were several identifiable forms of ME, none following rules agreed upon by everyone but basically intelligible across a wide spectrum of speakers and readers. ME vocabulary straddled the old and the new, still retaining OE words that subsequently dropped from PDE —such as "wite" and "guerdon"—and veering toward forms soon recognizable in PDE.[15] Even as it shifted away from its Germanic roots, ME used OE strategies of word formation (compounding and affixation) to import words from other languages into its semantic field.[16] ME retains some (but not all) of OE's rules for

---

gest. Consequently, I will follow her lead in my discussion of the complex politics surrounding these issues and deal with one very limited aspect of the trans experience, one that involves medical intervention and sees gender as fluid and non-binary. This experience contrasts with the experiences of those in the trans community who embrace gender binaries and see medical interventions as correcting a mistake.

15 Seth Lerer, "What was Medieval English?" in *Imagining Medieval English: Language Structures and Theories, 500–1500*, ed. Tim William Machan (Cambridge: Cambridge University Press, 2016), 15–33, citing 31.

16 Simon Horobin and Jeremy Smith, *An Introduction to Middle English* (Oxford: Oxford University Press, 2002), 79.

creating tense, tending more toward so-called "weak verb" formations rather than "strong verb" formations. The same is true for plurals, moving to "s" suffixes, which make plurals almost indistinguishable from possessives until the apostrophe is introduced as a grapheme to mark possession. Middle English retains much of the unhomogenized evidence of its centuries of linguistic accretions, the nature of which varied from region to region. This transvernacularity incorporates and deploys the development of language across time, making it one of the factors that lends each utterance so much polysemantic and polysyntactic possibility.

As a corollary to these historical ruptures, Middle English coexisted intimately with other languages that shaped and influenced it. Throughout the medieval period, Middle English was one of several languages spoken in England, and it was not the primary written language. French was the principal written vernacular used in commerce, law, and politics; and Latin was the language of the church, of learning, and of international communication. In this context, ME did not develop as an autonomous linguistic phenomenon; instead, it was formed in a multilingual environment where "a shifting set of relationships" created meaning "through a constant process of contrast, discrimination, overlap, and rivalry."[17] For example, when Old French words like "entente" entered the ME semantic field through the common law courts, they came loaded with legal connotations not found in the French context. In this milieu of mixed and repurposed languages, code-switching and multilingualism would have been the norm for Middle English readers, writers, and speakers. For them, translating, transposing, appropriating, and misappropriating were standard linguistic habits, again leading to polysemantic and polysyntactical wordplay. As a result, merging its vocabularies, structures, and orthographic features with those of French and Latin, ME did not carry a heavy baggage of "correctness." Paradoxically, PDE, the language deemed more orderly than ME, is a highly irregular language because of these first two characteristics. Modern English could have taken many different forms under different circumstances. What is now standard English results from centuries of choices and changes, nothing predetermined or required.

Throughout the medieval period, there were no efforts to impose standards for "correct" English; strictures did not appear until the eighteenth century (with Samuel Johnson's *Dictionary* providing a prime example). For readers accustomed to PDE's widespread standardization, ME can seem confused, primitive,

17 Ardis Butterfield, *The Familiar Enemy: Chaucer, Language, and Nation in the Hundred Years War* (Oxford: Oxford University Press, 2009), 11–14.

unstable, inconsistent—compromised by its incompatible variety. Because English was not taught by educators nor widely used by bureaucrats, no authority such as schools or bureaucracies issued rules governing how the language should be correctly spoken or written. Despite there being no "standard language" against which statements could or should be measured, there was clearly a consensus among readers, writers, and speakers about the ways ME, in all its varieties, created meanings.[18] Depending on the particular purpose at hand, English vernaculars were adapted to fit the need. Consequently, "long sentences, unsure in their subordinate clauses and relative pronouns," and "idiosyncratic blends of form and lexicon"—constructions that repeatedly defy our ability to pin down a written expression to a single, stable meaning—allowed Middle English readers and writers to convey and comprehend complex meanings.[19] Because orthographic conventions in the late-medieval period remained very flexible—they depended on the regional preferences of scribes rather than on some agreed-upon universal convention—almost every written text displays an example of polysemy.

The weave of possible meanings caused by a lack of standardization was further fostered by the conventions of a manuscript culture that included irregular capitalization and minimal punctuation. Slashes seem to have been more attuned to metrical units than syntactical ones, and white space (or its absence) structured meaning. Although ME manuscripts allowed more free play and encouraged a wider range of meanings, manuscripts that seem to us untamed by modern conventions proved quite capable of revealing to readers what the scribes considered "well-formed English."[20] In fact, aural readings (which allowed a larger audience for each manuscript) lessened the ambiguity, with the lector's intonation and voice supplying punctuation and clarifications. That oral delivery has been replaced for PDE readers with texts that discourage the hermeneutic play by adding notes, glosses, emendations, punctuation, and all the other trappings of modern scholarly editions in order to tie down a meaning and make the text understandable to today's readers.

---

18 Tim William Machan, "Snakes, Ladders, and Standard Language," in *Imagining Medieval English: Language Structures and Theories, 500–1500*, ed. Tim William Machan (Cambridge: Cambridge University Press, 2016), 54–78 at 67.

19 Lerer, "What was Medieval English?" 15–33 at 31 and 33.

20 Tim William Machan, "The Metaphysics of Medieval English," in *Imagining Medieval English: Language Structures and Theories, 500–1500*, ed. Tim William Machan (Cambridge: Cambridge University Press, 2016), 3–12 at 5. To these conventions, we can add factors that do not come into play in Jos Charles's transpoetics: manuscripts often included such distinguishing "mistakes" as scribal errors (for example, eye-skips and misread minums) and scribal "adjustments."

Of course, the first two characteristics—diachronic accretion of outside influences and the synchronic multicultural environment—remain attributes of PDE, though they are too often recognized and labeled as "irregularities" rather than as inherent features of English's historical development. The second two—lack of standardization and the conventions of manuscript culture—distinguish ME from PDE. Together, these four characteristics mean that each Middle English utterance is deeply defined by its relationships to other languages, other peoples, other understandings, other marks on the page.[21] This "architecture of associations" allowed Middle English to be "deeply ambiguous."[22]

When Jos Charles harnesses these four characteristics to transform Middle English into a vehicle for transpoetics, the resulting verse differs from other linguistic medievalisms.[23] She is not writing *in* Middle English (or even in a modified version of Middle English), a much different technique from the one used by Paul Kingsnorth, who resurrected and modified Old English in his 2014 novel *The Wake*, set in the years immediately following William of Normandy's 1066 invasion. In order to create a linguistic atmosphere not occluded by the language of the French invaders, Kingsnorth created what he calls a "shadow tongue." With this "pseudo-language," Kingsnorth seeks to "convey the feelings of the old language by combining some of its vocabulary and syntax with the English we speak today."[24] In important ways, the novel's language is limited by its invocation of OE: he predominately prefers words available to or derived from OE; he does not use non-OE letters (such as <k>, <v>, <j>, and <q>); he prefers OE orthography over PDE spellings; and he mutates PDE words to make them feel OE.[25] He explains that he aligned the novel's language with the world and people it depicts in order to convey "the sheer alienness [*sic*] of Old England."[26]

The Middle English in Jos Charles's lyrics works in a significantly different manner. Rather than being written *in* Middle English, the lyrics mimic the malleability and fluidity of Middle English. Though the lyrics reach back to fourteenth-century English for another way of creating meaning, they do not do so in order to evoke another time and place or to create an archaic feel. Jos Charles's use of

21 Lerer, "What was Medieval English?" 18.

22 J. D. Burnley, *A Guide to Chaucer's Language* (Basingstoke: Macmillan, 1983), 155.

23 Other examples include Caroline Bergvall's *Meddle English* (2012), Seamus Heaney's translations and poetic oeuvre, and J. R. R. Tolkien's Middle Earth trilogy.

24 Paul Kingsnorth, *The Wake* (London: Unbound, 2014), 353. Though Kingsnorth's novel was initially funded through crowdsourcing, it did not remain an outlier for long. It was longlisted for the 2014 Man Booker Prize and won the 2014 Gordon Burn Prize.

25 Kingsnorth, *The Wake*, 353–55.

26 Ibid., 356.

Middle English brings together two languages separated by 600 years to illustrate a possible mode of reading and creating meaning that assumes "a world of subsequent texts in which history had played out quite differently."[27] Similarly, I will argue, her use of Middle English does not convey either "the sheer alienness" or the irrationality of the transgender experience. Instead, the inherent ambiguity of Middle English and the arbitrary development of PDE provide a fertile ground for growing new meanings that, in turn, allow her to bypass those linguistic and cultural strictures imposed on the transgender experience by PDE and its modern users.[28] As we will see, because Jos Charles seeks to communicate generously, her use of ME is neither profligate nor unpredictable. Her desire to express a specific set of experiences prevents her from allowing language's linguistic variability to spin out of control.

Reading *feeld* encourages us to employ three reading modes: like a PDE reader, like an ME reader, and like both simultaneously. Returning to the musical analogy of hocket, the PDE and ME modes alternate to create a third mode, the complete sequential line that embraces the possibilities of the PDE and ME, while letting the resonance weave in a third strand of possibility.

As for the first mode, reading like a PDE reader is sufficient enough to gain an emotionally *felt* experience of *feeld*, even for those readers who expect the text to convey meaning through well-formed sentences that follow grammatical conventions and use regularized spelling. Although these readers might be initially frustrated when unfamiliar words appear and their definitions cannot be found in a dictionary (which might list alternate spellings, but only those deemed acceptable), these readers have the tools for reading *feeld* at this most rudimentary level. They already know to depend on contexts in order to distinguish meanings when words with different meanings and etymologies share the exact same spellings and pronunciations. In fact, accomplished readers of English verse know that, despite potential misunderstandings, one of the beauties of reading English literature is the ability to blur semantic distinctions. For example, when Shakespeare writes "Speak of my lameness, and I straight will halt" (Sonnet 89, l. 3), he asks us to hold in our mind both "stop" and "limp" when we read the word "halt." The most satisfying reading of this sonnet does not choose one meaning over the other but embraces them simultaneously, listens to how they speak to one another, and understands how their conversation cre-

27 Jos Charles, email message to author, August 29, 2019.

28 In making this argument, I will not (at least not at this particular moment) assume that fourteenth-century England was a transgender-friendly time and place.

ates a dense network of meaning for the poem. Similarly, a PDE reader of *feeld* intuitively knows how to handle homophones and puns.

Once PDE readers remember they have several techniques for apprehending a word with multiple semantic possibilities, they will be able to move beyond their frustration and confusion. First, as I noted above, PDE readers have long been accustomed to reading and understanding the syllepses, paronomasias, or wordplays inherent in a PDE word. Readers of *feeld* will find the 60 lyrics saturated with multiple nodes of homophones, such as "whole"/"hole"; "hart"/ "heart"; "stairs"/"stares"; and "reel"/"real." In the past generation, readers have added reading techniques honed by the proliferation of texting abbreviations. Girded with these skills, Jos Charles's readers will be able to multiply the possible syllepses because texting (and other electronic messaging) has taught them to ignore spellings. They know to reach for homophones whenever a lexeme doesn't appear to be a word. So, alongside the ampersand ("&"), they find "r," "i," "u," "1," "2," and "4." Not only do these phonemes represent the letters "r," "i," "u" as well as the numbers "1," "2," and "4," they also recall their homophones: "are" / "our," "I" / "eye," "you" / "ewe," "won," "to" / "too," and "for" / "fore." Traditional punning and contemporary texting have taught readers to read this way. Consequently, when readers without any facility with ME encounter what appears to be a misspelling, they can read "feeld" as "field" and thereby weave a satisfying understanding of Charles's poetry.

This PDE reading strategy is probably best understood by experiencing the poems aurally, the method that prevailed throughout the Middle Ages. By listening to Charles's reading of the poems (I recommend her recorded reading at the Chicago Humanities Festival), the series' poetic structure is discernible.[29] Listened to, rather than seen, the text presents its obscurity as syntactical rather than orthographic or semantic. Thus, when she reads aloud "LVII. tonite i wuld luv," she's done the work of translating for the reader, and nothing disruptive or jarring or alienating occurs. This oral PDE reading provides one of the most immediate and moving moments in the sequence, recounting both the short life expectancies of trans women (under 27) and the grief of losing so many beloved fellow travelers.

The second reading mode, reading like an ME reader, further enriches the process of creating meaning. To the nexus of PDE meanings any word and its homophones might have, we are asked to add ME words that no longer exist in everyday PDE. This requires knowledge of ME (or recourse to an ME dictionary). For

29 Recorded at the Chicago Humanities Festival, November 3, 2018, https://www.youtube.com/watch?v=Z3pMcmnc16M, accessed April 10, 2020.

example, to the strands of meaning for "reed" / "read," we can add ME "rēd," with meanings ranging across "advice," "permission," and "wisdom."[30] When "hands" is spelled "handes," the final "e" invokes the homophone cluster "hende" / "handy" that knits the meanings "courtly" with "grabby" and that forms the core of *The Miller's Tale*'s description of Nicholas (1.3199).[31] This echo occurs in "XXI. being graselesse" when the *persona* reminds herself that "i muste | re member / plese kepe ur handes | 2 urself/."[32] Or if we mind the virgules, the *persona* reminds the implied audience: "plese kepe ur handes | 2 urself/." Either way, "handes" carries with it the right to grab what they please that even the most refined and "well-mannered" men assume they possess. These (and over 40 other) homophone clusters invoking ME or pseudo-ME spellings provide a greater range of meaning for each word, each line, each lyric.

Beyond enriching each word's semantic possibilities, reading like an ME reader means encountering multiple syntactic possibilities, a phenomenon Tim William Machan has designated as "the metaphysics of medieval English: the language's structural traits [as well as] the sociolinguistic and theoretical expectations that frame them and make them real."[33] Unlike the vocabulary glosses current readers of many Middle English texts are now provided, fourteenth-century texts were not originally saddled with "contemporary notions of linguistic regularity and irregularity, error, and self-expression."[34] Of course, these ways of creating meaning can be found in any English verse, but *feeld* highlights distinctly ME methods for creating this syntactical multiplicity and ambiguity, features that guide us toward an understanding of a particular trans experience. For instance, we are encouraged to loosen up our readerly habits by the Middle English virgule, a punctuation feature that can often separate, frequently highlight, and sometimes end an expressed idea, all without creating hard boundaries. In the opening lines of the fourteenth lyric, we see the virgule working with "irreg-

30 *Middle English Dictionary*, s.v. "red (n.1)," accessed February 10, 2020, https://quod.lib.umich.edu/m/middle-english-dictionary/dictionary/MED36280/track?counter=1&search_id=11835734.

31 *Middle English Dictionary*, s.v. "hende (adj.)," accessed February 10, 2020, https://quod.lib.umich.edu/m/middle-english-dictionary/dictionary/MED20378/track?counter=1&search_id=11846668. Unless noted otherwise, all quotations and line numbers from Chaucer follow *The Riverside Chaucer*, ed. Larry D. Benson, 3rd ed. (Boston: Houghton Mifflin, 1987).

32 Charles, *feeld*, 21.

33 Machan, "Metaphysics of Medieval English," 4.

34 Ibid., 9. See also my article describing a series of exercises I assign to help students work beyond this tendency: "Teaching Chaucer in Middle English: A Fundamental Approach," in "Innovative Approaches to Teaching Chaucer," *Studies in Medieval and Renaissance Teaching* 22, no. 1 (Spring 2015): 21–32.

ular" punctuation and spelling to create an explosion of meaning: "its ther / inn | the feeld / the waye 2 inclose | & disclose a treee."[35] Each set of words within a virgule can stand alone, attach itself to previous words, precede the next set of words, or (as often happens) do all three simultaneously. The short passage can be read straight through, something like, "It's there in (or therein) the field the way to enclose and disclose a tree." Or we could put more pressure on the virgules, rendering the line as "It's there, in the field, the way to enclose and disclose a tree." Or we can heed the line ends as vectors of meaning-making and read the passage as something like, "It's their inn; the field, the way to enclose. And disclose a tree." Except for the punctuation that reinforces in the second instance that the important "there" is "in the field," the first and second readings follow the copula with a series of modifiers. The third possibility transforms the relationships so that "the field" is the tenor of the metaphorical inn that houses and exhibits the tree. The subtle shifts illustrated here bring out our knowledge of Middle English orthographic, manuscript, and reading practices; however, this approach provides a heavy-handed, very unsatisfying reading of the poem and perhaps a misguided reading of a trans experience.

To see how deft the poetic voice truly is in these poems, we must adopt a third reading mode, one that moves back and forth, reading across Middle English and Present-Day English. As much as we might want to join Kaveh Akbar's exclamation that Charles has gifted the reader with an "unprecedented syntax to accommodate an unprecedented experience," the truth remains that Charles draws on Chaucerian (and other literary) "anteseedynts" for her verse.[36] The past informs how she expresses and understands her "unprecedented experience." For this reason, we must train ourselves to think beyond the either/or construct of PDE or ME by exploring how those two reading modes engage with one another to create a new line of interpretive possibilities. We can begin by identifying new words using spelling and grammar conventions that combine the ones from ME and PDE, allowing them to create a new set of hermeneutical opportunities and creating the most expansive form of what translation theorists call "hyper-translation."[37] We are able to create these interpretive strands because, in Jos Charles's rendering via Middle English, transpoetics is a pedagog-

35 Charles, *feeld*, 14.

36 Charles, "Bowl of Oranges: An Interview of Kaveh Akbar."

37 Emily Apter, *Against World Literature: On the Politics of Untranslatability* (Brooklyn, NY: Verso, 2013). See also see Candace Barrington, "Hypertranslation and *Translatio Studii*," review essay in the special issue "Thinking Across Tongues," ed. Jonathan Hsy, Mary Kate Hurley, and Andrew Kraebel, *postmedieval* 8 (2017): 376–92.

ical poetics: more than finding multiple meanings, we are being taught to remove our cultural blinders.

To see how this pedagogical practice works, let's turn to the first poem of the series.

I.
thees wite skirtes / & orang
sweters / i wont / inn the feedynge marte /
    wile mye vegetable partes bloome /
    inn the commen waye / a grackel
    inn the guarden rooste / the tall
    wymon wasching hands /
        or eyeing turnups
/the sadened powres wee rub /   so economicalie /
    inn 1 virsion off thynges /
    alarum is mye nayme
            / unkempt & handeld
    /i am hors /
    i am sadeld / i am a brokn hors[38]

This lyric introduces us to the poetic "i" and the dilemmas she faces. It also introduces us to the poet's use of these three reading modes. We can schematize how the three modes create three different syntactic and semantic possibilities with the first three words—"thees wite skirtes."

Table 1: Three Reading Modes

Reading Mode	Syntactic possibilities	Semantic possibilities
PDE reader	A noun phrase: demonstrative pronoun—modifier—noun	These white skirts
ME reader	An independent clause: pronoun [with unclear antecedent]—verb—noun [direct object]	These [people/things] know skirts
Across PDE & ME	An independent clause: pronoun/substantive/verb phrase	This white [thing] moves [to the edges]

Understanding the hermeneutical possibilities requires a less schematic approach.

38 Charles, *feeld*, 1.

The least obvious—but most straightforward—reading is one gained by reading aloud phonetically, a mode reinforced by Charles's own readings available online. None of the first three words adheres to PDE orthography, yet all three sound like standard PDE words: "these," "white," and "skirts." The phrase easily translates to "these white skirts," with agreement between the plural demonstrative pronoun and the plural noun upheld. So, without any knowledge of Middle English, PDE readers can decipher this initial phrase without trouble, a trouble-free interpretation in accord with Charles's own performance. As she indicates in her Chicago Humanities Festival reading, she resorts to PDE pronunciations for two reasons: in order not to inflict an injustice upon Middle English pronunciation, and to make the meaning more accessible to her non-specialist audience.[39]

Although "thees" is an unattested form of ME "thēs," its homophonic quality would not impede the ME reader.[40] Likewise, "skirtes" would have been recognizable as referring to the lower part of a man's gown or woman's dress.[41] So far, the ME and PDE readers would have a similar understanding, though the PDE reader would have a more female-gendered sense of "skirtes." The interior word, though, would send the ME reader in a different direction: ME "wite" translates as "to know" or "to understand."[42] With the demonstrative pronoun "thees" and noun "skirtes" separated by the verb "wite," "thees" now has an ambiguous antecedent. Read in ME, then, this clause can translate to "these [people] know skirts." Who *these people* are remains uncertain. Perhaps they are the other women at the grocery store; or, equally likely, they are "the tall | wymon," perhaps even trans women, who have studied and learned gendered clothing habits that cisgendered women might dismiss as "natural."

Jos Charles's transpoetics goes beyond these two modes of reading by combining them, allowing the words to draw on both ME and PDE conventions of meaning-making. This third mode encourages us to see that "skirtes" can also be a singular verb that means "to avoid or to remain on the edges," and agreeing with "wite" (as a singular substantive of its homophone "[a] white [thing]").

---

39 Jos Charles: *feeld*, Chicago Humanities Festival, 2018.

40 *Middle English Dictionary*, s.v. "thēs (adj.)," accessed February 10, 2020, https://quod.lib.umich.edu/m/middle-english-dictionary/dictionary/MED45215/track?counter=2&search_id=11846668.

41 *Middle English Dictionary*, s.v. "skirt (n.)," accessed February 10, 2020, https://quod.lib.umich.edu/m/middle-english-dictionary/dictionary/MED40726/track?counter=1&search_id=11846668.

42 *Middle English Dictionary*, s.v. "witen (v.1)," accessed February 10, 2020, https://quod.lib.umich.edu/m/middle-english-dictionary/dictionary/MED52987/track?counter=3&search_id=11846668.

Note, though, that "skirtes" as a singular verb requires a singular subject, which is not available through either the PDE or ME readings. By invoking a playful engagement of PDE and ME with another, it is possible to hear "this" as a reading for "thees," resulting in "This white [thing] skirts (or moves [to the edges])." A further hypertranslation of this deceptively simple three-word phrase becomes a complex (yet highly ambiguous) statement about the ways clothing divides us and creates identity: these [people] know/understand white skirts; at the same time, the white [thing] avoids/keeps at the margins these [people]. That's a lot to pack into three words, but doing so is possible through a transpoetics using and moving across ME and PDE reading techniques.

When we apply these same techniques to the phrase "i wont," reading across ME and PDE brings us two possible meanings: "I want (I desire)" or "I won't (I will not [do/have that])." The syntactical object of "I want" can be the preceding "thees wite skirtes / & orang | sweters," thus "I desire these white skirts and orange sweaters." Or we can read the preceding "thees wite skirtes / & orang | sweters" as completing the verb phrase "I won't": "I will not know these skirts and orange sweaters." Unpacked as a hypertranslation, these lines can mean the following: I desire yet I will not have these white skirts, skirts known by these people, white skirts that keep these people on the margins. The sense of margins holding and defining the "i" is further abetted by the poem's left indentations that create a visual "wite" space that prohibits her entry, creates spaces where desires cannot be expressed.

I regret that this somewhat tedious exposition on two lines might make *feeld* itself seem tedious. It is not. As you can tell from the first lyric, Jos Charles has crafted a series of extraordinarily moving lyrics expressing the lived and felt experiences of a particular transgendered subject. Far from dull, they form a dramatic monologue channeling the pain and bravado associated with one of Chaucer's more memorable pilgrims, the Wife of Bath. In the last portion of this paper, I will move from this tight analysis of words and lines to larger sweeps inspired by Charles's other Chaucerian "anteseedynts."

By asserting her experience as a legitimate form of knowledge, Charles's "i" draws on the Wife of Bath, who declares the validity of "experience" in the absence of "auctoritee" (3.1). Indeed, this assertion—that "the embodied experience of the speaking subject" overrides the authority of those without the experience—is an important refrain in transgender studies.[43] Though somewhat diminished by its representation as a lower-case "i," the speaking subject announces early on her "wont": what she desires and what she will and will not

43 Stryker, "(De)Subjugated Knowledges," 12.

do. And the "i" appears in most of the lyrics, revealing her feelings and her actions. She tells us, "i am afrayde" and "i cant tell u how hapy i am | todaye"; she explains that "interpolation is a skirte | i ware"; and she exclaims "lorde i am 1 / lorde i am 2 / lorde I am infinate /."[44] Though she sets several scenes in hospitals and clinics, she makes Susan Stryker's words clear: "I'm a transsexual, and I'm not sick."[45] She refuses to be pathologized or dismissed in much the same way that the Wife of Bath resists being categorized by male clerics (3.9 and passim). Her experience continues to control the poetic series to the end, when it closes on a hopeful note. Like the Wife of Bath (in both her monologue and her tale), who ends her prologue claiming that a brighter world awaits her (3.822–25), the narrating "i" closes her lyrical series pronouncing that she "woake 2 see."[46]

In conjunction with this narrative "i," another important source of *feeld*'s affective power is its use of "u" and the audience that it implies. Like the embedded dramatic monologue in the Wife of Bath's *Prologue* (3.235–78), *feeld* repeatedly addresses a "u" who has tried to keep her within predetermined cultural roles. In her *Prologue*, the Wife of Bath announces that she will perform for her audience of pilgrims the diatribe that she delivered to her husbands. Repeatedly she says "thou seyst"—over 40 times—to reinforce that the shrewish behavior she exhibits is in truth the shrewish behavior others have projected on her. In fact, she laments that her husbands forced her into her behavior. If only they had treated her kindly and generously, she would have gladly enjoyed sex with them rather than use the "marital debt" as a commodity to be brokered and exchanged for her own financial security. Charles's *feeld* moves the "thou seyst" from the sphere of marital debt, that medieval formula of clearly defined sexual obligations, to the terrain of gender definition. Although the persona is speaking to an undisclosed "u," the reader is always implicated in the address. Like the "u" who wants all this to be clearly defined, who wants the final say in gendered identity, the reader often longs for hermeneutical clarity, for the fog of orthographic and syntactical confusion to lift, for the apparent gibberish to move into the realm of comprehensible mystery. Like the "u," we want to say, "I want to understand you, but you're not following the rules. Just follow the rules. They are easy enough to understand." Our task is to set these demands aside and to strive, as Rita Felski encourages us, "for a greater receptivity to the multifarious and many-shaded moods of texts."[47] And the courtesy we afford texts, Charles asserts, is the courtesy we should afford

---

44 Charles, *feeld*, 6, 39, 10, 34.
45 Stryker, "(De)Subjugated Knowledges," 1–2.
46 Charles, *feeld*, 61.
47 Rita Felski, *The Limits of Critique* (Chicago: University of Chicago Press, 2015), 12.

the transgendered subject. We must, unlike the Wife's older husbands, allow "ourselves to be marked, struck, impressed by what we read."[48] We must, in other words, be akin to Jankyn who submits to his wife's "soveraynetee" (3.818), who allows himself (at least in the Wife's account) to be remade by the Wife. We are bade to inhabit the text under the sovereignty of "i" in order to learn about multifarious possibilities of embodiment.

In addition to the Wife's voice, Charles's series also makes use of the equine imagery in the Wife's *Prologue*. The Wife tells us that she "hadde alwey a coltes tooth" (3.602), an expression of her sexual appetite. She also tells us that "as an hors I koude byte and whyne" (3.386), referring to her resistance to her husband's claims of lordship. As Jeanne Provost has argued, the Wife uses this metaphorical comparison to create an escape clause for herself. Like the recalcitrant horse she compares herself to, she can act against the best interests of the one who claims her as chattel property by forcing him to accept responsibility for her misdeeds.[49] If her husbands want to treat her like chattel property, then she will be like a horse whose misdeeds—its reckless kicking and stomping—have consequences that redound on its owner, not the horse. Her means of emancipation is by granting herself the freedom of the misbehaving, sexually profligate horse and by placing all the blame on her husbands.

The "i" of *feeld* takes that twofold metaphorical association with horses and converts it into a vehicle for expressing a twofold dilemma the trans woman faces: in order to own her gender identity, she must give herself over to processes controlled by "wharing masckulin economyes."[50] At the center of this struggle, as we learn in "XI. we knu a historie off," her transition depends upon "estrogyn" derived from "the urin | concentrat off pregnynt mares," known as Premarin. This synthetic estrogen compound derived from mare urine is responsible for her body's being able to present female characteristics. The horse—or more specifically the estrogen extracted from pregnant mares—allows the trans woman to present as female. Horses become the metonymic vehicle for the trans woman in *feeld*. Knowing this linkage helps us understand better the first lyric's final two lines: "i am hors / | I am sadeld / i am a brokn hors."[51] Reading across PDE and ME, the first three words can read "I am hoarse" or "I am Horse" (recalling the

---

48 Felski, *Limits of Critique*, 12.

49 Jeanne Provost, "Vital Property in *The Wife of Bath's Prologue and Tale*," *Studies in the Age of Chaucer* 38 (2016): 62 and 72; Candace Barrington, "Chaucer," in *The Cambridge Companion to Medieval English Law and Literature*, ed. Candace Barrington and Sebastian Sobecki (Cambridge: Cambridge University Press, 2019), 144–45.

50 Charles, *feeld*, 11.

51 Charles, *feeld*, 1.

1970s feminist anthem "I am Woman") or "I am Horse, the one who speaks for other trans women but made inaudible by speaking." At the same time, her trans experience has saddled and broken her. As we learn from the other lyrics, the trans experience isn't limited to just the medical interventions (which can be dangerous and uncomfortable and lengthy) or to the period either before or after the medical intervention. She has also been broken by the gender strictures that marginalize her, deny her, and threaten her life.

The most extensive reference to horses comes in "XLIII. how 2 cont," which I provide in full here.

how 2 cont
mye partes / hussbanded
2 a feeld off partes / kno
the pathe u cleeve is
not ur owne / u whos pryde
is a brocken hors / who
trods downe mye falts 2
seesond cropse / considre a lone
mye hoof / its metalld
shoe / & weape
/ i am a horsman 2[52]

This lyric states the paradoxes of the trans body. Her whole/holed body has been reduced to a "feeld of parts." The intensely personal decision to "cleeve" some of those parts does not belong exclusively to the trans woman. Or at least that decision has been claimed by others, even though it belongs to her. Here, the "u" seems to be those who stake a claim in the decisions made by the trans woman, who enforce their values through violence and hostility. If we take the "who" as a second modifying clause for "u," then the clause "you trod down my faults to seasonal crops" reduces trans identity to a sinful, passing phase that will soon go away. With "considre," we read the main verb for "u" as an imperative: "consider solely my hoof and its metal shoe and weep." Look, she entreats. Look at what has been nailed to me. Weep for what I have endured. Like you, I am made of parts. Some of my parts come from a horse.

In response to this anguishing call, the poetic series closes on a rather optimistic note. The antepenultimate lyric, "LVIII. preshus," immediately follows the somber count of dead trans women. It ends with a multi-faceted promise: "it meens wee can change"—that gender transitions are possible and that attitudes toward trans women can change, but we must keep in mind that all those

52 Charles, *feeld*, 43.

changes are "wee," collective and minuscule. By the penultimate lyric, the "i" has become akin to Moses, able to see the Promised Land but not enter it: "this is not | its seeson / i wil | herold the seeson."[53] Here, she eschews hope delivered in bad faith, offering instead hope that what the "i" has is good. If not Moses's glimpse of the Promised Land, the vision that the "i" has at the end is a day filled with promise of the "hole whorld | off thynges befor me," a day for speaking to her "husbande," a day for realizing that it is "*bettre 2 be a thynge | than a gathrer off thynges*," a day that awakes to seeing "1 plum leef hang."[54]

As this brief analysis has shown, Jos Charles's *feeld* draws on its Chaucerian antecedents in multiple ways. Primarily, though, it invites its readers to read like Middle English readers, and it creates a lyric voice that draws on the voice of the Wife of Bath. Charles asks us to traverse between then and now, bringing to bear reading skills operative in both eras as we read *feeld*. The reader is charged with determining the best way to traverse the two terrains, to explore the relationships that exist across words, to embrace both the old norms and the seemingly deviant. We can see that distinctive aspects of ME, such as the thou/you distinction that PDE has lost without much detriment to effective communication, means that other changes can happen, such as employing "they" as singular, without causing English to collapse into a morass of incomprehensibility. In this traversal, Charles's *feeld* doesn't ask us to remain in the late-medieval period. She situates her "feeld" in an affective space that Trigg and Prendergast have identified as "neo-medievalism": "a meta-medievalism that borrows, uses, and deploys other medievalisms rather than claiming any direct connection to the Middle Ages."[55] That is, Charles doesn't ask readers to occupy a late-medieval English space. Instead, she uses linguistic medievalism to create an affective space which allows the readers to feel—to touch and emotionally understand—a certain trans experience by immersing themselves into a destabilizing experience that ends up being remarkably familiar.[56] Charles's lyrical series allows cisgendered readers to feel the discomfort often associated with transgendered subjectivity. In her verse, readers recognize certain aspects of the terrain but are always looking for a translation that renders the lived experience easier, more recognizable, more natural, more transparent, and more legible. Readers are given, instead, a difficult—yet kindly delivered—lesson in the arbitrary nature of cultural

53 Charles, *feeld*, 60.

54 Charles, *feeld*, 61.

55 Thomas A. Prendergast and Stephanie Trigg, *Affective Medievalism: Love, Abjection and Discontent* (Manchester, UK: Manchester University Press, 2019), 8–9.

56 Eve Kosofsky Sedgwick, *Touching Feeling: Affect, Pedagogy, Performativity*, 2nd ed. (Durham, N.C.: Duke University Press, 2004).

mechanisms that define gender. By making visible the arbitrariness of linguistic meaning-making, the transpoetics of *feeld* achieves what advocates have long demanded: making "visible the normative linkages we generally assume to exist between social role and embodied gender."[57]

57 Stryker, "(De)Subjugated Knowledges," 3.

Daniel C. Remein

The Time Mechanic and the Theater: Translation, Performativity, and Performance in the Old English of Karen Coonrod's *Judith*, W.H. Auden, and Thomas Meyer

Translation in the Orbit of Performance

I would like to begin with reference to an experimental theatrical production based on the Old English poem *Judith*, as given in a partial workshop performance at the MIT Center for Art, Science, and Technology in March of 2019. The piece, titled *Judith*, is a "Music/Text/Chamber/Hybrid/Opera" with a libretto by Karin Coonrod and a score by Paul Vasile. The piece adapts the Old English poem *Judith*—itself an adaptation of the Deuterocanonical/Apocryphal Biblical book into Old English poetry—into the unstable space of experimental theatrical performance. Performed with a small number of both professional and accomplished amateur singers and instrumentalists in an unadorned auditorium, the production renders the poem in a highly anti-absorptive, stylized manner that heterogeneously incorporates translated and untranslated passages of Old English poetry as sung voice and digitally projected text.[1]

The Old English *Judith* is already a text anxious about translation and preoccupied by gender and sexuality. As Haruko Momma explains, "it is interesting that *Judith*'s complexity comes from its apparent simplification of the Latin

1 *Judith: Music/Text/Chamber/Hybrid/Opera from the Anglo-Saxon Epic*, workshop performance, libretto by Karin Coonrod, music by Paul Vasile, MIT Center for Art, Science and Technology, Cambridge, MA, March 5, 2019. Arthur Bahr (medievalist at MIT) and Liesl Smith served as consultants on the Old English. As I write this, the piece is not yet complete, as the writers' plans for another workshop to complete the work during March 2019 were thwarted by the Covid-19 pandemic. I thank my undergraduate honors thesis advisee, Ellis Hampton, for his insightful conversation with me about this performance. I also wish to thank the anonymous readers within and outside of this volume for their comments and suggestions, and Erica Weaver for discussing aspects of this essay with me. I offer my gratitude to David Hadbawnik for seeing this volume into print, and for catalyzing critical attention to the subjects of this book over a period of many years.

https://doi.org/10.1515/9781501511189-006

source material."[2] The Old English poem effaces its source-text's investment in religious difference by restructuring the narrative and omitting reference to Jewish dietary laws, the Temple cult, and circumcision—omissions that are "rounded off" by dilating on scenes of feast and battle, and which invoke less the ancient Near East than the world of *Beowulf*.[3] Along with these "domesticating" translative moves, as Mary Dockray-Miller points out, by *not* eliminating the character of Judith's maid along with other characters from the source-text, the poem portrays a "cooperative community of women."[4] The Old English text thus accedes to a certain mode of translating gender and sexuality (from Latin Christian texts about the ancient Jewish world into the Old English literary world) in a way that we might mark as queer:

> Judith is not described as a wife or widow (or even, technically, virgin) because her sexuality is not limited to a heterosexuality defined by her relationship with a man. Judith demonstrates a sexuality and satisfaction of desire that goes beyond the paradigm of two lovers, heterosexual or homosexual, to encompass different generations and a multiplicity of bonds, with men, with women, with mothers, with children, whether or not related by blood.[5]

Registering this queerness in the structure of her production in a manner that may also invoke an axis of Trans*-ness, Coonrod's libretto accounts for the third-person narrator of the Old English poem by inventing a "Bard" to perform the diagesis, whom Coonrod describes as "a kind of Tiresias 'they' character, a man and woman, ancient and modern"[6] (performed in this instance by Srinivasan Raghuraman, an MIT graduate student in the Theory of Computation also trained in Carnatic Vocal music).

At the climactic moment of the narrative, in which Judith delivers a prayer before beheading Holofernes, she sings in Old English while a translation of the text is projected on the back wall. Following this moment, a prolonged, slow-paced scene unfolds in which translation and source-text occupy the space of avant-garde theatrical performance—as voice and text—as the Bard narrates the beheading (itself not pantomimed), "speak-singing" in a high-pitched

2 Haruko Momma, "Epanalepsis: A Retelling of the Judith Story in the Anglo-Saxon Poetic Language," *Studies in the Literary Imagination* 36, no. 1 (2003): 59–73, 59.
3 Momma, "Epanalepsis," 60–61.
4 Mary Dockray-Miller, "Female Community in the Old English *Judith*," *Studia Neophilologica* 70, no. 2 (1998): 156–72, 165.
5 Dockray-Miller, "Female Community," 171. On Ælfric, by way of comparison, see Mo Pareles, "Jewish Heterosexuality, Queer Celibacy? Ælfric Translates the Old Testament Priesthood," *postmedieval* 8, no. 3 (2017): 292–306, 302.
6 Private correspondence with Karin Coonrod, January 9, 2020.

chant while both the Old English text and a Present-Day English translation of the text are projected on the back wall (the former in a font very closely resembling the miniscule of an Old English poetic codex).[7] Throughout this sequence, the chorus hums gravely and distressingly.

Along with the specific latencies of the Old English text that this performance throws into relief (a topic for another essay), it is also remarkable in that it places, as text, the translation of Old English poetry quite literally within the formal space of embodied dramatic performance—and within a space we might call "avant-garde" or "experimental." This performance thus provokes questions worth asking about the relationship between translation and performance in the queer medievalisms of modern and contemporary poetry. How might historical conventions of dramatic performance—whether in the context of a source-text or a translation—shape the practice and function of translating medieval texts within queer modern poetics? How might the historical, concrete possibility of a formalized use of either source-text or translation as a performance script condition its translation? How might the inescapably performative trajectories of texts not explicitly marked for formalized performance nonetheless pull translation into the dynamics queried above? This essay cannot provide answers to all these questions, either as general theory or as particulars of literary history. In an attempt to generate the kind of critical terrain in which to phrase such questions, what follows will turn to twentieth-century poet W. H. Auden's poem known as "The Watershed" and contemporary poet Thomas Meyer's translation of Ælfric's *Colloquy on the Occupations* from his 1979 book *Staves Calends Legends*. First, however, I will briefly consider where the questions posed above might intersect with the translation poetics of mid-twentieth-century poet Jack Spicer (whose figure of the "time mechanic" provides the context for this collection), and the place of performativity in foundational queer theory.

Translation, Performance, Spectral Sexuality

In a famous discussion of the basic problems of translation that appears in his book *After Lorca*, post-war twentieth-century poet Jack Spicer exhorts that "a poet is a time mechanic not an embalmer."[8] I would like to pause on this

7 "Speak-singing" is Coonrod's description (private correspondence). The insular miniscule-resembling font may be Pater Baker's "Beowulf". It should be noted that the final form of this piece may differ from this workshop performance.

8 Jack Spicer, *After Lorca*, in *My Vocabulary Did This to Me: The Collected Poetry of Jack Spicer*, ed. Kevin Killian and Peter Gizzi (Middletown, CT: Wesleyan University Press, 2000), 122.

maxim, allowing Spicer's "time mechanic" to calibrate, if somewhat indirectly, these questions about translation and performance in the queer medievalisms of modern and contemporary poetics. A central figure in the gay coterie of the so-called "Berkeley Renaissance" (along with Robin Blaser and Robert Duncan), the later San Francisco Renaissance, and the loose grouping of the "New American Poetry" from the post-war period, Spicer was also a student of the Middle Ages under philologist Arthur G. Brodeur and historian Ernst Kantorowicz (having completed all his coursework, but never a thesis, for a PhD at Berkeley).[9] Spicer's work is at home in the fundamentally disclosive turn away from symbolist thought (and the reinterpretations of the legacy of Romanticism) that Charles Altieri long-ago identified as a hallmark of a broad spectrum of American post-war poetries.[10] But it is also consistently auto-marginalizing and oppositional to both adjacent avant-gardes and even his own companions—hostile to the expressivism of the beats, intensely skeptical of the attempt to construct a "public" voice that Blaser and Duncan would take from the work of Charles Olson, and dismissive of the New York poets Frank O'Hara and John Ashbery with whom he simply did not get along.[11] As Daniel Katz argues, "Spicer fails to fall comfortably on either side of most of the structuring poetic oppositions of his time."[12] His corpus (both the work of an "unabashedly gay poet" and marked by irremediable moments of misogyny and anti-Semitism) positions the poetic act as "a process of becoming less human, less alive, less distinctive, less oneself."[13] This positioning—which eventually takes the form of a theory of "dictation" in which an alien, spectral, or haunting "Outside" uses the poet like a radio receiver to write the poems—marks an attack on property, markets, and subjectivism, but also contributes to "an obsessive assault on what he saw as poetic expediency or fashion [that] is also an assault on the notion of the 'timely' itself."[14] Spicer's above-cited assertion takes its place among the workings of a corpus

---

9 For Spicer's authoritative biography, see Lewis Ellingham and Kevin Killian, *Poet Be Like God: Jack Spicer and the San Francisco Renaissance* (Hanover, CT: Wesleyan University Press, 1998), 65, 71, 75.

10 Charles Altieri, "From Symbolist Thought to Immanence: The Ground of Postmodern American Poetry," *boundary 2* 1, no. 3 (1973): 605–42.

11 See Michael Davidson, *The San Francisco Renaissance: Poetics and Community at Mid-Century* (Cambridge: Cambridge University Press, 1989), 151; Miriam Nicholls, *Radical Affections: Essays on the Poetics of Outside* (Tuscaloosa: University Alabama Press, 2010), 141, 173–75; Daniel Katz, *The Poetry of Jack Spicer* (Edinburgh: Edinburgh University Press), 4; Ellingham and Killian, *Poet Be Like God*, 65, 71, 75.

12 Katz, *The Poetry of Jack Spicer*, 4.

13 Ibid., 4, 10.

14 Ibid., 5.

that can thus, as Katz puts it, "displace the historicity of both the poet and the poem in ways which trouble the implicitly temporal claims of any avant-garde"—playing to the "ghostly" logic of "an avant-garde whose time can never arrive."[15] So the figure of Spicer's "time mechanic" directly faces the effort to plot a literary history of medievalism—a queerly never-yet that is also an unfashionable long-gone—in avant-gardes since World War II.

The exhortation appears in one of several letters addressed to a deceased Federico García Lorca that Spicer includes in his book. In the context of his letter, Spicer's claim modulates alike the economy of poetic diction and the ontology of poesis itself:

> It is very difficult. We want to transfer the immediate object, the immediate emotion to the poem—and yet the immediate always has hundreds of its own words clinging to it, short-lived and tenacious as barnacles. And it is wrong to scrape them off and substitute others. A poet is a time mechanic not an embalmer. The words around the immediate shrivel and decay like flesh around the body. No mummy-sheet of tradition can be used to stop the process. Objects, words must be led across time not preserved against it.
>
> I yell "Shit" down a cliff at an ocean. Even in my lifetime the immediacy of that word will fade. It will be dead as "Alas." But if I put the real cliff and the real ocean into the poem, the word "Shit" will ride along with them, travel the time machine until cliffs and oceans disappear.
>
> ...
>
> Words are what sticks to the real. We use them to push the real, to drag the real into the poem. They are what we hold on with, nothing else. They are as valuable in themselves as rope with nothing to be tied to.
>
> I repeat—the perfect poem has an infinitely small vocabulary.[16]

Any *poesis* here depends on the poem's fundamentally translative capacity.[17] But as a mechanic, rather than a priestly embalmer, a poet cannot simply "scrape off" all the pesky and unnecessary words, "short lived and tenacious as barnacles," that cling to "the immediate" when the poet tries to transfer it into the poem (the so-called "original" poem issuing from this inaugural extra/infra-linguistic translation of world into poem).[18] Despite wanting "an infinitely small vocabulary" in which words and their historical contingencies get out of the way of the real, the poet cannot (despite Spicer's well-known interest in

15 Ibid., 6.

16 Spicer, *After Lorca*, 122–23.

17 And see David Hadbawnik, "Time Mechanics: The Modern Geoffrey Chaucer and the Medieval Jack Spicer," *postmedieval* 4, no. 3 (2013): 270–83, at 275, which similarly points out Spicer's conflation of poet and translator.

18 Spicer, *After Lorca*, 122.

magic) behave as a cleric preserving the sacred against history—for, "no mummy-sheet of tradition can be used to stop the process."[19] David Hadbawnik explains that for Spicer, "[t]o deny the particularities of a historical moment in relation to poetry is, indeed, to burden poetry's language with an eternity of meanings, essentially rendering it meaningless and allowing the invisible real to which it is attached to slip away in the process."[20] The time mechanic does not play elite acolyte to a sacred body in a fiction of transcendence and sovereignty (not to mention political theology), but, merely, tinkers with a time machine.[21]

Spicer's insistence in *After Lorca* on a poetics in which, in Daniel Katz's terms, "the poem is part of and penetrated by the real" (even as it enacts "a poetics of meditation, rejecting proximity ... in favor of a relationship constituted by difference and absence") does suggest that part of the point of this discussion is the impossible challenge to comprehend it literally.[22] However, to the extent that our phenomenal experience of time is not mechanical (setting aside its measurement by the mechanical clock), not subject to manipulation by humans bearing temporal wrenches and ratchets, we implicitly take the sense of "time mechanic" as figurative—perhaps as metaphor, perhaps even as catachresis. Spicer is clarifying the *role* of the poet, a part the poet figuratively takes up, puts on, performs. This performative dimension of the time mechanic contributes to Spicer's often-remarked opposition to what he calls "the big lie of the personal," which, as Katz notes, cannot be reduced to a "disinterested impersonality."[23] To generate the kind of fundamentally translative poetry Spicer is after, the poet must, in some sense, play the part of, dress up as, a technician (and here, there is surely a fraught class politics worth elaborating elsewhere). By opposing the time mechanic, as a secular office, to that of the priest (the reference to mummification implicitly placing the sinister "embalmer" within a loose allusion to popular

19 Ibid., 122–23.

20 Hadbawnik, "Time Mechanics," 275.

21 See Lori Chamberlain, "Ghostwriting the Text: Translation and Poetics of Jack Spicer," *Contemporary Literature* 26, no. 4 (1985): 426–42, at 426, where Chamberlain similarly opposes Spicer's theory of translation to religious, specifically Platonic models, focusing on the secondary, parasitic role of the translator. Spicer's need to explicitly reject the priestly role here is the result of his strategic conflation of poet and translator.

22 For example, Katz, *The Poetry of Jack Spicer*, 56–57. The attempt to read this literally is also useful and elsewhere I do attempt a more literal reading of this discussion. See Daniel C. Remein, "Robin Blaser, Jack Spicer, and Arthur Brodeur," *postmedieval* 6, no. 2 (2015): 174–90.

23 Katz, *The Poetry of Jack Spicer*, 59. This point is anticipated in Chamberlain, "Ghostwriting the Text," 426–42, where she notes Spicer's comment on the "big lie of the personal," but also that "[at] the same time, however, Spicer's poems *are* very personal" (432–33).

conceptions of ancient Egyptian funerary cults), Spicer implicitly underscores the especially performative function of the role (this, in some tension with the ostensibly non-performative fact of actual skilled labor). Not a "maker," the office of poet is a performative one;[24] in part, an element in a drama in which the poet plays the role of a technician or a maintenance-worker, in part, a rhetorical situation in which the poet's speech acts (in J. L. Austin's famous sense of the "performative," in which to say something is to *do* something) must persuasively accomplish the upkeep of the slippery and uncertain relationship between language and the real through time.[25]

It is not incidental, then, that Hadbawnik's exploration of Spicer and Geoffrey Chaucer as "time mechanics" proceeds through a reading of Spicer's most nearly-completed (if never produced during his lifetime) theatrical adaptation of Chaucer's *Troilus and Criseyde.*[26] Hadbawnik's analysis implicitly places Spicer's thought on translation in the vicinity of medievalism, dramatic performance (in the sense of dramatic theatricality), and the performative of speech act theory.[27] Here, and in what follows, the sense of "performance" strategically oscillates between that of theatrical doing and that of "the performative" in the philosophy of language.[28]

The time mechanic's refusal of the role of the embalmer also raises the possibility that at least some of the other players in this drama are no longer living; hence Spicer's often-remarked characterization of poetry, elsewhere in the *After Lorca* letters, as how the dead write to each other.[29] What the poem translates itself into and what the translation as a time machine translates across time both

---

24 On the complicated relationship of Spicer's poetics to the famous Pound dictum to "make it new," see Hadbawnik, "Time Mechanics," 273.

25 See J. L. Austin, *How to Do Things with Words* (Oxford: Oxford University Press, 1962), 6–7.

26 Hadbawnik, "Time Mechanics." In Spicer's *Troilus* "the characters act like stand-ins for his developing poetics" (278). Spicer's *Troilus* was turned down by the now well-known Boston Poet's Theater Group (see Ellingham and Killian, *Poet Be Like God*, 75), but was later performed in truncated versions by both the Buffalo Poets Theater (February, 27, 2010), and its San Francisco counterpart (during the 2000s). My thanks to David Hadbawnik for this information.

27 Hadbawnik, "Time Mechanics," 278: "In Spicer's *Troilus*, the characters act like stand-ins for his developing poetics."

28 Strictly speaking, the latter would (according to Austin) exclude dramatic performance, be it literary or theatrical, as "parasitic." See Austin, *How to Do Things With Words*, 22. However, following Jacques Derrida's intervention in speech act theory, "[p]arasitism does not need literature or the theater to appear," as the structural iterability of the performative and its attendant temporality already harbor the possibility of the parasitic. See Jacques Derrida, *Limited Inc.*, ed. Gerald Graff, trans. Samuel Weber and Geoffrey Mehlman (Evanston, IL: Northwestern University Press, 1988), 89.

29 Spicer, *After Lorca*, 134.

require a spectral logic, wherein—to borrow Katz's terms for the relationship of the dead to the poet in *After Lorca*—"the alterity of company is both negated and preserved."[30]

Feminist translation theorist Lori Chamberlain locates Spicer's approach to translation in opposition to Platonist, representational, and expressivist models, positing an impersonal erotics of linguistically conditioned belatedness that inevitably invokes just such a ghost. Chamberlain identifies the "after" of *After Lorca* as "the operative term" for its translational poetics, not only in a temporal sense, but as the logic of "the writing's desire," thus invoking a spectral erotics after (in the sense of "in pursuit of") the dead.[31] As Chamberlain explains, "the go-between, shuttling between Eros and Thanatos, is, in Spicer's language, the ghost, the sign of the crossover between life and death."[32] This belatedness is implicit in the figure of the time machine and the role of the poet as its technician—bearing speech whose illocutionary effects persuasively tinker with the relationship of language to time so as to arouse the desire of the ghost, to seduce the ghost into riding the time machine. Chamberlain goes on to discuss the relationship of these erotics to gay male desire in Spicer's community of gay poets at mid-century,[33] but queerness here is also conditioned by a sexuality other than that of the living human. The mode of survival offered by poetry, by translation—never the preservation of an origin(al) or the continuity of a presence—is here contingent on a spectral erotics in which the poet has a role to play whose indirect effects facilitate the desires of the ghost.[34] Rephrased as readerly praxis, this double-haunting, at once of and by both an erotics and a temporality, means that, as Chamberlain explains, "Spicer's theory of translation finally demands that we read it intertextually, acknowledging the sexuality of the subtext."[35]

This critical lexicon veers away from the transparent in part because of the potential strangeness of translative poetics enunciated not from their systematic

30 Katz, *The Poetry of Jack Spicer*, 59.

31 Chamberlain, "Ghostwriting the Text," 436.

32 Ibid., 426.

33 Ibid., 436–37.

34 Framing it as a mode of survival, living on, Chamberlain positions Spicer's theory as "remarkably similar" to that of Walter Benjamin's famous essay "The Task of the Translator"; but see by way of comparison, Hadbawnik, "Time Mechanics," 275, which points out Spicer's divergence from Benjamin's construction of an "original" and his differentiation between poet and translator. And see David Hadbawnik, "Differing Intimacies: *Beowulf* Translations by Seamus Heaney and Thomas Meyer," in *Dating Beowulf: Studies in Intimacy*, ed. Daniel C. Remein and Erica Weaver (Manchester: Manchester University Press, 2020), 232, which points out Benjamin's failure to escape the language of "fidelity and license" that imply a so-called "original."

35 Chamberlain, "Ghostwriting the Text," 437.

elaboration in the form of a treatise, but from their performance in Spicer's poetry. As such, in what follows, these terms will apply unevenly, incompletely overlapping the descriptive functions of close reading, leaving slippages that I take not as a liability of the angle of approach, but on the contrary, as its generative potential. Jacques Derrida's famous hauntological injunction, to "live with ghosts, in the upkeep, the conversation, the company, or the companionship, in the commerce without commerce of ghosts," emerges in a reading of Marx and inexorably leads to a question of the labor of the specter and the spectrality of labor.[36] Having observed of the ghost that, despite its non-presence in the present, "the thing *works*," Derrida is left then to ask, "[w]hat is work?"[37] Spicer's injunctions analogously prompt the question of how we should understand this performative labor as a performance of sexuality (and again, Spicer's formulation of the poet appropriating proletarian labor calls for a further critique beyond what I can provide here), and, as its condition, how (or if), precisely, one should understand the sexuality of the ghost. If, "in order to write poetry, the poet must be a dead man,"[38] how (without recourse to a neo-Gothic necrophilia) do we phrase the question of the sexuality of the dead? The cases that follow do not answer these questions, but furnish us with examples of their terrain to the extent that they do not enact *translatio* in the traditional sense of carrying-across so much as they accomplish performances that, when felicitous, constitute the tinkering (summonings, arousals, exorcisms, conjurations) with whatever might allow the back and forth (between past and present, one text and another) of the erotics of ghost.

Secret Agents, Performativity, and Translations of Gender

In a previous reading of W. H. Auden's poem beginning "Control of the passes" (later titled "The Secret Agent") as a translation of the Old English poem known as "Wulf and Eadwacer," I describe a certain kind of potentially queer translation of the medieval as an an-economic "queer mixing of times and languages *as a mixing of sexualities*."[39] In this respect, it is interesting to note that however

36 Jacques Derrida, *Specters of Marx*, trans. Peggy Kamuf (New York: Routledge, 2006), xvii–xviii.

37 Derrida, *Specters*, 9, italics in original; and see 10, 58–60.

38 Chamberlain, "Ghostwriting the Text," 433. And see Katz, *The Poetry of Jack Spicer*, 58: "for Spicer one is only a poet to the extent one is dead."

39 Daniel C. Remein, "Auden, Translation, Betrayal: Radical Poetics and Translation from Old English," *Literature Compass* 8, no. 11 (2011): 821–22, emphasis in original.

much the poetry of Auden (a late modernist gay poet whose corpus spans his early Oxfordian Marxism to his later commitments to the Episcopal Church, Niebuhrian Christianity, and an orientation towards critics like Lionel Trilling)[40] may have never taken a position more radical than "a mild contrapposto,"[41] it was nevertheless (and not entirely incidentally) important to Spicer's poetic development. As Ellingham and Killian note, Spicer "had loved and imitated Auden's great 1930s lyrics since he had first discovered them as a teenager," and as late as Auden's reading at the San Francisco Poetry Center in the mid-1950s, he was important to the queer poetry scene.[42] Auden's aforementioned crypto-translation of an Old English elegy in the guise of a lyric allegorizes closeted modern(ist) gay male desire with the secrecy of a spy narrative—the poem itself acting as a "double agent," not betraying the original, but handing over the present "to the heterogeneity of a *pre-*."[43] An additional attention to performativity would only come naturally to this Derridean phrasing of a queer translation of the medieval, and might thicken attention to Auden's medievalism, especially by rendering gender a more explicit term in the analysis (for starters, Auden's poem, gendering its character with the pronoun "he," translates one of the only Old English elegies that stages the voice of a woman—so marked only by a feminine adjectival ending—into a narrative of modernist masculinities at the cost of risking an erasure of women from Old English literary history).[44]

Performativity may seem ancillary to traditional, representational conceptions of translation in terms of equivalency and fidelity, or to the potential queerness of translation apart from the sexuality and/or gender of the translator or the "content" of the source-text. But we should remember the foundational place of the performative within Queer Theory (including its pride of place in the two lead articles of the inaugural issue of *GLQ*, by Eve Kosofsky Sedgwick and Judith

---

40 For a condensed summary of Auden's biography, see Richard Davenport-Hines, "Auden's Life and Character," in *The Cambridge Companion to W. H. Auden*, ed. Stan Smith (Cambridge: Cambridge University Press, 2004), 15–24.

41 This is David Antin's indictment in an essay from the inaugural issue of the journal *boundary 2*. David Antin, "Modernism and Postmodernism: Approaching the Present in American Poetry," *boundary 2* 1, no. 1 (1972): 105.

42 Ellingham and Killian, *Poet Be Like God*, 54.

43 Remein, "Auden, Translation, Betrayal," 817, 820, 821–22; Derrida, *Specters*, 33, quoted in Remein, 822.

44 On the erasure of women from OE literary history in the case of "Wulf and Eadwacer," see the pioneering essay by Marilynn Desmond, "The Voice of Exile: Feminist Literary History and Anonymous Anglo-Saxon Elegy," *Critical Inquiry* 16, no. 3 (1990): 572–90.

Butler, respectively).[45] Further, we should recall the way that the temporal structure of the performative and its capacity for queerness also describe a process cognate to that of translation. As Butler writes, citing Derrida's intervention in Austin's theory, performative speech acts are fundamentally repetitions—a citational practice—that "are never simply replicas of the same" by virtue of their iterability:

> If a performative provisionally succeeds (and I will suggest that "success" is always and only provisional), then it is not because an intention successfully governs the action of speech, but only because that action echoes a prior action, and *accumulates the force of authority through the repetition or citation of a prior, authoritative set of practices.* What this means, then, is that a performative "works" to the extent that it *draws on and covers over* the constitutive conventions by which it is mobilized. In this sense, no term or statement can function performatively without the accumulating and dissimulating historicity of force.[46]

Even echoing the conventions of the "impossibility" of translation ("success" is always provisional) and of the necessarily contradictory effort to plot translations in terms of accuracy or fidelity (*draws on and covers over*), the performative also traces the shape of translation in the convergence of performativity as both "speech acts" and "theatricality" (hence, "the embodying or performing of gender norms and the performative use of language," as "modes of citationality" within a horizon of compulsory interpolation).[47]

Precisely such performativity conditions the horizon of queer translation in another poem which appears in the same 1930 collection as "Control of the passes"/"The Secret Agent," and which Auden would later title "The Wanderer" after its most salient Old English source-text. Opening with the line, "Doom is dark and deeper than any sea-dingle," the poem renders the famously hallucinatory

---

45 For example, Judith Butler, *Gender Trouble: Feminism and the Subversion of Identity* (New York: Routledge, 1990), especially 128–41, and "Critically Queer," *GLQ* 1, no. 1 (1993): 17–32. Eve Kosofsky Sedgwick, "Queer Performativity: Henry James' *The Art of the Novel*," *GLQ* 1, no. 1 (1993): 1–16. Butler's essay also appears in revised form in Judith Butler, *Bodies that Matter: On the Discursive Limits of "Sex"* (New York: Routledge, 1993). Of course, the risk of Butler's intervention here is its difficulty comprehending the *core* importance of gender for some people (including many Trans* people), since it mounts, after a fashion, a critique of identification in general, admitting only its political exigency. My thanks to Mo Pareles for multiple conversations on this point.

46 Butler, "Critically Queer," 18–19; citing Derrida, "Signature, Event, Context," in *Limited Inc*, 1–24.

47 Butler, "Critically Queer," 22.

perception of sea-birds mingled with memories of a friendly hall in the Old English source-text in terms of the pain and desire of a closeted sexuality:[48]

> There head falls forward, fatigued at evening,
> And dreams of home,
> Waving from window, spread of welcome,
> Kissing of wife under single sheet;
> But waking sees
> Bird-flocks nameless to him, through doorway voices
> Of new men making another love.[49]

The fact that it was first published as the chorus from a now-lost play by Auden,[50] a point not noted often enough, underscores that the poem's translative operations include the possibility of an embodied—and ineluctably gendered—formalized dramatic performance (of a specifically male, closeted sexuality), in which gender becomes inflected and transformed by the translation between historical discourses of heroic masculinity, that of the "new men," and whatever modern reader's/performer's body it may interpolate. A model of medievalism which takes the text of "Wulf and Eadwacer" or "The Wanderer" as a kind of script for these performances (the felicitous result of which would be a modernist poem) thus requires a more supple attention to the possibilities of the translations of gender within the horizons of queer medievalism. And here, the very phrase "translations of gender" should remind us that Transgender Studies has generated its own approaches to the relationship between translation practices, translation theory, and Trans* experience and praxis.[51] As A. Finn Enke explains, "[t]ranslation is a nec-

---

48 On the "allegory of the closet" in this and other early Auden poems, see Richard R. Bozorth, "Auden: love, sexuality, desire," in *The Cambridge Companion to W. H. Auden*, ed. Stan Smith (Cambridge: Cambridge University Press, 2004), 175–87, at 181–82.

49 W. H. Auden, *Poems* (London: Faber and Faber, 1930), 43.

50 John Fuller, *W. H. Auden: A Commentary* (Princeton: Princeton University Press, 2000), 78; Auden, "Chorus from a Play," *New Signatures* (1932): 33. And see, Chris Jones, *Strange Likeness: The Use of Old English in Twentieth-Century Poetry* (Oxford: Oxford University Press, 2006), 89–95, for an early queer reading of this poem.

51 The literature here is extensive and diverse, and pulls directly on premodern studies. For example (non-exhaustively), Arielle A. Concilio, "Pedro Lemebel and the Translatxrsation: On a Genderqueer Translation Practice," *TSQ* 3, no. 3–4 (2016): 462–84; Emily Rose, "Keeping the Trans in Translation: Queering Early Modern Transgender Memoirs," *TSQ* 3, no. 3–4 (2015): 485–505; Jyl Josephson and Þorgerður Einarsdóttir, "Language Purism and Gender: Trans* Activists and the Icelandic Linguistic Gender Binary," *TSQ* 3, no. 3–4 (2016): 376–87. This last especially speaks to translation from languages, like Old English, with a tripartite system of grammatical gender. And see A. Finn Enke, "Translation," *Keywords*, *TSQ* 1, no. 1–2 (2014): 244. From essary and profoundly hopeful act for those who trans gender, for we have been taught that transgender is marked by dysphoria, a word from the Greek that means difficult to bear, difficult to carry."[52] I do not presume to place this essay under the sign of Transgender Studies, but given, as Enke argues, that "[t]ransgender highlights the labors of translation," and that "[t]ranslation is the skin of transgender,"[53] placing the translation of the medieval in the vicinity of performance would necessarily draw on and owe a debt to such work.

Ghosts in the Crux: A Spectral Old English Script

Read as performances that take medieval texts as their scripts, Auden's translations of the medieval proliferate beyond what critics have previously noted. Take, for example, another poem that, like "The Secret Agent," originates in Auden's early modernist psychomachia project, *The Megalopsych* (much of which constitutes his 1928 and 1930 *Poems*).[54] Eventually given the title "The Watershed" in his *Collected Poems*, the poem is one of the two earliest examples of Auden's work that he continued to include in publications beyond the 1930 *Poems*, and was composed at his parental home in Harborne in the immediate wake of his return from a 1927 trip to Yugoslavia.[55] It is the poem that, for the editor and bibliographer of Auden's standard texts, Edward Mendelson, "marks the divide between his juvenilia and the work of his maturity ... when he found his own voice."[56] Given that, so far as I can tell, extant studies of Auden's medievalism have so far overlooked this poem, I want to devote a little space to demonstrating how it can be understood in relationship to a particular Old English source-text, namely, the poem conventionally known as *The Ruin*, from the tenth-century Old English Exeter Book manuscript.

---

the side of translation studies, see Douglas Robinson, *Transgender, Translation, Translingual Address* (London: Bloomsbury, 2019).

52 Enke, "Translation," 242.

53 Ibid., 243.

54 See W. H. Auden, *Juvenilia: Poems, 1922–1928*, ed. Katherine Bucknell (Princeton: Princeton University Press, 2003), 199–270; Katherine Bucknell, "Introduction," in Auden, *Juvenilia*, xlviii.

55 Fuller, *Commentary*, 8; Auden, *Juvenilia*, 219 (commentary); Bucknell, "Introduction," li.

56 Edward Mendelson, *Early Auden, Late Auden: A Critical Bibliography* (Princeton: Princeton University Press, 2017), 40. Note that this text combines Mendelson's formerly separate volumes of *Early Auden* and *Late Auden*. And see Bucknell, "Introduction", li.

Auden's poem, comprised of two asymmetrical stanzas (the first longer by six lines)—opens with enigmatic syntax that falls away into a description of "Auden's sacred landscape among the lead mines of Alston Moor:"[57]

Who stands, the crux left of the watershed,
On the wet road between the chafing grass
Below him sees the dismantled washing-floors,
Snatches of tramline running to the wood,
An industry already comatose,
Yet sparsely living. A ramshackle engine
At Cashwell raises water; for ten years
It lay in flooded workings until this,
Its latter office, grudging performed,
And further here and there, though many dead
Lie under the poor soil, some acts are chosen
Taken from recent winters; two there were
Cleaned out a damaged shaft by hand, clutching
The winch the gale would tear them from; one died
During a storm, the fells impassable,
Not at his village, but in wooden shape
Through long abandoned levels nosed his way
And in his final valley went to ground.[58]

Unlike other pieces included in Auden's 1930 *Poems*—whose medievalism Chris Jones has analyzed in detail—here Auden has left no salient shibboleth to direct us back to an Old English poem, whether as allusion or as source-text.[59] As Jones also chronicles, Auden's later poems and plays also carry plenty of explicit allusion to or fragmentary direct translation from medieval sources.[60] But even without a direct moment of conventional translation, the texture of the 1930 *Poems* (as a sequence of drama and lyric densely infiltrated by poems from the Exeter Book) triangulates the lines of "The Watershed" into signs of the poem's translative affinity with that manuscript. As "[a] poem concerned only with borders,

---

57 Fuller, *Commentary*, 8.

58 W. H. Auden, *Poems* (London: Faber and Faber, 1930), 56. I cite here the 1930 text of the poem. Unlike "Control of the passes," no significant revisions seem to have taken place (other than adding a title) between this and later collected versions of the poem. Between the *Megalopsych* and the *Poems* there are only minor changes to punctuation that do not bear on the present reading. See, by way of comparison, W. H. Auden, *Collected Poems*, ed. Edward Mendelson (New York: Vintage, 1991), 32–33; *Juvenilia*, 218.

59 On the more clarion allusions of "Paid on Both Sides" and "The Wanderer" to *Beowulf*, *The Wanderer*, and *Sawles Warde*, see Jones, *Strange Likeness*, 79, 84, 113. And see Fuller, *Commentary*, 32, 34, 78.

60 Jones, *Strange Likeness*, 68–121.

separations, finality, cruxes, a poem where even nature makes decisions, chooses between possibilities,"[61] the poem most generally signals its affinity for Old English verse with syntax and paronomasia that take on a riddling function.[62] Mendelson's summary of the problems is apt:

> [I]s *Who stands* interrogative or declarative? What is the missing grammatical link between that phrase and the next? [I]s *the crux* a crossroads or a dilemma? Does *left of* mean "remaining" or "to the left side"? And is *the watershed* a divide on high ground where waters separate, or a basin on low ground where waters gather ... By the end of the poem all these questions are resolved—and the crux proves to be both a crossroads and, by implication, a dilemma—but the opening refuses to give up its meaning.[63]

John Fuller similarly treats the opening of the poem like a riddle with a topographical and cartographical solution: "Perhaps the solution is that the crux is Killhope Cross: keeping it to your left while standing on the A689 'between the chafing grass', you do indeed look down towards the scars of the leadmining process above Nenthead."[64] Auden's correspondence with his friend Christopher Isherwood additionally underscores the riddling nature of the narrative at the end of this first stanza. The lines elliptically refer to a funeral that was delayed when a man died eight miles from his village because weather made "the fells impassable"—finally accomplished only because the coffin was carried back part-way through the mines.[65] As Auden reluctantly explains to his friend, "I don't understand your perplexity over the funeral. In his new shape ['in wooden shape'] means, of course, his coffin. The shape of the coffin should justify 'nosed.' The deliberate association of the process with animals is obvious."[66] Of course, the necessity of such an "explanation" betrays that Auden's riddle is not "obvious."

Some of what Mendelson characterizes as "blank verse lines" with apparently irregular "awkward cadences" can be resolved as perfectly fine specimens of Old English metrical patterns, relying on words with stress on an initial root syllable, complete with caesura ("snatches of tramline | running to the wood"), toleration of spondee ("wet road"), and variable numbers of unstressed elements (take, for example, "Snatches of tramline running to the wood" [/xx /x | /x

---

61 Mendelson, *Early Auden, Later Auden*, 40.
62 The final third of the Exeter Book consists almost entirely of riddles. And see John D. Niles, *Old English Enigmatic Poems and the Play of Texts* (Turnhout: Brepols, 2006).
63 Mendelson, *Early Auden, Later Auden*, 41.
64 Fuller, *Commentary*, 9.
65 Fuller, *Commentary*, 10; Auden, *Juvenilia*, 219.
66 Auden, *Juvenilia*, 219.

xx/]).[67] In light of these more subtle marks of the Old English poetic corpus, and the Exeter Book in particular, other details yoke Auden's text more specifically to *The Ruin*, famously enigmatic in its fragmentary extant state, and nestled in among the larger sequence of riddles in the latter part of the manuscript.[68] The germane details are not individually conspicuous, but, taken together, register an atmosphere in which *The Ruin* haunts Auden's text.

The Ruin opens with the description of a ruined Roman wall in a ruined Roman town (often presumed to be Bath):

> Wrætlic is þes wealstan,   wyrde gebræcon;
> burgstede burston,   brosnað enta geweorc.
> Hrofas sind gehrorene,   hreorge torras,
> hrungeat berofen,   hrim on lime,
> scearde scurbeorge   scorene, gedrorene,
> ældo undereotone.[69]

> Wondrously-adorning is this wallstone, demolished by "what happens,"
> the fortification-place broke open; the work of giants decomposes.
> Roofs are collapsed, towers dilapidated,
> decorated gates wrecked, hoar-frost on the mortar,
> rain-coverings gashed open, hewn away, withered,
> undermined with age.

For Joshua Davies, *The Ruin* and its translations, alone and together, constitute a "time-knot," posing questions like, "when is the now of a medieval text?" and, "[h]ow many nows might a medieval text possess?"[70] As Davies argues, the poem's poetics and material state (with huge lacunae from astonishing damage to the manuscript) conspire such that it "requires unriddling."[71]

In "The Watershed," this "time-knot" unspools into ruination in-process within a modern industrial landscape. As already noted, the "crux left of the watershed" can be "solved" as a crossroads to the left of a point of high ground; but even so, given the description of dereliction that follows, "left" still summons the sense of "what remains," while "crux" retains in its polysemy the philologi-

67 Mendelson, *Early Auden, Later Auden*, 41.

68 *The Ruin* occurs in a cluster of non-riddle poems (and Riddle 60) sandwiched between riddles 1–59 and (the presumably incomplete) 61–94.

69 *The Ruin*, in *The Exeter Book*, ed. George Philip Krapp and Elliott Van Kirk Dobbie, The Anglo-Saxon Poetic Records, vol. 3 (New York: Columbia University Press, 1936), 227–29, ll. 1–6a.

70 Joshua Davies, *Visions and Ruins: Cultural Memory and the Untimely Middle Ages* (Manchester: Manchester University Press, 2018), 8, 29, 18, 38.

71 Ibid., 25.

cal and paleographical sense of an illegibility. And while "watershed" may indeed refer to topography, we might also read it as a literal compound word describing the pumping engine, personified below as an ungrateful servant, itself only barely rescued, and, we gather, only temporarily given reprieve from ruin: "for ten years/ It lay in flooded working until this,/ Its latter office, grudgingly performed."

In any case, this "ramshackle" pump and this metonymically fragmentary "crux" are at best hazy in their outlines. But this half-ruined description of a ruin registers the mechanisms of *The Ruin* at work in Auden's text, summoned and effective within it without being present to the poem in Auden's modernist present. In Davies's account, *The Ruin* "is less interested in creating a detailed image of the building than investigating what meanings it holds in the present and held in the past and how those meanings are generated."[72] As a constative statement, Auden's topographical and architectural description is nothing like an "equivalent" of that in the Old English text—whether in terms of referent or individual lexemes. However, its performative force would seem to summon the specter of *The Ruin*'s descriptive functions and arouse them to work in the modern text.

The ruins of *The Ruin* are described as having already reached a ruined state, but, as Davies argues, "rather than providing a detailed description of the site, the poem focuses its attention on the processes by which the scene of destruction was created."[73] These processes of ruination, although not precisely present, nor represented, also obliquely haunt both the referents of Auden's poem and its riddling poetics of present participles. Auden's sketch of "the wet road between the chafing grass" may gesture to the erosive processes, currently active if not yet complete, which literally under-eat (*underetan*) the wrecked structures that appear suddenly in view in the opening lines of *The Ruin*. Furthermore, we might take "chafing" as a subtle catachresis, whose figurative misuse further displaces the process of wearing-down that it describes from proper presence while yet setting it to work.[74]

In *The Ruin*, this decay is also ascribed to a process involving human mortality and the disappearance of skilled labor for construction and maintenance:

---

72 Ibid., 25.

73 Ibid., 24.

74 Unless Auden invokes a British regionalism of which I am unaware, the PDE use of the verb "chafe" in the sense of rubbing and abrading (versus the mostly obsolete sense of to heat or to figuratively excite) with respect to subjects other than human skin is rather rare, as is this awkward usage, whether it is taken as reflexive or passive. See *Oxford English Dictionary*, s.v. "chafe (*v.*)."

Betend crungon
hergas to hrusan. Forþon þas hofu dreorgiað,
ond þæs teaforgeapa tigelum sceadeð
hrostbeagas hrof.[75]

The repairers fell,
the populations to the soil. Because of that these
buildings are derelict and the ochre vaults shed
their tiles.

A pattern of chiasmic nominal variation on terms for the earth's unforgiving grasp syntactically locks the dead in the soil:

Eorðgrap hafað,
waldend wyrhtan forweorone, geleorene
heardgripe hrusan.[76]

The earth-grasp holds
rulers, builders, rotten, vanished—
the solid-grip of the soil.

The Ruin refuses to scrape off the words that cling to its realities, allowing terms for soil, dirt, and the earth (*hruse* and *eorðe*, as above, as well as the phrase *lamrindum beag* (ring of clay/soil-crust))[77] to proliferate as the poem locates dead human bodies within the locking hold of their referents.

Accordingly, Auden's poem tethers itself to these words not by providing "equivalents" but by letting them operate in the processes of his poem without being properly present. Take, for example, the aforementioned account of a coffin that finally "went to ground" by means of a riddling zoomorphic "process" (in the sense of linear movement), through the grip of the mine levels. Even more focused on ruination as process, the structures in Auden's poem are not yet fully crumbled like those of the ancient building industry that left behind the "work of giants." The tenuously repaired water-engine signals the fragile persistence of some *betend* (repairers, restorers), and with them, "[a]n industry already comatose, / Yet sparsely living." Sparsely living indeed, as in Auden's poem, "many dead/ Lie under the poor soil"—among them industrial laborers who died maintaining the mines ("two there were/ Cleaned out a damaged shaft by hand").

75 *The Ruin*, ll. 28b–31a.
76 Ibid., ll. 6b–8a.
77 Ibid., l. 17.

If one thing Auden's poem is *doing* is elegizing an industrial ruination of modern male proletarian bodies, it is haunted in this by *The Ruin*, which provides the modernist poem with a ghostly medieval script. What better place to look for specters, wraiths, apparitions, or ghosts, than a ruin? Almost nothing detailed in "The Watershed" could be construed in good faith as a translation of *The Ruin* according to the traditional criteria of "equivalency;" but *The Ruin* is nonetheless at work in the poem in some strange way. To the extent that Auden's poem is "after" (as belated/in-pursuit-of) *The Ruin* as Spicer is "after" Lorca—wooing the specters of the Old English poem—it accomplishes a certain kind of queer translation. This is not, I want to stress, a positive or systematic taxonomizing of the poem, but one way to comprehend it as a kind of translation and to account for the spectral conditions of its medievalism along with, as we will see, its spectral horizons of gender and sexuality, both medieval and modern.

Translation and the Ruins of Gender and Sexuality

The second, shorter stanza of Auden's poem continues to take *The Ruin* as a performance script, constituting a speech act whose illocutionary gravity conjures a spectral translation of gender and sexuality. This translation orients itself around at least three partly overlapping topoi: the gendering of labor, the interpolation and gendering of bodies within larger processes of ruination across time, and a mutual deforming of medieval and modern(ist) gender performances. Immediately, the imperative mood consolidates the performativity of the poem:

> Go home, now, stranger, proud of young stock,
> Stranger, turn back again, frustrate and vexed:
> This land, cut off, will not communicate,
> Be no accessory content to one
> Aimless for faces rather there than here.
> Beams from your car may cross a bedroom wall,
> They wake no sleeper; you may hear the wind
> Arriving driven from the ignorant sea
> To hurt itself on the pane, on bark of elm
> Where sap unbaffled rises, being spring;
> But seldom this. Near you, taller than grass,
> Ears poise before decision, scenting danger.

The first two lines provisionally resolve the main riddle of the first stanza as an extended vocative hail, topographically interpolating the unidentified, absent, and invisible addressee. In this, the entire poem becomes legible as a particular speech act: a warning.

But who speaks here? In the Old English *Ruin*, as Patricia Dailey's analysis would seem to suggest, the voice may remain unmediated, in an aporiatic relationship to the reader:

> Although the descriptive narrative of this poem appears to be a subject's meditation on a past, no subject appears as an authorial voice. The poem is haunted by the remains of a subject in a way that resembles the riddles before it in the Exeter Book.[78]

Alain Renoir similarly notes this spookiness, as the Old English poem "has a speaking voice but no speaker."[79] And in Auden's poem, the enigmatic opening lines of the first stanza already gave us a ghost. As Fuller puts it, "the sense of 'who' as 'whoever' is more than a mere grammatical sleight ... it sets up a ghostly protagonist in the poem of far greater weight than a hypothesis."[80] In addition to this protagonist, the warning of the second stanza conjures another spectral body, marking the gulf between the ghostly stranger's approach and the temporality of the ruination process. Mendelson explains:

> The spatial barrier between the land and the stranger is also a barrier in time. The land, "already comatose," is too aged, too marked by its "many dead," to join the stranger proud of his "young stock." The stranger can neither communicate with the past nor decide on a plausible future.[81]

This temporal knot cannot be untied or cut even as it both summons and forbids a particular modern body's access to this mingling of medieval and modern ruination. In this sense, the warned stranger constitutes a kind of palimpsest of this anonymous body (barred—for good or ill—from these modern processes of ruination) and the modernist poet (haunted by the medieval poem and the specters of its own ruins).[82]

78 Patricia Dailey, "Questions of Dwelling in Anglo-Saxon Poetry and Medieval Monasticism: Inhabiting Landscape, Body, and Mind," *New Medieval Literatures* 8 (2006): 175–214 (183).
79 Alain Renoir, "The Old English *Ruin:* Contrastive Structure and Affective Impact," in *The Old English Elegies: New Essays in Criticism and Research* (Cranberry, NY: Associated University Presses, 1983), 150. And see Davies, *Visions and Ruins*, 25.
80 Fuller, *Commentary*, 8.
81 Mendelson, *Early Auden, Late Auden*, 42.
82 On modernist texts as queer palimpsests of the medieval, see Peter Buchanan, "*Beowulf*, Bryher, and the Blitz: A Queer History," in *Dating Beowulf: Studies in Intimacy*, ed. Daniel C. Remein and Erica Weaver (Machester: Manchester University Press, 2020), 279–303.

This haunting, interpolating hail opens a cipher for translations of particular, historical discourses of gender and sexuality as they operate in the medieval poem and the modernist poem, in medieval and modern processes of ruination. *The Ruin* emphasizes the state of the ruined structures it describes by contrastively populating the gendered interiors of their past:

þær iu beorn monig,
glædmod ond goldbeorht geleoma gefrætwed,
wlonc ond wingal wighyrstum scan;
seah on sinc, on sylfor, on searogimmas,
on ead, on æht, on earcanstan,
on þas beorhtan burg bradan rices.[83]

where before many men—
happy-minded and gold-bright, adorned with radiance,
magnificent and full of wine—gleamed in war-ornaments;
looked upon treasure, upon silver, upon alluring-gems,
upon wealth, upon property, upon precious stone,
upon this bright city of a spacious kingdom.

Precious stones, property, war-gear—these instances of patriarchal, martial, homosocial male display glimmer as spectral apparitions among the crumbling walls,[84] now absent of any living human bodies. As Dailey argues, in this poem "[t]he past is constantly interpolated into the present as a coupling that ultimately cannot be disentangled."[85] From the position of the poem's speaker, each gem or war-ornament encodes nostalgic, aristocratic masculinities (following Davies, both those of early English perceptions of Romano-British society and those of an earlier moment in pre-Norman Old English speaking areas of Britain) against which those gender performances contemporary to the poem are tacitly, if ambivalently, measured.[86] As costume jewelry for a role only ghosts can now play, they thus haunt the speaker's own performance of gender and sexuality, beckoning and refusing entry to the ruins, interpolating that body (or the

---

83 *The Ruin*, ll. 32b–37.

84 On the complexity performance of heroic masculinity in Old English poetry, especially in terms of weapons and accoutrements, see Gillian R. Overing, "*Beowulf* on Gender," *New Medieval Literatures* 12 (2010): 1–22.

85 Dailey, "Questions of Dwelling," 184.

86 Davies, *Visions and Ruins*, 28, "the poem imagines both Anglo-Saxon and non-Anglo-Saxon communities occupying the ruins." And Eileen A. [Fradenburg] Joy, "On the Hither Side of Time: Tony Kushner's *Homebody/Kabul* and the Old English *Ruin*," *Medieval Perspectives* 19 (2005): 175–205, at 196.

poem's aforementioned spectral voice) into a nostalgic ideology in which the impossibility of its successful performance redoubles as its normative force.

By contrast, Auden's "Beams from your car may cross a bedroom wall,/ They wake no sleeper," shines an automobile headlight in on the private domestic space of the laborers who work the mines, on walls that display nothing. A flash of an abandoned house, perhaps one of the tiny cottages that once housed miners and their families in so-called "pit villages," this chance autopsy of that most intimate of modern spaces encodes modern absences. The bedroom may play host to the ghosts of the heteronormative proletarian couple, or, in a kind of double-absence of heteronormativity, a closeted, isolated, homosexual desire (or a dangerous intimacy) within the homosocial context of the community of mineworkers. This flash of headlight grants the stranger only a brief flicker of spectral vision into this "haunted house," marking, with a deep ambivalence, the stranger's exclusion from the absent intimacies of the bedroom and the processes of ruination in which they are imbricated. Classifying this poem among other early Auden "allegories of the closet" (including the aforementioned "The Secret Agent"), Richard R. Bozorth notes that it registers a "fascination with the idea that sexual marginality can lend itself to a subversive detachment from mainstream culture."[87] However subversive, the stranger is at least doubly detached from whatever spectral performances of gender and sexuality are now absent from the abandoned bedroom.[88]

In its fragmentarily preserved descriptions of Roman baths, *The Ruin* considers another space of intimacy ahead of all ruination:

> Stanhofu stodan, stream hate wearp
> widan wylme; weal all befeng
> beorhtan bosme, þær þa baþu wæron,
> Leton þonne geotan [.................]ofer
> harne stan hate streamasun
> [..........................
> .þæt hringmere hate ....
> .... þær þa baþu wæron.[89]

> Stone-structures stood, a stream flung heat,
> a broad jet; a wall embraced it all
> in its bright heart, where the baths were,
> hot in its chest/core. That was convenient.

87 Bozorth, "Auden: love," 181–82.
88 I extend my thanks to the anonymous reader internal to the volume and to Sarah Hamblin for comments that helped to clarify my observations in this paragraph.
89 *The Ruin*, ll. 38–46.

They let them gush out....
hat streams over grey stone
un[der?]....
    the ring-pool   hot ....
                where the baths were.

Although now cold, the baths are described in their once-lavish state, with a paronomasia that gives way to a personification of the bathhouse as the beating heart of a living body (one critic even leans on this moment to read the poem as a city-body riddle).[90] As Dailey notes, this focus on the once "living city" in the latter part of *The Ruin* has the effect of generating "an other time that is not successive, but performative."[91]

Answering this particular curtain call, against the figuration of "convenient" embodied intimacy and the comfort of the hot gushing water, Auden's poem is menaced by the exposed "ramshackle engine" bringing up water—whose former state "in flooded workings" must have involved stagnant muck. As Fuller notes, "[m]ining mother earth is symbolically presented as a male activity in very early Auden,"[92] and within a horizon of modernism and Auden's early engagements with Freudian psychoanalysis,[93] both mine-shafts and the water-engine may partake of a perhaps blunt trope of symbolic male penetration of a female landscape—Eliotic in its lack of reproductive fecundity, displacing the performance of gender and sexuality from private embodiment to industrial process of ruination.

Auden's poem is remarkable in employing substantive adjectives and indefinite pronouns ("many dead," "two," "one") to almost entirely avoid gendered personal pronouns or possessive adjectives, with the single exception of the "his" that describes the "way" of the dead man through the mines and toward final burial. But this single "his" also registers the tacit gendering of the mining operations as working-class male labor. The specific sense in which "[t]his land, cut off, will not communicate" (as, Mendelson puts it, "a place the miners cannot escape and the stranger cannot enter"),[94] is thus additionally haunted by a trans-

90 William C. Johnson, Jr., "*The Ruin* as Body-City Riddle," *Philological Quarterly* 59 (1980), 397–411. See, by way of comparison, Dailey, "Questions of Dwelling," 193.
91 Dailey, "Questions of Dwelling," 187.
92 Fuller, *Commentary*, 10.
93 On the complexity of Freud in Auden amidst his commitment to other theorists and, early on, to Marxism, see Rod Mengham, "Auden, Psychology, and Society," in *The Cambridge Companion to W. H. Auden*, 165–74; on Freud in Auden's medievalism, see Remein, "Auden, Translation, Betrayal," 821.
94 Mendelson, *Early Auden, Late Auden*, 42.

lation between at least two ruined, historical, homosocial masculinities: the martial, aristocratic elite of *The Ruin*, and the modern proletarian man of Auden's poem. The stranger is warned off/excluded from both. In this sense, the warning might be characterized as a kind of dialectical inversion of the queer historiographical touch that Carolyn Dinshaw influentially described in terms of "partial connections, queer relations between incommensurate lives and communities—relations that collapse the critical and theoretical oppositions between transhistorical and alteritist accounts, between truth and pleasure, between past and present, self and other."[95] Beyond the immediate implications of the poem's Freudian symbolic freight, the larger point is that a sexed and gendered embodiment remains at work in the specters of *The Ruin* which the performativity of Auden's poem is after.

Moreover, beyond the operations of Auden's poem that arise from the gendering of industrial mining, the ruined industrial landscape also raises the specter of a ghostly, inhuman sense of gender and sexuality—or at least a spectral indifference to the same. Haunted by *The Ruin*, the warning of Auden's poem serves to exclude the stranger not only from the performances of gender and sexuality at work in both the Old English source-text and the modern industrial landscape, but also from the spectral, non-human ruins of those performances of gender and sexuality. Following the apparition of the abandoned house, one can hear only the a-sexuality and non-gendered sound of the erosive wind (figured as a bird) which "hurt itself on the pane" of the empty bedroom window—indifferent to both the absences that haunt the house and the stranger's ambivalent detachment from those spectral intimacies. The sap that rises in the elm, which elsewhere in English literature (e. g., Chaucer's April showers or Eliot's "cruelest month") might encode heteronormative male virility, is here "unbaffled," indifferent to human sexuality, rising only because a non-anthropogenic Spring has arrived. The only living sentience left for the stranger to find, or not, is the non-human animal whose "Ears poise before decision, scenting danger"—only barely registered by this lightest of metonymic touches that peek up

95 Carolyn Dinshaw, *Getting Medieval: Sexualities and Communities Pre- and Postmodern* (Durham: Duke University Press, 1999), 35. This is *not* to suggest that the medieval or the medieval poem cannot be queer while modernity is or could be, or that only the relationship between the medieval and the modern (rather than the medieval "on its own") harbors that capacity. I am *not* suggesting that the medieval is not the proper province of queerness nor even that Auden was suggesting that queer people should not or cannot "enter" the medieval, but that the translational logic of his poem registers an ambivalence about both the medieval and this industrial scene in terms of its perceived simultaneous implication of and hostility to certain bodies and their performances of gender.

into the text. Were the stranger to approach instead of turning back, this quickest of creatures—read variously as a hare or (in connection with an earlier poem) a field mouse—will vanish, so that it might as well have been a ghost.[96] In the same stroke, the poem marks the gender and sexuality of the "stranger" who stands beside or approaches the processes of ruination as variably illegible, non-present, spectral, or of no interest to both the dwindling human community and its non-human environment. In this regard, it is interesting that Auden seems to have originally titled the poem "Rookhope." The word is a toponym (another village in county Durham). But in the context of the sustained medievalism of the 1930 *Poems*, it might be read as an irresistibly riddling *kenning*, referring to the "beasts of battle" trope of Old English poetry (in which the raven, the wolf, and the eagle are referenced as carrion-eaters in association with the aftermath of violence or when violent death is expected in a verse narrative). "The hope of the rook" might grimly mark an anxiety about distinctly human finitude, and/or an expectation of some sort of destruction or ruination.[97]

Both *The Ruin* and the "stranger" haunt the poem as queer spooks of translation—Auden's poem conjuring *The Ruin*, this spectral translation conjuring the stranger in turn. If *The Ruin* is, as Eileen A. Fradenburg Joy argues, "a poem about being bewitched by Otherness and a missed encounter with the foreign past, while also writing the strange past into the present in order to hold it and fix and render it *Heimlich*,"[98] Auden's re-performance of it evinces a nuanced, multivalent ambivalence, unsure of the "stranger's" embodied response to particular inscriptions of gender and sexuality, but ineluctably summoning, or at least implicating, sexed and gendered bodies—human and spectral—in the translative act determined as performance. If, in the process, *The Ruin* is transformed—weathered, eroded, its elements repurposed—much farther beyond what is traditionally legible as proper or "faithful" to "translation," it is not because the poem's genesis lies categorically outside of translation. Among other questions, as Dailey writes, *The Ruin* asks, "[h]ow does a poem dwell in time and space?"[99] Auden's poem phrases that question in terms of gender and sexuality in a modernist poem whose performativity allows it to be inhabited by ghosts of the medieval.

---

96 For example, Auden, *Juvenilia*, 14 (commentary); Fuller, *Commentary*, 11.
97 On the "beasts of battle" trope as a signal of animal communication from which humans are cut off, see Mo Pareles, "What the Raven Told the Eagle: Animal Language and the Return of Loss in *Beowulf*," in *Dating Beowulf: Studies in Intimacy*, ed. Daniel C. Remein and Erica Weaver (Manchester: Manchester University Press, 2020), 164–86.
98 Joy, "Hither Side," 187–88.
99 Dailey, "Questions of Dwelling," 182.

The case for calling this poem a "translation," even an "improper" translation, may seem weaker at first glance than that of Auden's "The Wanderer," or even "The Secret Agent." However, "The Watershed" does recall the kind of performative, textual intimacy that Chris Piuma poses as part of the activity of "dystranslation"—a "queer approach to translation" in which the translator plays the role of a relationship "broker" for the intimacies between texts.[100] Hadbawnik makes the case that "the notion of intimacy, as applied to translation, can ... break (or at least sidestep) the binary ... between 'accuracy' and 'creativity'" so often inflicted on translations from medieval texts.[101] The term *performance* —deployed to strategically conflate its senses relating to the action of conventionalized theatricality and the performative speech act—plots the erotics and intimacies of queer translation from the medieval along yet another axis.

Because of *The Ruin*'s fragmented state and non-narrative, non-personified mode of description, Fradenburg Joy argues, "the poem does not have a clearly delineated ideological coherence."[102] While Auden's poem may not participate in a univocally saturated ideology, as a translation that takes *The Ruin* as a performance script, it cannot possibly be outside of ideology in the strict Althusserian sense, since the performative, as a practice, as the very materiality of ideology, is *always* derivational, in an asymmetrical and reiterative relationship to the authority it re-cites.[103] Another way to comprehend this ambivalence that may seem in excess of that in its source-text without plotting it on a representational axis of "accuracy" or dismissing it as "adaptation," is to read it as a spectral (but sexed and gendered) body that constitutes one of the spatial dimensions of translation in the vicinity of performance. In an exploration of yet another attempt at "a new ontology of translation moving away from a hierarchy of fidelities and failures," routing Lawrence Venuti's famous concept of a textual remainder in translation through Elizabeth Grosz's readings of Irigaray's insistence on the irreducibility of sexual difference, Aarón Lacayo posits a

---

100 Chris Piuma, "The Task of the Dystranslator: An Introduction to a Dystranslation of the Words of the 'Pearl' Poet," *postmedieval* 6, no. 2 (2015): 120 – 126 (120, 124 – 25). Part of the brilliance of Piuma's term also lies in its grammatological underpinnings; namely the canny, perhaps untranslatable "misspelling" of the prefix *dis-* in such a way that it does not alter the pronunciation of the word, rendering it—on the model of the infamous *a* in Derrida's *différance*—irreducibly *written* and so implicating grammatological logics in the problems and pleasures of translation. The term itself is thus only dystranslatable.

101 Hadbawnik, "Differing Intimacies," 228.

102 Joy, "Hither Side," 190.

103 See Butler, *Bodies that Matter*, 3.

"queer mode of translation" with a "sexual—that is, corporeal" remainder.[104] "The Watershed" enacts translation as a mode of corporeality, one that implicates a body that may be non-human and spectral, poised on the threshold of a performance that may or may not "succeed." Indeed, it is about the success of a whole set of performances that Auden's poem harbors such strong ambivalence, not least of which is its success as a translation.

Schoolbook Re-citation: Old English Performance in Translation

The question of what is "lost in translation" between medieval and modern thus pales in interest to the question of *what else* is translated when we consider the translation in question as a speech act. In the final phase of this essay, I want to gesture to the spatial and corporeal dimensions of dystranslation and its spectrality that become increasingly salient as such performativity becomes increasingly, and sometimes, quite strangely, literalized.

Take, for example, contemporary poet Thomas Meyer's inclusion of his translation of Ælfric's *Colloquy on the Occupations* within his 1979 book, *Staves Calends Legends.*[105] Unlike the translations of Auden's 1930 *Poems*, Meyer's translation is not at all cagey about its relationship to its source-text or its status as a translation. It is not a case of translation by subtly seducing the ghosts of an old poem to inhabit a new one. However, as we will see, Meyer's source-text already functions as a script for a kind of early medieval theatrical pedagogy, throwing the performative dimensions of translation into high relief and summoning yet another sort of sexed and gendered spectral corporeality.

The *Colloquy* is a Latin text from early medieval England that survives in three copies, one of which includes an interlinear Old English translation.[106] The text stages a dialogue between a master and a group of monastic students who play the parts of laborers of various types (e.g., an oxherd, a fisher, a hunter, a fowler, etc.), answering questions about those occupations as well as their own monastic vocation. Although the text cannot be reduced to its most narrow

104 Aarón Lacayo, "A Queer and Embodied Translation: Ethics of Difference and Erotics of Distance," *Comparative Literature Studies* 51, no. 2 (2014): 215–30, 226, 219, 223–25.

105 Thomas Meyer, *Staves Calends Legends* (Charlotte, NC: The Jargon Society, 1979).

106 The surviving manuscripts are Oxford, St. John's MS 154; London, British Library, Add. MS 32246; and London, British Library Cotton Tiberius MS A.iii.

didactic functions,[107] it serves in part as a schoolroom aid to learning Latin. The copy that survives with an accompanying Old English translation underscores this point and perhaps lends credence to its modern use as an introductory reading in Old English textbooks and courses.

A prose schoolroom text, most likely encountered by a poet in modernity as an exercise rather than as a literary composition—these qualities render the *Colloquy* an unlikely and curious selection for translation and inclusion in a book of late-modernist poetry from the late 1970s.[108] Moreover, the text is not meant for univocal reading, whether for an audience or in private contemplation. As Katherine O'Brien O'Keeffe notes, it is a text meant "to be memorized and then performed in interaction with others,"[109] a point Erica Weaver pushes further in arguing that such texts "allow us to retrace a particular kind of theater."[110] In Weaver's reading, the *Colloquy* is quite literally a "script" that activates the performativity of the literal pedagogical space it defines—part of a "community theater" that renders legible the extent to which not only individualized and interiorized forms of "attention," but also "dispersed attention—even intentional distraction … can also help to constitute the thinking subject."[111]

Meyer's translation, which is presented without any paratextual or dramatic cues, appears about half-way through a collection of mostly fragmentary (what Meyer might call "intermittent") lyric poems.[112] The collection takes up an avant-garde medievalism from a variety of source-texts, starting even with the book's epigraph, taken from the opening lines of *The Dream of the Rood:* "hwæt ic swefna cyst secgan wylle/ hwæt me gemætte to midre nihte" (listen, I want to speak about the best of dreams/ what I dreamed in the middle of the night).

---

107 For example, Katherine O'Brien O'Keeffe, *Stealing Obedience: Narrative of Agency and Identity in Later Anglo-Saxon England* (Toronto: University of Toronto Press, 2016), 95–96; Joyce Hill, "Winchester Pedagogy and the Colloquy of Ælfric," *Leeds Studies in English* 29 (1998): 137–52.
108 The reading of Meyer as a latter-day modernist is the poet's own suggestion and is in keeping with his association with Basil Bunting, the English concrete poets, the Objectivists, etc., who already, as Peter Nicholls has suggested, complicate the *terminus ad quem* of English-language Modernism. See Thomas Meyer and Patrick Morrisey, "Interview with Thomas Meyer," *Chicago Review* 59, no. 3 (2015): 116–17; and Peter Nicholls, "Modernisng Modernism: From Pound to Oppen," *Critical Quarterly* 44, no. 2 (2002): 41–58.
109 O'Brien O'Keeffe, *Stealing Obedience*, 106.
110 Erica Weaver, "Performing (In)Attention: Ælfric, Ælfric Bara, and the *Visitatio sepulchri*," *Representations* 152, no. 1 (2020): 17; and see Irina Dumitrescu, *The Experience of Education in Anglo-Saxon England* (Cambridge: Cambridge University Press, 2018), 62, 76–78.
111 Weaver, "Performing (In)attention," 4, 16–17.
112 Meyer and Morrisey, "Interview," 116.

Meyer's book is additionally marked by a continuity with the New American Poetry (especially the Black Mountain School) and the influence of British contributors to mid-century International Concrete poetry. The volume's rather handsome book-arts materiality, with tight, square-ish dimensions, is typical of the early books published by the Jargon Society—a press run by Meyer's late longtime partner, Jonathan Williams. A line drawing by concrete poet John Furnivall furnishes the book with a frontispiece. Consolidating these elements, Meyer's reflection on his own initials in notes on the front jacket flap calls attention to an interest, encoded in the book's title, in concrete inscription and its relations to temporality and the "counting" of prosody: "The lines that make up an M or a T are staves, and to count calends—new moons—I mark down one, two, three, four staves and a fifth to cross off winter."[113] In precisely positioned type on unnumbered pages, the book cultivates an elegant, concrete-inflected, lyric mode—even when playing out jokes on the professional jargon of Old English studies, as in the typographically underscored wordplay on *kenning* and *futhork* on the last page of the sequence "Solstice Hymn, Loom Song:"

here near the road
this stone shall stand
the distance that bounds
the common range of vision

$$\frac{\text{kenning}}{\text{inkling}}$$

$$\frac{\text{futhork}}{\text{hayfork}}$$

from these staves' prongs
harvest fodder to pack your
heart's loft & store your
brain's barn for the winter.[114]

Elaborating the medieval conditions for an unlikely modernist poetic diction, the verse plays the enigmatic quality of the kenning, as a trope, against (all at once) the physical characteristics of an inked glyph, the cognitive and embodied characteristics of an intuition, the physical shape of the *futhork* (the "row" of runic characters), and the physical shape of a farming tool.

---

113 Meyer, *Staves Calends Legends*, front jacket flap.
114 Meyer, *Staves Calends Legends*, n.p.

The discrete and sustained translation of the *Colloquy* thus appears distinct from the rest of the book, in which medievalism in the form of references to Old and Middle English and Old Norse narrative, poetry, and myth, are infused into the lyric fabric—in part the result of Meyer's early project to translate Old English medical and medico-magical texts out of Thomas Oswald Cockayne's *Leechdoms, Wortcunning, and Starcraft of Early England* (1866) at the suggestion of the late poet Gerrit Lansing.[115]

Perhaps deepening the apparent incongruity of the *Colloquy*'s pedagogical role-play and Meyer's highly textual lyric, Meyer himself seems to demure before a performativity determined within a horizon of theatricality:

> My work is meant to be public however intimate it seems. That's its artifice. I feel an obligation to read in public because the voice, the actual sound of the poet, pertains significantly. Though the idea of performance makes me shy: tipping over the edge from "reading" to "performing" moves the event from presentation to attraction.[116]

But the title Meyer gives his translation, "Pro Doctrina Quam Nescire (Aelfric's Colloquy)" (the Latin can be read as "for study [rather] than ignorance/stupidity"), obliquely references the dialectic of pain, pleasure, and pedagogy that opens a horizon of monastic performativity in the text when the master asks: "Will you be flogged for learning?" (Uultis flagellari in discendo? / Wille bespungen on leornunge?).[117] The young male students respond: "We prefer to be flogged for study than for stupidity. But we know you are gentle & will not give us welts unless we give you cause" (Carius est nobis flagellari pro doctrina quam nescire. Sed scimus te mansuetum esse et nolle inferre plagas nobis, nisi cogaris a nobis / Leofre ys us beon bespungen for lare þænne hit ne cunnan. Ac we witun þe bilewitne wesan ond nellan onbelæden spincgla us, buton þu bi togennyd togenydd

---

115 See David Hadbawnik and Thomas Meyer, "Interview with Thomas Meyer," in *Beowulf: A Translation*, trans. Thomas Meyer (Brooklyn: punctum books, 2012), 261–62; Meyer and Morrissey, "Interview," 126. A non-exhaustive list of such elements that make it into *Staves Calends Legends* include charm-like references to agriculture, bees, and birds, (e.g., "Bee & spicer/ rowan, pimpernel/ sinegreen/ cold iron"), narrative of Vikings in early medieval England (e.g., "& Vikings invated, settled the land/ bringing their gods") including references to Viking paganism ("& Yggdrasil grows sideways"), and a poem titled "Starcraft, Runes," which includes references to the Egil of *Egils saga*, a Rune poem, and further references to early medieval Scandinavian paganism.

116 Meyer and Morrisey, "Interview," 119.

117 Meyer, *Staves Calends Legends*; G. N. Garmonsway, ed., *Ælfric's Colloquy* (Liverpool: Liverpool University Press, 1978), 18, ll. 7–10. Cited here with the Latin text and the Old English "main text." Abbreviations are silently expanded and orthography regularized.

fram us).[118] This, as Irina Dumitrescu phrases it, "conventional, if rather wishful, treatment of corporal punishment,"[119] implies a performativity that functions as a heuristic for learning—one that constructs, as Weaver argues, attention or attentiveness as "the crucial stage direction that enables all the others to unfold."[120]

This performativity is doubly linked to learning and to translation as constituent elements of poesis in both the early medieval context and in Meyer's larger corpus, which includes a number of other translations.[121] As Meyer explains in an interview conducted by Hadbawnik and included in the volume of his *Beowulf* translation, "[h]ook, line, and sinker, at a young age, I swallowed Pound's dicta: translating is how you learn to write a poem."[122] Moreover, in a discussion of the "the initial impulse that kickstarts the poem" in an interview for the *Chicago Review*, Meyer again links translation and learning: "what I'm suggesting is that the learning (experience or 'tradition') fires the need for transmission, which results in text. Both are instances of translation and poem."[123] The formulation is remarkable in modeling modernist lyric as fundamentally translative in a manner that echoes the medieval concept of *translatio studii* (the translation/transmission of learning).

In the case of Meyer's translation of the *Colloquy*, the source-text already links its performativity to a knot of learning and translation with a distinctly queer trajectory. As O'Brien O'Keeffe explains, both Ælfric's *Colloquy* and his *Grammar* are concerned with "the training of boys in the monastic *familia*, both to initiate the young into Latin textual culture and to reproduce the textual community of the Benedictine reformed monastery."[124] Drawing especially on Carol Braun Pasternack's critical framing of early medieval monastic chastity in terms of sexual orientation, Mo Pareles locates the queerness of monastic sexuality and affectivity not in a general non-normativity nor a homoaffectivity, but in precisely this mode of "absolute orientation away from biological reproductivity and its secular institutions, and the formation of other durable kinship and affective structures."[125] As Pareles argues, in Ælfric's larger corpus, especially

118 Ibid.

119 Dumitrescu, *The Experience of Education*, 66–67.

120 Weaver, "Performing (In)attention," 17.

121 For example, Meyer, *Beowulf*; Thomas Meyer, trans., *Daode Jing* (Chicago: Flood, 2006).

122 Hadbawnik and Meyer, "Interview," 270.

123 Meyer and Morrissey, "Interview," 115.

124 O'Brien O'Keeffe, *Stealing Obedience*, 107.

125 Pareles, "Jewish Heterosexuality," 294–98. And see Carol Braun Pasternack, "The Sexual Practices of Virginity and Chastity in Adhelm's *De Virginitate*," in *Sex and Sexuality in Anglo-Saxon England: Essays in Memory of Daniel G. Calder*, ed. Pasternack and Lisa M. Wester (Tempe: ACMRS, 2004), 93–120.

his translations of the Old Testament, this construction of chastity, monastic maleness, and asexual reproduction depends on an ideology of supersessionist translation in which "heterosexuality is outmoded by aligning sexual difference with Jewish-Christian difference."[126] Initiating young male students (*pueri/cildra*, in Meyer's translation, "boys") into the monastic same-sex community, the theatricality of the *Colloquy* thus performs precisely such queer translations.

Meyer's text then *re-translates* this translation. Invoking the Latin text for the title of the piece suggests a reliance on the Latin as a source-text; but, the proliferation of Old English medievalism elsewhere in the book, and the fact that most modern readers of the *Colloquy* probably encounter only the Old English (not the Latin) text (usually in the context of an Old English textbook), may leave readers of Meyer's *Colloquy* certain that it is a translation, but not entirely sure of which text. The unstable early medieval script, already performing gender and sexuality in/as translation, thus generates another unstable script in modernity.

This framing results in a double-dystranslation—of source-text and its translative knots, and of the bodies that it summons into performance in modernity—as when the master asks the students to answer questions about their own monastic life:

> How do you like this speech, boys?
>
> It pleases us well, although you discuss things deep
> & over our heads. Speak in terms we know so we can
> understand what you say.

The downright conspicuous modesty of the teacher's question calls for attention, as the monastic construct of learning-translation-sexuality rings differently when re-cited as a script for poetry informed by various modernist avant-gardes in the late 1970s. The early medieval teacher's invitation for the young students to consider how rhetoric and inward understanding pertain to their Latin lesson easily becomes a meta-poetic question about diction in the context of a gendered audience. The determination of this audience as "boys" might resonate with a folksy teacher addressing younger male students, but also might play as a vernacular boast in an all-male context or as a question about poetry in a twentieth-century queer literary community. In this way, the script that interpolates early medieval speakers into a community of learning and translation inseparable from queer, non-biological, all male, modes of reproduction, is dystranslated by the very modern bodies it summons to perform it in/as translation.

---

126 Pareles, "Jewish Heterosexuality," 298, and see 302–3.

On its face, Meyer's *Colloquy* may appear less "dystranslative" than Auden's "The Watershed." The gap between script and performance in Auden's text is perhaps more obvious. Auden's poem re-cites *The Ruin* without any pretense toward the "embalming" against which Spicer writes. The queerness of such translation stems in part from the spectral erotics that govern an ambivalent performance linking processes of ruination, gender, and modes of production—the performative effect of which is the implication of a queer body haunted by the place of gender and sexuality in both medieval and modern ruins. But while Meyer's text seems to translate much more conventionally (if still making strategic, understated interventions), it also conjures/follows the work of a spectral, gendered, corporeality operating in the different and partial connections between modern queer malenesses and early medieval queer male celibacies. This working in turn raises the specter of dystranslating the gendered space of a modern body in reciting this translated medieval script. Here, as opposed to Auden's "The Watershed," we are much closer to a translational enactment of Dinshaw's partial, historiographical touch that rejects the choice between "mimetic identification with the past or blanket alteritism" as a false dilemma.[127] In Auden's poem, the body of the modernist stranger—warned away from performances of gender and sexuality implicated in processes of ruination (heteronormative, homosocial, antique, medieval, and modern)—is dystranslated by the possibility of a spectral inhuman gender and sexuality. In Meyer's text, just the possibility of the modern bodies implicitly summoned to perform it dystranslate the source-text with another kind of spectral corporeality altogether. Although there is more to say about this than space allows here, in Coonrod's *Judith*, the deterritorialization of literary translation within a formalized space of dramatic performance would seem to achieve something similar even as it embraces a kind of theatricality assiduously avoided by Meyer's poetics.

Not corporeal performance alone, divorced from the dynamics of text and the protocols of textual translation, but such an embodied performance of the medieval in a dialectical orbit with textualized translation translates the space of performativity itself in its sexual and gendered dimensions.[128] After all, as Spicer writes, "[w]ords are what sticks to the real. We use them to push the real, to drag the real into the poem. They are what we hold on with, nothing

127 Dinshaw, *Getting Medieval*, 34.

128 Here I am responding to an argument made by Carolyn Dinshaw that linked performance and translation in the case of a theatrical/dance performance of the trial of John/Eleanor Rykener in which Dinshaw urged that literary scholars consider performance as a way to move *away* from text. Carolyn Dinshaw, "Doing Medieval Sex Work in the 21st Century: John/Eleanor Rykener and the Last of the Cockettes," lecture, GW MEMSI, March 2, 2017.

else."[129] The logic here is that of an impure phenomenology on a translative trajectory—one that sets the pure immanence of the body in classical phenomenology into a dialectic with the inescapably deconstructive textual time mechanics of re-citation. This logic is already at work in corners of Merleau-Ponty's *Phenomenology of Perception*, in which the belonging-to-space of the body summons and shapes it as much as it risks interpolation by a textualized script:

> I am not in space and time, nor do I think space and time; rather, I am of space and time; my body fits itself to them and embraces them. The scope of this hold measures the scope of my existence; however, it can never in any case be total. The space and time that I inhabit are always surrounded by indeterminate horizons that contain other points of view.[130]

As "indeterminate horizons," the spectral corporealities summoned by the re-citation of a medieval source-text—in Meyer's *Colloquy* as well as in Coonrod's *Judith* and Auden's "The Watershed"—dystranslate the sexual and gendered space of the modern performing body. In these cases, it is a question of how the medieval inscribes the space and corporeality of performance as well as the trajectory of performavity—and how one positions performance in both the present and the past with respect to those inscriptions. Re-citation thus emerges as a crucial element of the time mechanic's queer potential. Although hardly a surprise to queer theory, whose objects of epistemology and practice have long comprehended this, it should further texture how we comprehend the place of translation in the queer medievalisms of modern and contemporary poetics.

129 Spicer, *After Lorca*, 123.
130 Maurice Merleau-Ponty, *The Phenomenology of Perception*, trans. Donald A. Landes (London: Routledge, 2012), 141.

Sean Reynolds

Translation for the End Times: Peter O'Leary's *The Sampo*

> What do you do when your world starts to fall apart? I go for a walk, and if I'm really lucky, I find mushrooms.
>
> – Anna Lowenhaupt Tsing

The post-apocalyptic genre has today become the domain of anthropologists. In one of the great post-apocalyptic books of the last decade, *The Mushroom at the End of the World*, anthropologist Anna Lowenhaupt Tsing sets out on a quest to answer the question: "what manages to live in the ruins of the world we have made?"[1] She selects the Japanese wild mushroom matsutake—located in deciduous forests across every continent of the Northern Hemisphere—as a case study for understanding how growth is possible within the wake of anthropogenic global ecological catastrophe.

What makes the mushroom a worthwhile case study subject for post-apocalyptic models of growth? This fungus thrives in forests disturbed and decimated by humans. Like rats and cockroaches, it flourishes within "the environmental messes humans have made."[2] By tracing both the folk traditions and global capitalist market surrounding the wild mushroom, she offers us a model of "fungal ecology" that may allow us "to better understand the promise of cohabitation in a time of massive human destruction."

Tsing warns, though, that the mushroom should not be read as an image of ecological hope. It is categorically different from the symbol of the shoot sprouting up from the stump of Jesse. Rather, the mushroom signals merely how we might live with (or "put up with") our hopeless propensity toward ecological destruction. The time for hope and optimism has already passed. Tsing characterizes optimism as an attitude proper to the twentieth century. In the prologue to her book, she provides an unflinching assessment of how the predicament of a human in 2015 is irreconcilable with that of a human in the mid-twentieth century. I want to quote from it directly for the reason that she mentions poets specifically as individuals who need to update their outlooks:

---

1 Anna Lowenhaupt Tsing, *The Mushroom at the End of the World: On the Possibility of Life in Capitalist Ruins* (Princeton, NJ: Princeton University Press, 2015), 2.

2 Tsing, *The Mushroom at the End of the World*, 4.

https://doi.org/10.1515/9781501511189-007

> The world's climate is going haywire, and industrial progress has proved much more deadly to life on earth than anyone imagined a century ago. The economy is no longer a source of growth or optimism; any of our jobs could disappear with the next economic crisis ... Precarity once seemed the fate of the less fortunate. Now it seems that all our lives are precarious—even when, for the moment, our pockets are lined. *In contrast to the mid-twentieth century, when poets and philosophers of the global north felt caged by too much stability,* now many of us, north and south, confront the condition of trouble without end.[3]

Are poets confronting "the condition of trouble without end"? Or, are we still rehearsing modernist anxieties?

In his recent collection, *Earth is Best*, poet Peter O'Leary also argues that, amidst ecological crisis, mushrooms may point the way forward, for literature and humanity. The mushroom of O'Leary's eye is not the matsutake, however, but the *Amanita Muscaria*, "the legendary fly agaric,"[4] also called "toadstool." In a series of 33 "Amanita Odes," O'Leary probes the saprotrophic roots of the fungal life, looking for a pattern that might offer us direction. More directly relevant to Tsing's concerns, however, O'Leary also provides a remarkable afterword in the form of a manifesto called "Mycopoetics," that is, a poetics modeled on mushrooms. The manifesto opens with the same urgency and alarm as Tsing's book:

> The Earth is in crisis. Anthropogenic climate change has altered the atmosphere, primarily with the excessive introduction of carbon dioxide ... The evolutionary fact that defines human culture ... is that we burn shit to get its energy. Realistically ... the likelihood of this changing for the better is remote.[5]

The problem this poetics attempts to answer is not how to create, or how to innovate, or how to break off from our inheritance. The question mycopoetics addresses is this: what do we do about all of this toxic waste we have created? Mycopoetics is about getting rid of existing material: "Mycelium is a saprotroph, a devourer of dead matter. Without decay and the breaking down of dead matter, our ecosystem would cease to function. It would become inert."[6] The way O'Leary translates this function over to the field of poetry is uncomplicated:

> The archetype of the mycelium extends to language. In fact, to me language is the thing that most resembles the communicating properties of mycelium ... poetry is rife with toxins. That sounds like a criticism. It's not. In fact, it's as things should be. Like mycelium, poetry

3 Tsing, *The Mushroom at the End of the World*, 1–2.
4 Peter O'Leary, *Earth is Best* (New York: The Cultural Society, 2019), 105.
5 O'Leary, *Earth is Best*, 101.
6 O'Leary, *Earth is Best*, 104.

> processes toxins: poisons in language, poisons in thought, poisons in the imagination. Poetry is the noxious, gnostic contagion Robert Duncan conceived it to be.[7]

Similar to Tsing, O'Leary adopts the mushroom as an ambivalent symbol of concerns unique to the twenty-first-century poet. To understand this poetics better, though, we must trace its spore back to a model of translation, specifically back to O'Leary's 2016 imagist epic *The Sampo*, itself a "translation" of the Finnish epic the *Kalevala*.

I hope to argue that the mushroom—or saprotrophic growth more generally—also offers a model for a twenty-first-century response to our inheritance, an inheritance that is replete with humanity's abuse of the natural world. A fungal relationship between past and present is most directly comprehensible within the context of translation, for, there, the roles of dead material and fungal decomposition find direct analogs in the source text and the translation.

Looking at O'Leary's *The Sampo*, I will attempt to tease out two different currents. One is the action of a medieval epic poem. The other is the action of an ecological subplot of catastrophic proportions. This subplot is introduced by the translator—or rather, to use the mycological term, it is "inoculated" by the translator. Following this inoculation, we are able to witness the unfolding of a saprotrophic relationship between source text and translation—wherein the mycelia of the translator eat the original up from the inside out. This fungal relationship will, perforce, confuse any normative model of translational reproduction and, in the end, show itself to be of a very queer nature.

Inoculating the Spores of an Ecological Subplot

As a translator, O'Leary approached the *Kalevala* with no previous knowledge of the Finnish language, a fact he readily attests to in his "Afterword" to *The Sampo*. He explains that he relied on the consultation of three different English language translations with the occasional supplement of a Finnish lexicon. In this sense, O'Leary approaches the *Kalevala* as a stranger. In another way, O'Leary has an intimate familiarity with the source text. The heroic adventures of the epic took purchase in his imagination from adolescence, when the story was adapted and illustrated in Time Life's *Enchanted World* series. It is easy to see how this story could appeal to a young audience. It has everything you could want out of the fantasy/adventure genre. There is Väinämöinen, the grey-bearded

7 Ibid., 107.

Wizard Poet who battles against Louhi, the hag sorceress from the dark, cold North Country. And what do they fight over? The Sampo: an enigmatic "magic mill," source of wealth, first forged by the great smith Ilmarinen, friend and comrade of Väinämöinen.

The *Kalevala* is best understood as an attempt to piece together an epic, rather than an epic proper. Organized into 50 "runes" or Cantos, it is "essentially a conflation and concatenation of a considerable number and variety of traditional songs, narrative, lyric, and magic." It tells the stories of the legendary people known as the Kaleva, who inhabited an area known as Karelia, which extended from Eastern Finland to Russia's White Sea. In order to create a mostly coherent narrative of the adventures of Väinämöinen, O'Leary extracts parts from across a range of over 30 runes and repackages them into four sequential sections (which I will continue to refer to as "runes"). For the purpose of opening context, I will provide a brief synopsis of the first three runes, which contain the bulk of the action. I will reserve the fourth, epilogistic rune for an in-depth analysis later in the chapter.

- In the first rune, "Forging the Sampo," the wizard Väinämöinen transports Ilmarinen into the North Country, in the hopes that he will be able to forge a magical mill called the Sampo for Louhi, a villainous sorceress. Ilmarinen agrees to forge the Sampo for Louhi only on the condition that he can marry her beautiful daughter; however, after Ilmarinen successfully forges the mill, the daughter refuses to leave with him.
- In the second rune, "Pike and Harp," Väinämöinen and Ilmarinen sail back up to the North Country with a plot to recapture the Sampo from Louhi, who has hidden the mill deep within a mountain. Their voyage is impeded by a colossal predatory pike, whom Väinämöinen slays with an astral sword. From an assortment of the pike's bones, the wizard constructs a harp, which becomes his most beloved possession.
- The third rune, "Stealing the Sampo," opens with the heroes' arrival in the North Country and their confrontation with the sorceress Louhi and her army. By means of his new harp, Väinämöinen is able to lull her army to sleep, leaving the heroes free to descend into the center of the mountain from which they extract the Sampo. Making their escape by boat, Väinämöinen's crew begins to celebrate prematurely with song, offending the ears of a giant crane, whose bellows awaken Louhi and her army. Louhi summons the divinities of air and water whose tempests rattle Väinämöinen's ship until his beloved pike-bone harp is tossed overboard, never to be recovered. The longest and most fast-paced section of the book concerns the ensuing maritime battle between Väinämöinen and Louhi over the fate of the

Sampo, which culminates in Louhi's fantastic and vindictive dismemberment of the mill. No victor emerges. All is lost.

Into this narrative, O'Leary inoculates a covert ecological plot. At times this plot becomes as large as biomes, at others it as small and hidden as fungal spores. Initially, the ecological—or climatological—preoccupations of *The Sampo*'s narration merely bloom ornamentally within the storyline of the main protagonists. For example, in the opening rune, Ilmarinen leads Väinämöinen into the woods to find the perfect spot to construct an oven in which he may forge the Sampo. Note the extent to which O'Leary transfigures this walk into a mushroom hunt:

And with that, setting off
Into the woods.

Crimson flesh. Fleecy remnants on the caps.
    Pushing through the pine duff.
Leading Ilmarinen. Deeper into the trees.
Lucid-looking amanitas.
Sifts of light. Bright red dottles.
His attention. Expanded.
Sweet wandering. A day. Then days.

There. Huge. A stone. Streaked with color.
    Hematite.
Troop of amanitas. In a circle around it.
Rhizomorphs.
...[8]

Here the reader may merely sense that he or she is being told a story by a narrator who happens to also be a naturalist. At its least invasive, *The Sampo* adds to the *Kalevala* a heightened awareness that the conflict between the heroes of the Kaleva and the North Country is entangled within a larger conflict between two climate zones, each containing a distinctive cast of flora. In the North we have the *Taiga*, the artic boreal forests, a biome of which our century and the last has witnessed rapidly shrinking. In the South, where Väinämöinen and Ilmarinen reside, we have the subarctic climate. Between them stands a very real dividing line, an ecotone north of which the deciduous can no longer grow and the coniferous (firs, spruces, pines) reign.

At the terminus point between these two climates, the mountain birch tree stands sentinel. The ascendance of the birch tree to the position of major protag-

---

8 Peter O'Leary, *The Sampo* (New York: The Cultural Society, 2016), 16.

onist marks the most radical departure made by O'Leary's adaptation from the *Kalevala*. As a character, it actually both opens and closes the book. The first rune, "Forging the Sampo," opens with the wizard fleeing from the frozen North and reaching, by means of reindeer sleigh, his deciduous homeland:

> Absorbed by the snowy fields. Hiss of his sledge.
> Cutting birchwood runners.
> Deerskins. Elks' antlers. Clean cold he rolls
> through
> And there: at last. A birch tree.
> Stripped of leaves. Mycophoric birch. Branches
> witching outward.
> This specimen: sorcery's northmost sign. Polished
> wedge of wood rubbed smoother still.
> Birch. *Koivu*. In his pocket. Talismanic sympathy
> of the southerly
> woods …[9]

In this particular scene, the birch tree seems to be an addition entirely unique to O'Leary. He even provides it with the heroic epithet–*Mycophoric*–*fungus-bearing*. In the 1989 translation of Finnish scholar Keith Bosley, we are only told that Väinämöinen rides "by swamps and by lands / by wide open glades," until he reaches "Kalevala's heath."[10] The function of the birch tree is particular to O'Leary's narrative–it is the inoculation of a secondary, translational storyline within the "grounds" of the source text (*Kalevala*). Indeed, we are only introduced to the hero Väinämöinen secondarily through his metonymic relationship to the birch talisman he rubs in his hands. We are further signaled to read the birch tree as a character, or persona, by the fact that it is accompanied with its Finnish name, *Koivu*–the birch, like Väinämöinen, deserves to have its proper name untranslated, and capitalized at that.

Once Väinämöinen has returned home, he begins to sing a song of joy. In Bosley's translation, we are told simply that "he sang a spruce topped with flowers / topped with flowers and leaves with gold."[11] In contrast, O'Leary inserts a section of trochaic tetramer about the birch trees:

> Väinämöinen. Singing spruces.
> Into life. And birches crowned in

---

9 O'Leary, *The Sampo*, 3–4.
10 Elias Lönnrot, *The Kalevala*, trans. Keith Bosley (Oxford: Oxford University Press, 1989), 104.
11 Lönnrot, *The Kalevala*, 105.

golden leaves all shining. Birches
lords of evening's shadow brighter.[12]

I bring attention to the trochaic tetrameter because this is, in fact, the meter in which the Finnish *Kalevala* was composed. (The popularity of the *Kalevala* in the nineteenth century was such that Longfellow was inspired to bring the meter into English for his epic *The Song of Hiawatha.*) These four lines are the only entrance of the meter in *The Sampo*—leading to an irony in which O'Leary departs from the source material (by adding more birches) for a stanza that uniquely signals back to the source material.

My comparisons of *The Sampo* against other, traditional translations are in no way intended to be valuative—my goal is only to establish that the ecological and climatological preoccupations of *The Sampo* are a subplot inoculated by the twenty-first-century translator.

These ecological preoccupations in the narration bloom larger as the narrator turns to describing the magic mill. The irony of transfiguring the story of the Sampo into an imagist epic is that the Sampo itself is an unimaginable object. We are not quite sure what it looks like, or what the entirety of its powers entails. Its name remains untranslated, as it has no other iteration. Here is what O'Leary says in his afterword about the identity of the Sampo:

> The Sampo itself is a deeply coveted object of mysterious power and provenance. Typically, it is described as a magic mill, grinding out salt, corn, and even coins. But that description doesn't quite suffice. Over the years, some have speculated that it is a treasure chest, or the ritual replica of an arctic world pillar that carries the sky on top of which is the Pole Star itself. The Finnish poet Paavo Haavikko even proposed that it was a fabulously wrought mint stolen by the Vikings from Byzantium.[13]

The most important function of the Sampo within the plot is that it sets characters into motion—the action it's actually performing is of little consequence to the story. In O'Leary's hands, though, the cryptic mill assumes a much more tangible imagining. He goes on to explain:

> And yet these explanations feel insufficient too, because the Sampo has obviously organic features—including great roots it extends deep into the earth—behaving at times as esoterically and as plenteously as a mushroom, a theory that R Gordon Wasson ventures in *Soma: the Divine Mushroom of Immortality.* Whatever the Sampo is, everybody wants it.

12 O'Leary, *The Sampo*, 5.
13 Peter O'Leary, "Afterword," in *The Sampo*, 106–7.

O'Leary approaches the Sampo with the precision of a taxonomist. From the morphological descriptions provided by the *Kalevala*, this is not a far leap to make. The Sampo is said to have a domed lid, beneath which grows a network of roots that could easily call to mind the mycelium of a mushroom. Let's examine O'Leary's first description of the Sampo, which comes immediately after the mill has been forged by Ilmarinen:

> There. After three days. In the bottom of the
>   furnace.
> The Sampo. Forming. Like a pyromantic morel.
>   In the ashes.
> Its many-colored cap. Lustrous and waxy. Fuse of
>   force pushing it from the flame
> Into life.
>
> And Ilmarinen. Flexing his fist on the shaft of his
>   hammer.
> And with his tongs pulling the Sampo. From the
>   heart of the fire.
> Shaping for the maiden this vivid form
> Its intricate interlocking lid. Its image of the
>   starry sphere.
> Its mirror of the underworld channels.
> Its forest of root systems
> Its agarical jewels.[14]

Any comparison of this passage against that of a translation source text would be pointless. The taxonomic and mycologic nomenclature, this is entirely original to *The Sampo*. First, the Sampo's emergence is compared to that of the morel—a mushroom known for thriving in the wake of forest fires—with multicolored "cap" or *pileus*, the bloom. It proceeds to establishes a deep and complex root system analogous to the mycelium "root" structure of fungi. Finally, it sprouts jewels that are "agarical," or agaric, a term referring to "the fleshy or fruiting part of various fungi."[15] O'Leary then turns nomenclature up a notch in the closing of the stanza:

> From the Sampo
> An energy emerges

---

14 O'Leary, *The Sampo*, 21.

15 *Oxford English Dictionary*, s.v. "agaric (*n.* and *adj.*)," accessed June 3, 2021, https://www.oed.com/view/Entry/3796?redirectedFrom=agaric#eid.

Whose radiolarian saprophytes
Nourish the earth they suture.[16]

From the first emergence, O'Leary identifies the Sampo as having fungal "saprophytes"—that is, an organism that feeds off of decay (*sapro-* from the Greek for *rotten*)—piercing and expanding below the earth's surface.

Väinämöinen, the shaman poet, and Ilmarinen, the smith, gift the Sampo to Louhi, the sorceress hag of the North Country, on the condition that Väinämöinen can marry Louhi's beautiful daughter. When Louhi places the great mill at the center of the Copper Mountain, O'Leary again makes special note of the mycelium roots and their rhizomatic structure:

Nine fathoms deep she quests. Into the
    mountain's heart.
Where the Sampo's reef-like salamandrine roots
begin their tapping.[17]

The climax of the narrative action in The Sampo comes in the third rune, "Stealing the Sampo," as Väinämöinen recaptures the Sampo and is hunted by Louhi and her army, who ultimately destroy the Sampo in the sea. Immediately after wresting it from the earth and taking it aboard his ship, Väinämöinen reaffirms its mycological features as he tells Ilamerinen: "This Sampo. With its sacronymic amanite lid. / To the Misty Island / To its headland."[18]

Much in O'Leary's description of the aftermath of the final sea battle with Louhi suggests that something akin to an anthropogenic natural disaster has occurred. Here is O'Leary's description of the scene in which Väinämöinen gathers together the ruins of the Sampo:

Väinämöinen. Earth's ward. Feeling it. Earth's ancient aura ...

Morning mist perfuming him. In an aerosol
Of light. Shaking the seeds of the Sampo like spores of
Dusky weather over the patterns of trenches in the open earth
he's made. Everywhere plumes of shook dust.[19]

After positioning Väinämöinen as the "ward" of the Earth, O'Leary then provides a pretty grim picture of how he has treated it. The atmosphere around him is

16 O'Leary, *The Sampo*, 22.
17 Ibid.
18 Ibid., 53.
19 Ibid., 86–87.

"aerosol"; fungal spores flutter in grim weather patterns; below them are the gaping wounds of the earth, aftermath of war.

The mushroom is literally and symbolically crucial right here, as fungal growth flourishes in the wake of this mass destruction. Tsing seizes on this in her study of disturbance-based ecologies:

> When Hiroshima was destroyed by an atomic bomb in 1945, it is said, the first living thing to emerge from the blasted landscape was a matsutake mushroom ... Grasping the atom was the culmination of human dreams of controlling nature. It was also the beginning of those dreams' undoing. The bomb at Hiroshima changed things. Suddenly, we became aware that humans could destroy the livability of the planet—whether intentionally or otherwise. This awareness only increased as we learned about pollution, mass extinction, and climate change.[20]

O'Leary's translation takes the narrative culmination of the Kalevala and transposes it onto this "culmination of human dreams of controlling nature." The dismemberment of the amanitic Sampo (a mushroom cloud in the sky, of sorts) and its scattering into the aerosol winds brings to its fullness the action of the heroes —this is the ultimate, horrific climax of their power. What sorts of fungal spores will blossom in the fourth and final rune?

The Breaking of the Mill as Anthropogenic Climate Change

To fully appreciate the ecological ramifications (and ecological catastrophe) of the destruction of the Sampo in O'Leary's translation, we may need to forage deeper into the coding of this mechanism—namely in its participation of the archaeo-astronomical mytheme of the "Heavenly Mill." If the Sampo-as-mushroom overinvests ecological imagery into the narrative conflict, the mytheme of the quern-stone imports a climatological catastrophe. Such a reading of the *Kalevala* was controversially put forth by Giorgio de Santillana and Hertha von Dechend in their 1969 study *Hamlet's Mill: An Essay Investigating the Origins of Human Knowledge and Its Transmission Through Myth*. Here de Santillana and Dechend trace the recurrent narrative unit of a heavenly mill across Indo-European and Uralic mythology, concluding that it offered a "coded" prehistoric knowledge of astronomy. The identity of this knowledge is the most controversial part of their argument: that the heavenly mill—and its repeated destruction—displays

20 Tsing, *The Mushroom at the End of the World*, 3.

an ancient understanding of axial precession. "Axial precession" need only, for our purposes, be given this reductive definition: the change of the orientation of the Earth's axis, or a wobble at its pole, that takes approximately 26,000 years to perform one full rotation. This polar wobble is the reason Earth's equatorial plane moves in relation to the sun, but it also implicates greater climatological shifts. The precession "alters the strength of summer sunlight in the high Arctic, causing great ice sheets to shrink or grow and affecting global climate as a result."[21] This wobble, for de Santillana and Dechend, mythologized a primeval catastrophe—"a kind of cosmogonic 'original sin' whereby the circle of the ecliptic (with the zodiac) was tilted up at an angle with respect to the equator, and the cycles of change came into being."

The study enters in through the Old Norse predecessor of the Danish "Hamlet," the Old Icelandic "Amlódhi," a melancholy young boy of "high intellect" who was "dedicated to avenge his father," but whose narrative centered on the turning of a millstone:

> Amlódhi was identified, in the crude and vivid imagery of the Norse, by the ownership of a fabled mill which, in his own time, ground out peace and plenty. Later, in decaying times, it ground out salt; and now finally, having landed at the bottom of the sea, it is grinding rock and sand, creating a vast whirlpool, the Maelstrom (i.e., the grinding stream, from the verb mala, "to grind"), which is supposed to be a way to the land of the dead.

This template reappears in the character of Frodhi from the Prose Edda, who owned a magic millstone called Grotte, "the crusher," which was able "to grind out gold, peace and happiness." Like the Sampo and the mill of Amlódhi, the Grotte met with catastrophe. In greed Frodhi indentured two Maidens to grind out gold for him day and night until the point when the mill was stolen aboard a ship by the sea-king, Mysingr. He commanded the Maidens to grind him out salt through the night until it sunk the boat, together with the mill, to the bottom of the sea.

The recurrent damage of the magic millstone is more important to de Santillana and Dechend than any property of the mill itself. Given the "starry inscriptions" reported on the lid of the Sampo, it is difficult not to indulge their claim that the destruction of the mill represents a primeval incongruity of the earth and sky—that the spinning of the world is off-kilter. O'Leary's translation not only betrays his knowledge of this astronomical mytheme, but also unpacks it more explicitly to and for his source text. Immediately following the destruction

---

21 "Earth's Orbit Cannot Explain Modern Climate Change," Climate Feedback, https://climatefeedback.org/claimreview/earths-orbit-cannot-explain-modern-climate-change/.

of the mill and its disappearance into the sea, Louhi explains the climatological ruin that will befall the Finns:

> Whatever you grow,
> whatever you plow,
> whatever you sow,
> whatever this broken Sampo's magic emplenishes,
> I'll ruin
> I'll devise endless, recurrent ruination for it—[22]

The response Väinämöinen then gives in *The Sampo* is interesting to compare against that of the traditional translation by Bosley. *The Kalevala* introduces Väinämöinen's response with a simple tag:

> Then the old Väinämöinen
> put this into words:
> No Lapp sings at me, no man
> of Turja shoves me around!

He proceeds to conclude his dismissal of Louhi's threat with the following lines:

> raise a bear from the heath
> from a thicket a fierce cat
> from the wilds a hollow-hand
> and from beneath a sprig a gap-tooth
> for Northland's furthest lane, for
> where the North's herd treads!

Informed by the argument of de Santillana and Dechend, we can better understand the additions made in O'Leary's version. Here is how the shaman-poet's response is introduced:

> Then Väinämöinen. Feeling weary. But feeling the
> ancient earth moving
> very slowly under him. Saying,
> "Spells from the North Country. Weak little
> whispers to me ..."[23]

22 O'Leary, *The Sampo*, 83.
23 Ibid.

And Väinämöinen concludes by telling Louhi:

> A hail of steel. Is all you'll harvest.
> And the bear you weird. From the shadows of the
> pines. Her jaws
> lined with vicious teeth. Menacing. Preying.
> On Sariola's cattle. I've seen it. Up from the
> ancient earth. A vision.
> Revolving around me.[24]

A distinctive trait of O'Leary's poem is the homogeneity of vocabulary among characters and the narrator. They are all working in the same direction. Above, the narrator and Väinämöinen share a preference for the term "ancient earth"—an epithet more outstanding when a character uses it in reference to his own (futural) prophetic vision. Its implication regarding the originary shift of the earth beneath the stars is clear. However, what O'Leary more subtly suggests is Väinämöinen—after stealing the Sampo—has not merely authored the earth's axial shift, he is also the very center of this shift. The earth moves under him. The celestial vision of the bear and cattle is now revolving around him. Given the vast implications of an axial shift, it is striking that O'Leary should give such an emphasis on the very place and person of Väinämöinen here.

Mushrooms and the Modernist Inheritance

In the "Afterword" to *The Sampo*, O'Leary lays out the lineage for the poetic style of his imagist epic:

> I adapted a technique borrowed from the poetry of Thomas Meyer, especially his poem "Rilke," but more generally in his books *Coromandel* and *Kintsugi*. To these models, just as to the *Kalevala* itself, I have made modifications and changes to suit the purposes of my poem. But just so, my poem could not exist without these examples.[25]

According to O'Leary, he adopted from Meyer's work a style of "rotoscoping,"[26] which allows the rapid sequential presentation of static images to become animated. To state the obvious, the central problem of creating an "imagist epic"

24 Ibid., 85.
25 O'Leary, "Afterword," 111.
26 Peter O'Leary, discussion with author, January, 2020.

is how to make activity happen. I want to pursue further the influence of Meyer's "Rilke," which is itself a translation:

> Help me! Who would hear. The terrible. Citizens. Angelic.
> Orders. And if they did and held me I would die.
> To their hearts. In the beauty. At the beginning. The
> Terror. Its first twinges.
> Takes our breath and we begin. We
> survive. Survive because it waits and will
> not strike. Every angel. The Terror. Every angel.[27]

What O'Leary refers to as the "rotoscoping" is the flourish of splices introduced by an exuberantly excessive periodization. Every clause, every word, becomes a hinge point for motion. As O'Leary writes, "From this seemingly limiting mode of expression, Meyer coaxes impressive flexibility. New thoughts act like verbs; full sentences receive rewarding complements after completion. And there's a feeling of movement that pervades."[28] The method is somewhat paradoxical: by introducing periods between subject and predicate, between a verb and its object, the momentum intensifies.

The style that O'Leary adopts in *The Sampo*, however, goes much further than Meyer's in the direction of decomposing syntax into a paratactic sequence of discrete parts. O'Leary shows a much stronger aversion to finite verbs, and most especially the paring of subjects and finite verbs. Instead, O'Leary's subjects usually stand in proximity to an assortment of participial phrases. Consider the following passage from "Stealing the Sampo," in which the fragments are scattered by the storming seas before Väinämöinen's eyes:

> Billows. Wild, rocking directed movement.
> Väinämöinen. Feeling ancient. And purposeful.
>   Following the floating fragments
> of the Sampo. Tossed on the lake waves to the
>   nearing shore.
> Tumbling over the breakers. Onto the sandy
>   shoreland.[29]

27 Cited in Peter O'Leary, review of *Kintsugi*, by Thomas Meyer, *The Volta* (2012), www.thevolta.org/fridayfeature-kintsugi.html.
28 Ibid.
29 O'Leary, *The Sampo*, 80.

We do not hear the "Väinämöinen. *Felt* ancient" or the "Sampo. *Tumbled* over the breakers." The use of participial phrases invests actions with an autonomy that allows them to stand apart from a subject. However, the separation only serves to intensify the momentum of their interactions. As O'Leary describes it, the "cross-cutting" between subject and verb generates an effect akin to "electricity from an exposed wire, the poem begins spraying out this energy as it moves forward, even if [I am using] a seemingly abrupt technique."[30]

Just as quickly, though, can O'Leary repurpose this technique toward the solemn or elegiac. For example, he deploys the same splicing in the opening of the fourth and final rune, in order to depict a distraught Väinämöinen in the wake of losing his harp:

> Väinämöinen. His Mind.
> Moving at the pace of a driven breeze. Testing the
> branches
> of the birches and oaks on the headland. Music.
> It's time for music. But his smashed kantele—
> sunk in the waters. "My joy. It's gone. To the rock
> caves
> the salmon and lake pike cool in
> shadows and murk
> more deeply obscure.[31]

The rune begins with a doubled subject, in which the Wizard is dissociated even from his own mind. What is "moving"? What is "testing"? All is lost in the gaps. He remembers with a pang his lost harp, and the dash substitutes for a copulative verb: breakage substitutes for being.

The imagist thread—especially in the ascendance of the subjectless verb—obviously enough leads back to Ezra Pound and *The Cantos*. In explaining what can be gained by the cross-cutting of subject and verb, O'Leary points directly to a most prescient passage from foundational Imagist text *The Chinese written character as a medium for poetry:*

> A true noun, an isolated thing does not exist in nature. Things are only the terminal points, or rather the meeting points of actions, cross-sections cut through actions, snapshots. Neither can a pure verb, an abstract motion be possible in nature. The eye sees noun and verb as one. Things in motion, motion in things.[32]

30 O'Leary, discussion.
31 O'Leary, *The Sampo*, 91.
32 O'Leary, discussion.

O'Leary takes the modernist preoccupation with dangling action and repurposes it toward a rather straightforward, sequential, and easy-to-follow narrative.

The Rupture in which Translation Itself Is Translated

Having established the style that dominates nearly the entirety of *The Sampo*, I want to address its sudden, cataclysmic interruption in the fourth and final rune. It is a rupture in meter, tone, diction, and subject matter. It is, however, the most moving and important section of the book. It is the climax of the mycological translation, which blossoms in the wake of the narrative climax.

As mentioned above, the fourth rune opens with a grieving Väinämöinen, who is coming to terms with the loss of his harp: his one-of-a-kind, irreplaceable treasure:

> Pleasure. Lost to me.
> Pleasure from my harp, my jawbone harp, lost.
> Pleasure from the harp I made. Gone.[33]

Then, within the nadir of our hero's despair, a most curious thing happens: the poem switches into ballad meter. We get 17 stanzas of English rhyming ballad meter, beginning:

> And Väinämöinen wanders then
> Into the bright-lit woods
> To cross a swollen rivulet
> That marks the springtime floods.
>
> There is no shadow he would claim.
> The one across his heart
> Suffices to deprive him of
> The workings of his art.

From a traditionalist's standpoint, this is a formally impeccable section. However, more than just meter changes. Grammatically, we begin seeing subjects paired to finite verbs. The startling shift sets the stage for the tender scene to come. Väinämöinen hears, interrupting his own lament, the weeping of the other main protagonist of *The Sampo:* the birch tree.

33 O'Leary, *The Sampo*, 94.

Then up ahead he hears a groan.
It is a birch tree weeping.
Lamenting. Speckled branching tree.
Whose saps and resins seeping

The wizard Väinämöinen rubs
along his finger's edge.
He lifts it up; it smells of life
And takes him to the verge

Of where a song might still be drawn
From nature's shining brow.
"Oh beauteous birch tree shedding tears—
Wherefore weepest thou ..."[34]

The reason for the tree's tears is both deeply personal and global in character: the birch has been mistreated by humans. They come and rip off its long white strips of bark. Children, as they are wont to do, carve their names into it with knives. Then adults come and strip off more layers "to make a plate or a cup."[35] Then it's the basket-weavers taking their share, followed by the young girls who cut down its branches "to bind them up / to make their summer brooms."[36]

In the wake of the cataclysmic battle of the elements that closed the third rune, we are now floating in what feels like an elegiac, pathos-heavy afterword. The birch tree laments being overly instrumentalized for human ends. It is unclear why the birch tree offers these laments. Is it requesting a quick death? Is it looking to Väinämöinen for solutions or consolations? Regardless of the

---

34 Ibid., 95–96.

35 Ibid., 96–97.

36 In Väinämöinen's encounter with the self-pitying birch tree, I cannot escape the sense that O'Leary is also translating Dante's testimonies of the condemned, further signaling the reader that the final rune takes place in some world of the dead. More specifically, I recall Dante's walk through the murky and leafless forest in Canto XIII of the Inferno—The Wood of Self-Murderers—where desperate souls neither live on nor die, encased in the trunks of thorn trees. It was here that Dante plucked a twig and heard the plaintive voice ask: "Why manglest thou me? Hast thou no spirit of pity?" This tree (containing the soul of a former advisor to Caesar) goes on to explain the origin of his condition, and the condition of all those who commit suicide:

When the fierce soul leaves the body from which it has uprooted itself ... It falls into the wood, not in a place chosen for it but where fortune flings it. It sprouts there like a grain of spelt and rises to a sapling and a savage tree; then the Harpies feeding on its leaves, cause pain and for the pain an outlet.

tree's wishes, Väinämöinen offers it a solution. He will cut down the tree and craft it into a harp to use. The diction he employs in this proposal is crucial:

> Then Väinämöinen says in turn,
> "Oh birch tree, weep no more.
> A joyful future comes for you
> Because you hide the spoor
>
> Another saprophytic life
> Begins to mushroom from.
> To you will come transfigured life
> In everlasting form."[37]

The mushroom imagery first attached to the Sampo has now reappeared in Väinämöinen's plans for a new wooden harp. O'Leary employs a pun as Väinämöinen says the birch tree hides within it a "spoor"—it is the trail that he can follow, but it is also one of the hidden *spores* inside the substrate of the birch tree that had been scattered in the winds and over the earth following the destruction of the Sampo by Louhi. We hear no reaction from the birch tree. However, this appears to be a perfect solution for Väinämöinen. After all, Väinämöinen will get not only a new harp, but also a new proxy-mushroom, to replace the proxy-mushroom of the Sampo. The problem with the last harp, made of a pike's jawbone, is that it is one-of-a-kind. The wooden harp, on the other hand, can be replicated and mass-produced. The optimism of the ending rests on the hero's assumption that there *is* an everlasting supply—a position that the translation, with its furtive spores, has eaten away at from the inside out.

If the climax of the epic narrative came with the destruction of the Sampo at the close of rune four, the climax of O'Leary's translational action arrives in Väinämöinen's proposal of a "saprophytic" afterlife to the birch tree. Here is where O'Leary resituates Väinämöinen's magical manipulation of the natural world into the contemporary Anthropocene, where humans do not just manipulate the natural world, but control it; and not just control, but feast off its rotting.

Moving From a Seed-Based to a Spore-Based Translation

At any point when the birch tree appears in *The Sampo*, we are alerted to the poem's translated-ness—that there is an "original" Finnish substrate out from

---

37 O'Leary, *The Sampo*, 98.

which O'Leary's poem is blooming. In that sense, the birch tree destabilizes the coherence, or self-sufficiency, of the translation. We saw this previously when O'Leary gave the birch tree the Finnish name *Koivu*, and briefly approximated the trochaic tetrameter of the Finnish. This culminates in the introduction of the ballad meter and Väinämöinen's dialogue with the birch tree. The ballad stanzas do not merely provide the poem with a variant rhythm; they break the epic open. They insert an external duration that is foreign to the poem as we have come to know it up until that point.

However, I argue that this interruption *makes* the entire translation, insofar as it shows how *The Sampo* is being made. In Väinämöinen's dialogue with the birch tree, the *Kalevala* ceases to be represented, and, in its place, the act of translation itself appears. Let's return again to the first words Väinämöinen speaks to the birch tree after hearing its crying: "Oh beauteous birch tree shedding tears—Wherefore weepest thou." Where is that language coming from? It is as though another dimension has cracked open inside an imagist poem. And indeed that is exactly what is happening. O'Leary has taken the line directly from F. W. Kirby's 1907 translation of the Kalevala—one of the four translations that O'Leary cites as having "relied on" in his composition of *The Sampo.*[38] All the cards are turned—this is how the translator is translating. The scene represented in ballad meter is much more than a hero speaking to a birch tree. It opens up a space in which the relationship between translation and source text can be described—using a mycological model of spores and saprotrophy.

Much of O'Leary's method of translation owes an inheritance to the modernist lineage of the "poet's version," and I want to define this inheritance before I close by arguing for O'Leary's queer mycological revision of the modernist lineage. The greatest indebtedness *The Sampo* owes to the advances in translation undergone during literary modernism is the way in which it capitalizes on the translator's limited knowledge of the source language. O'Leary explained:

> I found that the unfamiliarity [of the Finnish language] to almost anyone who would encounter it, including and maybe especially myself, was advantageous in that I didn't feel any obligation to try to be true to it. If I were true to it, nobody would be like, "This is remarkably true."[39]

In his 1992 article "Theorizing Translation," the Ezra Pound scholar Thomas H. Jackson explains how, during the twentieth century, the difficulties presented by a translator's gaps in knowledge was compensated for by a reconfiguration of

38 O'Leary, *The Sampo*, 111.
39 O'Leary, discussion.

how language performs. In the modernist's confrontation with foreign words, he will immediately "reject the notion that [this foreign] language is a system of signifiers designating some more or less corresponding array of signifieds."[40] Instead, he reassures himself of "the conviction that language is a mode of energy, is a behavior, is a form of life, and that what counts is not something we clumsily rationalize as 'content' or 'meaning' but the life in it, the potential for energizing human beings."[41] As Steven Yao set out in his book *Translation and the Languages of Modernism*, the twentieth century gave rise to the poet who "repeatedly engaged in translation, and sometimes achieved remarkable results, with partial, imprecise, faulty, and sometimes even no formal understanding of the languages in which the texts they translated were originally written."[42] Similarly, Ronnie Apter characterizes the trajectory of twentieth-century poetic translation by its increasing willingness to "exaggerate, delete, or sacrifice" the literal sense of the source text in order to carry across an equivalent to the original's "overall impression."[43] In place of literal meaning, the primary component to be carried over into the translator's native tongue was the original's "life," "energy," or "living breath."

If W. S. Merwin could translate from over a dozen languages; if his mentor Pound could translate from at least ten; if Robert Hass can go from Czesław Miłosz to Basho to Neruda; if Jerome Rothenberg can translate Navajo, then German and Hebrew. This is only because of a deeply optimistic reorientation of the translator's task, which has eliminated the fear and possibility of loss. With an eye toward what the original could contribute to the contemporary, the creative poet-translator ceases to regret "what is lost in translation" by narrowing in on a doubled gain: 1) the original "nourishes" the contemporary, translating language with the "sustenance" it needs, and 2) the translator brings the original "back to life" in a modernized, new poem.[44] We can begin with a passage taken from Pound's 1920 essay collection *Instigations*, which reads: "Even though I know the overwhelming importance of technique, technicalities in a foreign tongue cannot have for me the importance they have to a man writing in that tongue; almost the only technique perceptible to a foreigner is the presentation of content as free as possible from the clutteration of dead technicalities …

40 Thomas H. Jackson, "Theorizing Translation," *SubStance* 20, no. 1 (1991): 88.
41 Jackson, "Theorizing Translation," 88.
42 Steven G. Yao, *Translation and the Languages of Modernism: Gender, Politics, Language* (New York: Palgrave Macmillan, 2002), 11–12.
43 Ronnie Apter, *Digging for the Treasure: Translation after Pound* (New York: Peter Lang Publishing, 1984), 12.
44 Apter, *Digging for the Treasure*, 133, 160.

and from timidities of workmanship."[45] Recounting his first encouragement toward translation by Pound, Merwin writes similarly about the guiding principle of liveliness: "I still approach translation as a relatively anonymous activity in which whatever in the result may appear to be mine comes there simply because that is how the language ... sounds most alive to me."[46]

Jackson Mathews writes that, by the end of the twentieth century, "Every saddened reader knows that what a poem is most in danger of losing in translation is its life."[47] However, as translation turned from the "dead technicalities" of signifiers, to a base principle of spirit or energy, their theories of translation, observes Thomas A. Jackson, "tend to be couched in figuration and metaphor and analogy, whereas ideally, explanations should be definite and straightforward."[48] The metaphors tended along the following biological tropes: seeds, germination, embryos, offspring, and sexual reproduction. Tony Barnstone, the American poet-translator who studied under Robert Hass, writes:

> I came to Chinese poetry originally as an American poet learning how to make the image. Like many other American poets, I was led to China by my interest in Ezra Pound, William Carlos Williams, and other modernist poets who developed and modified their craft in conversation with the Chinese tradition. I came to China, in other words, to learn how to write poetry in English. This is also how I came to translation: as a way of extending the possibilities of poetry written in English ... A translation, after all, is the child of parent authors from different cultures, and however assiduously the translator attempts to remove his or her name from the family tree, the genetic traces will be found in the offspring.[49]

Rosmarie Waldrop, one of the poets that Jackson cites as having most "satisfactorily" theorized creative translation, writes:

> Perhaps we can turn the idea of the afterlife of a work of literature toward biology and consider translation as the offspring of the original, less handsome than the parent, but true kin. (This analogy, which also does not bear to be pressed very hard, has curious implications for the time gap that often exists between the original publication and the translation and that compounds the cultural differences.) The first task of the translator would be to find the "genetic code" of the work, to get from the surface to the seed which, in our

45 Ezra Pound, *Instigations of Ezra Pound* (New York: Boni and Liveright, 1920), 4.
46 Ed Folsom, "W. S. Merwin on Ezra Pound," *The Iowa Review* 15, no. 2 (1985): 71.
47 Jackson Mathews, "Third Thoughts on Translating Poetry," in *On Translation*, ed. R. Brower (Cambridge, Harvard University Press: 1959), 69.
48 Jackson, "Theorizing Translation," 88.
49 Tony Barnstone, "The Poem behind the Poem: Literary Translation As American Poetry," *Manoa* 11, no. 2 (1999): 66.

> terms, would mean getting close to the nucleus of creative energy that is at the beginning of a poem.[50]

The break O'Leary makes from the modernist lineage of poetic translation hinges on the translation of this very metaphor, moving from the sexualized reproduction of seeds into the catastrophic, reductive, and furtive growth of fungal spores.

Mycological Translation; and What Is so "Queer" about It?

Fungus offers a path forward to speak about translation in a way that destabilizes tropes such as lineage, conception, offspring, reproduction, etc. In O'Leary's *Sampo*, we have seen how his ecological sub-plot constantly threatens to undermine and disrupt the primary epic narrative concerning the adventures of heroes. How do we describe such a relationship between source text and translation? The model of offspring, reproduction, and new life does not quite work here. Would it not be more fitting to say that *The Sampo* has inoculated something inside the Finnish epic that eats it from the inside out?

To return to Anna Tsing, she argues that capitalism has pathologized fungi as a deviant murmur within the consistent "pulse of progress"—particularly as it came to the efforts of commercial logging and the conversion of forests into agricultural plantations. With the rise of the U.S. timber industry and scientific forestry in the mid-twentieth century, the need for scalability and standardization transfigured the landscape. She paints the picture thusly:

> Unwanted tree species, and indeed all other species, were sprayed with poison. Fires were absolutely excluded ... Thinning was brutal, regular, and essential. Proper spacing allowed maximum rates of growth as well as mechanical harvesting. Timber trees were a new kind of sugarcane: managed for uniform growth, without multispecies interference, and thinned and harvested by machines and anonymous workers.[51]

Fungi were not just the nuisance of the farmer, they were "the enemy of civilization and, later, progress." Tsing later takes this point in an interesting direction, by suggesting that fungi's greatest potential for disruption lies within the fluidity

---

50 Rosmarie Waldrop, *Dissonance (If You Are Interested)* (Tuscaloosa: University of Alabama Press, 2004), 139.
51 Tsing, *The Mushroom at the End of the World*, 41.

and non-normativity of its methods of reproduction. Consider the queerness latent in her description of spores:

> Both in forests and in science, spores open our imaginations to another cosmopolitan topology. Spores take off toward unknown destinations, mate across types, and, at least occasionally, give rise to new organisms—a beginning for new kinds. Spores are hard to pin down; that is their grace ... In thinking about science, spores model open-ended communication and excess: the pleasures of speculation.[52]

The mycologist Patricia Kaishian takes these implications much further in her recent article, "Science Underground: Mycology as Queer Discipline." For Kaishian, "mycology is queer insofar as it is disruptive, collective, transformative, revolutionary" and its role within taxonomy and horticulture has been, from the beginning, to destabilize binaries such as parent and offspring:

> Mycology disrupts our mostly binary conception of plants versus animals, two-sex mating systems, and discrete organismal structure, calling upon non-normative, multimodal methodologies for knowledge acquisition. Mycelium is the web-like network of fungal cells that extends apically through substrate, performing sex, seeking nutrients, building multispecies and multikingdom symbioses. ... *Mycology is queer at the organismal level.* Fungi are nonbinary: they are neither plants nor animals, but possess a mixture of qualities common to both groups, upending the prevailing binary concept of nature. It is rare for a fungus to have only two biological sexes, and some fungi, such as Schizophyllum commune, have as many as 23,000 mating types. When two compatible fungi meet, their mycelia will fuse into one body, sexually recombine, then remain somatically as one as they continue to live, grow, and explore in their environment.[53]

If the language of reproduction is to be so embedded in discussions of translation, might we be able to queer it by introducing destabilizing and saprophytic tropes of mycological reproduction? Could this be the more appropriate model to proceed with in the wake of capitalism and the ruins of climate catastrophe? The distinction would be far more than semantics. If we say, as I have argued, that the relationship between the mushroom and the birch tree is an analogy of the relationship of translation to source text, there are important implications. The crux is that the mushroom does not carry the "genetic code" of the birch tree out from which it grows (to use the language of Waldrop). It also means—in the saprophytic sense—that translation is contributing to the decay of the source text. If passing along genes guarantees legacy in the heteronormative tra-

---

52 Ibid., 227–28.

53 Patricia Kaishian and Hasmik Djoulakian, "The Science Underground: Mycology as a Queer Discipline," *Catalyst: Feminism, Theory, Technoscience* 6, no. 2 (2020): 1–26.

dition, the mushroom translation establishes the end of a line. Queer theorist Lee Edelman has pointed out the way in which American consumerism and capitalist growth depends upon an ideology of "reproductive futurism": a continually deferred promise of healing, which he most often finds invested in the image of the Child or Offspring. Within an ideology of reproductive futurism always looking to affirm a social order hypostasized "in the form of its inner Child," the most threatening political position an individual can adopt is one which intends no future; Edelman identifies such a position with a "queer politics."[54] The offspring represents a symbolic delay—communicating to us that the next generation will solve the effects of all we have dropped into the sea and all the birch trees we have cut down.

54 Lee Edelmen, *No Future: Queer Theory and the Death Drive* (Durham: Duke University Press, 2004), 3.

Katharine Jager

The Harlot and the Gygelot: Translation, Intertextuality, and Theft in Medbh McGuckian's "The Good Wife Taught her Daughter"

The Northern Irish feminist poet Medbh McGuckian's *The Currach Requires No Harbours* (2007), her ninth book of poetry, contains several "translations" of other texts.[1] McGuckian has long borrowed from other texts and used unattributed quotations in her work, a practice understood critically as a feminist means of resisting the singularity of meaning, wherein her appropriative diction is "neither static nor monological, but metamorphic and dialogical."[2] While some poems in *Currach*, like "Anne Glyd, Her Book, 1656," or "Bright Star, I Say That Thou Art Dust," use titling to suggest links to an earlier primary text, McGuckian's free verse "The Good Wife Taught Her Daughter" does not. The poem was first published in 2006 in *Poetry* magazine, and their website's "More About This Poem" attached tab, which often explains origins and textual history, is empty except for McGuckian's biography.[3] To a twenty-first-century reader unfamiliar with McGuckian's source texts, the poem might seem to be an original composition whose syntax and repetition fit seamlessly into McGuckian's broader poetic concerns with feminist language play, dreams, and what Carmine Starnino has described as "an exploratory seeping forth of sounds."[4] To medievalists familiar with conduct literature, however, McGuckian's "The Good Wife" obviously excerpts and translates several Middle English texts concerned with the behavior and comportment of late-medieval mercantile women:

Note: Thank you to Sarah Salih for reading an earlier version of this essay and providing vital information. And thank you to Claude Jager-Rubinson, Jude Jager-Rubinson, Thomas Jager-Cash, and Griffin Jager-Cash for "not bearing to be quiet."

1 Medbh McGuckian, *The Currach Requires No Harbours* (Winston-Salem, NC: Wake Forest University Press, 2007), 24.
2 See Shane Alcobia-Murphy, *Sympathetic Ink: Intertextual Relations in Northern Irish Poetry* (Liverpool: Liverpool University Press, 2006), 281.
3 This can be found at https://www.poetryfoundation.org/poetrymagazine/poems/48969/the-good-wife-taught-her-daughter. It is longer, by a couplet, than the version published in *Currach*.
4 Starnino, "Beyond Heaney?: Five Irish Poets Who Are Changing Irish Poetry," *Poetry* (November 2008): 155.

https://doi.org/10.1515/9781501511189-008

the conduct poem "How The Good Wife Taught Her Daughter," the prose *The Book of Margery Kempe*, the Paston *Letters*, the *Book of the Knight of the Tower*, and *Le Ménagier de Paris*, among others.[5] It also deploys—without attribution—Sarah Salih's analysis of this literature, the essay "At Home; Out of the House."[6]

I argue that McGuckian's "The Good Wife" occupies an intertextual, queer, post-structural, and postcolonial space that can accommodate at once the present and the past. It does so, however, by means of a falsely binary, retributive form of justice that situates Salih's scholarship as oppressor and McGuckian's *poeisis* as a triumph of the oppressed. In its translation of different Middle English texts to create a new, Modern English remix of both, McGuckian's "The Good Wife" is a poem which Tejaswini Niranjana might argue "does not re-present an 'original,'" but which instead "re-presents that which is always already represented."[7] In other words, "The Good Wife" is an intertext, one whose translation practice of blending, excerpting, and mixing genres necessarily involves the "translation, deformation, displacement" at the heart of postcolonial subjectivity.[8] McGuckian has noted that the process of stitching together her source material into a new whole is "like getting a blood transfusion into your system."[9] Her practice of citational borrowing cannot be divorced from questions of history,

5 See for instance George Shuffelton, ed., "How the Good Wife Taught Her Daughter," in *Codex Ashmole 6: A Compilation of Popular Middle English Verse* (Kalamazoo, MI: TEAMS, 2008); Lynn Staley, ed., *The Book of Margery Kempe* (New York: W. W. Norton and Co., 2000), https://d.lib.rochester.edu/teams/publication/shuffelton-codex-ashmole-61.; Norman Davis, ed., *Paston Letters and Papers of the 15th Century* (Oxford: Clarendon Press, 1971); Rebecca Barnhouse, *The Book of the Knight of the Tower* (New York: Palgrave Macmillan, 2006); and Georgine E. Brereton and Janet M. Ferrier, eds., *Le Ménagier de Paris* (Oxford: Clarendon Press, 1981).

6 Sarah Salih, "At Home; Out of the House," in *The Cambridge Companion to Medieval Women's Writing*, ed. Carolyn Dinshaw and David Wallace (Cambridge: Cambridge University Press, 2003), 124–40. Both Shane Alcobia-Murphy, "'Nobody Knows What is In Them Til They Are Broke Up': Medbh McGuckian's Feminist Poetry," *Études Irlandaises* 37, no. 2 (2012): 97–111, and Kenneth Keating, "Medbh McGuckian's Source Texts and the Challenge to Authorial Identity in 'The Good Wife Taught Her Daughter,'" *Irish Studies Review* 23, no. 3 (2015): 310–30, analyze "The Good Wife" and its relationship to Salih and the primary sources she uses. Both essays are discussed at length below.

7 Tejaswini Niranjana, *Siting Translation: History, Post-Structuralism and the Colonial Context* (Berkeley, CA: University of California Press, 1992), 9.

8 Niranjana, *Siting*, 46.

9 See Shane Alcobia-Murphy and Richard Kirkland, "Interview with Medbh McGuckian," in *The Poetry of Medbh McGuckian: The Interior of Words*, ed. Shane Alcobia-Murphy and Richard Kirkland (Cork: Cork University Press, 2010), 194–207, at 199.

colonial power, and inherited language. Her poetic work takes place in a language that is both hers and not hers. She notes that:

> English isn't my native language or my mother tongue. English is this huge empire of signs, that because I'm not able to write or speak in Irish, I have the texts as a resource for my pleasure or my taking. It's my only way of asserting my rights; it's a way of getting back my freedom in the language.[10]

McGuckian makes a strange claim here, noting that she is unable to speak or compose in Irish, but that English is neither her native language nor her mother tongue. English functions instead for McGuckian as "this huge empire of signs," one that exists outside of her own voice and which she is only partially embedded within. She trawls within this empire for the stuff of her poetry, in a language that is hers and not hers.

English texts and manuscripts have long been associated with patrilineal power, and so McGuckian's appropriation of what she calls "the flowers of poetry" serves as a kind of postcolonial feminist act of resistance.[11] In this way, her reuse of Middle English texts is consonant with Diane Watt and Roberta Magnani's argument for a queer philology that focuses less on an unbroken Bloomian line of transmission and more on "the fissures, lapses, and gaps" between and among texts that allow new forms and identities to appear.[12] McGuckian's oeuvre, in its magpie-like collation of other sources, exemplifies these "fissures, lapses, and gaps." In this way, she also serves as the feminist, postcolonial inheritor of twentieth-century American poet Jack Spicer's idea that the poet is a "time mechanic, not an embalmer," someone who takes other languages, histories, words, and reshapes them into something new.[13] Yet this approach to poetic composition may best function, in an ethical sense, only with the language of the long dead and the anonymous. As Spicer argues, "words are what stick to

---

10 Alcobia-Murphy and Kirkland, "Interview," 199.

11 McGuckian says, "I just take an assortment of words, though not exactly at random, and I fuse them. It's like embroidery." See Shane Alcobia-Murphy, "'My Cleverly Dead and Vertical Audience': Medbh McGuckian's 'Difficult' Poetry," *New Hibernia Review/Iris Éireannach Nua* 16, no. 3 (2012): 67–82, at 73. She also notes that her practice has developed over time, and that "gradually I became more and more at ease at going into a book and finding these flowers of poetry and making, as you know, my first notebook, then my second notebook and then writing my poems." See Alcobia-Murphy and Kirkland, "Interview," 196.

12 See Diane Watt and Roberta Magnani, "Towards a Queer Philology," *postmedieval* 9 (2018): 252–56, at 256.

13 This notion builds upon David Hadbawnik's "Time Mechanics: The Modern Geoffrey Chaucer and the Medieval Jack Spicer," *postmedieval* 4 (2013): 270–83.

the real. We use them to push the real, to drag the real into the poem."[14] There are "real" words in McGuckian's "The Good Wife." But we cannot read the poem simply as a "time mechanical" remix, free of ethical constraints. McGuckian's poetic practice depends on mining historical, anonymous, and pseudonymous primary sources, but it also depends on mining research produced by living scholars. The "real words" that McGuckian drags into her poem are not simply neutral source material. They are the products of a critical essay written by a real person, whose labor has gone unattributed.

A New Tissue of Past Citations

In his "Theory of the Text," Roland Barthes famously argues that "bits of code, formulae, rhythmic models, fragments of social languages, etc., pass into the text and are redistributed within it, for there is always language before and around the text."[15] This post-structural concept of intertextuality, a blending of sources into a new compositional whole, should not "be reduced to a problem of sources or influences," because all texts are made of other texts and voices. McGuckian's poems might be read as intertextual mashups, or "a new tissue of past citations," one where ancient poems and half-remembered essays are included in the composition of the poem.[16] In this sense, intertextuality can function as a productive hybrid space, one constituted by the postmodern relationship between McGuckian's original source texts, by the new poem she produces out of those texts, and by the reader herself. Scholarship on McGuckian's body of work has primarily followed this theoretical vein, using theories by Barthes and Kristeva[17] with occasional gestures towards Deleuze and Guattari,[18] to conceptualize her appropriation of primarily twentieth-century source material. McGuckian's intertextual use of writings by Kristeva, Mandelstam, Tsvetaeva,

14 See Jack Spicer, *My Vocabulary Did This to Me: The Collected Poetry of Jack Spicer*, ed. Peter Gizzi and Kevin Killian (Middletown, CT: Wesleyan University Press, 2008), 122–123.

15 Roland Barthes, "Theory of the Text," in *Untying the Text*, ed. Robert Young (London: Routledge, 1981), 31–47, at 39.

16 Barthes, "Theory," 39.

17 See Robert Brazeau, "Troubling Language: Avant Garde Strategies in the Poetry of Medbh McGuckian," *Mosaic* 37, no. 2 (2004): 127, and Shane Alcobia-Murphy, "Intertextual Relations in Medbh McGuckian's Poetry," in *Back to the Present, Forward to the Past: Irish Writing and History Since 1798*, ed. Patricia A. Lynch, Joachim Fischer, and Brian Coates (Amsterdam: Rodopi, 2006), 271–85.

18 See Richard Kirkland, "Medbh McGuckian and the Politics of Minority Discourse," in Alcobia-Murphy and Kirkland, *Interior*, 147–61.

Sexton, Heaney, and Frost has also been extensively charted by Shane Alcobia-Murphy and Leontia Flynn.[19] Others have examined her political position as a postcolonial writer.[20] Few scholars, however, have examined McGuckian's use of medieval and early modern source material through either a descriptive or a critical lens. None has read her work within a postcolonial framework that accommodates her use of historiography and considers the ethical implications of appropriating scholarship that is itself explicitly feminist. This is an unusual *aporia*, given McGuckian's status as a feminist Northern Irish writer and her recent use of historical sources.

McGuckian's practice of composition involves first constructing a binary poem-making apparatus in a notebook, with the "original" text on one side and her own new poem, made of bits and pieces of the original, on the other.[21] Her source texts often include biography, prose, journals, and criticism; only recently has she begun to use other poems as constitutive material. These sources are only rarely attributed, and indeed as Shane Alcobia-Murphy has argued, McGuckian's poetry might best be understood as using "concealed quotation," an invisible layering together of other texts and referents to create a new aesthetic whole.[22] The "quotations" buried within the body of McGuckian's seemingly original poems often work against syntactic and grammatical meaning, which can make her work weirdly inaccessible. It is difficult to parse a through-line of sense in her lyrics, and reviewers of McGuckian's early books were hostile to this obfuscatory style, arguing that "if lines are so arbitrary that they mean more or less anything, then necessarily they mean more or

---

19 See Leontia Flynn, "Reassembling the Atom: Reading Medbh McGuckian's Intertextual Materials," in Alcobia-Murphy and Kirkland, *Interior*, 77–93. Shane Alcobia-Murphy identifies McGuckian's source texts in his "My Cleverly Dead and Vertical Audience," and "'Signs of the Still Recent War': Medbh McGuckian and Conflict," *Irish Studies Review* 20, no. 2 (2012): 115–33.
20 Of particular interest are Michaela Schrage-Früh, "Speaking as the North: Self and Place in the Early Poetry of Medbh McGuckian," in Alcobia-Murphy and Kirkland, *Interior*, 22–40; Maureen Fadem, *The Literature of Northern Ireland: Spectral Borderlands* (New York: Palgrave Macmillan, 2015); and Shane Alcobia-Murphy, "Lest We Forget: Memory, Trauma, and Culture in Post-Agreement Northern Ireland," *The Canadian Journal of Irish Studies* 39, no. 2 (2016): 82–107.
21 See Alcobia-Murphy and Kirkland, "Interview," 196, for further discussion of this method. Shane Alcobia-Murphy discusses McGuckian's side-by-side practice in his "My Cleverly Dead," and "Signs of the Still Recent War."
22 See Shane Alcobia-Murphy, "'You Took Away My Biography': The Poetry of Medbh McGuckian," *Irish University Review* 28, no. 1 (1998): 110–32, at 122.

less nothing."[23] In order to comprehend her work, reviewers claimed, "we must be able to explicate her gnomic tendency, prove that she is not writing nonsense verses or being willfully obscure."[24] However, questions of meaning cannot be separated easily from gendered notions of literary authority, historically predicated upon patriarchal rivalries and influences. The male, heteronormative *auctor* makes sense to an audience expecting a single, originary voice of genius who is directly responding to his rival predecessor.[25] But McGuckian's use of multiple voices and sources, her resistance to creating a single claim for meaning, offers a decidedly complicated and queer example of poetry. To read McGuckian on her own "gnomic" terms is to resist implicitly this phallocentric emphasis, and to immerse oneself completely within a sea of language. There is no single, canonical source text in McGuckian's poem to which she pays proper homage. Rather, she uses multiple sources that themselves are referring to other sources, in an allusive hall of mirrors. Her poems "operate at another remove," according to Leontia Flynn, and use a variety of related sources and texts, all speaking at once to each other.[26] This is not to say that McGuckian's work is merely citational, a kind of hollow sampling, but that her practice calls into question authority itself.

"The harlot is talkative and wandering"

"How the Good Wife" shares themes with a similarly titled poem, "The Good Housewife," from McGuckian's 2008 *My Love Has Fared Inland.*[27] In both poems, historiographic essays constitute the original source text that McGuckian

---

23 Patrick Williams's review of *On Ballycastle Beach*, quoted in Leontia Flynn, "Reassembling the Atom: Reading Medbh McGuckian's Intertextual Materials," in Alcobia-Murphy and Kirkland, *Interior*, 177.

24 Michael Allen, review of *On Ballycastle Beach*, quoted in Flynn, "Reassembling," 177.

25 Watt and Magnani critique this notion and its historical use in manuscript studies, arguing that "as long as manuscript studies and philology in general continue to be dominated by masculinist discourses of rivalry, the field will remain elitist and conservative, as it will focus on ring-fencing privilege and its default identity: white, able-bodied, straight, male, and Christian." See Watt and Magnani, "Towards," 256.

26 Flynn, "Reassembling," 178.

27 See Medbh McGuckian, "The Good Housewife," in *My Love Has Fared Inland* (Oldcastle: Meath, 2008), 64–65. "The Good Housewife" uses as its source text a letter from Francesco Datini to his wife Francesca, among other primary sources found in Mary Rogers and Paola Tinagli, eds., *Women in Italy, 1350–1650: Ideals and Realities* (Manchester: Manchester University Press, 2005). For further discussion of McGuckian's use of this source text, see Alcobia-Murphy, "Nobody."

appropriates. She uses excerpts from these essays verbatim to create postcolonial, translational lyrics, composed in rough blank verse English stanzas, whose construction calls into question the very nature of authority and history. In the case of "How the Good Wife," Middle English popular verse and prose are translated into a Modern English lyric. Niranjana has argued that translation is "brought into being in the colonial context in a complex field structured by law, violence, and subjectification, as well as by determinate concepts of representation, reality, and knowledge."[28] The language of the colonized is often quite different from the colonizer, even if they end up speaking technically the same words. When these words are inflected by a historical past that exists outside of these colonial constraints, however, new possibilities are made available. Postcolonial translation complicates our received notions of what knowledge is and how it is transmitted; it borrows, begs, and steals from past words to create new poetry. It can present this new poetry as contemporaneous, even if it is culled from history. Indeed, Niranjana posits that "Perhaps post-colonial theory can show that we need to translate (that is, disturb or displace) history," and McGuckian's "How the Good Wife" might offer a way of thinking through the displacement engendered by postcoloniality.[29] Her combination of Modern English historiography and early English texts creates a strangely dreamlike Northern Irish lyric concerned with feminine subjectivity and social surveillance.

Given McGuckian's own tutelage under Seamus Heaney—indeed, it was Heaney who christened the explicitly Irish spelling of McGuckian's first name—it is not surprising that she turns to medieval sources for her poetry.[30] Heaney famously mined the Neolithic and the medieval past for poetic material. Like McGuckian, a Northern Irish Catholic raised in a monolingual, English-speaking colonial culture, Heaney's poetry also lives in the interstice between literary and political history. In the introductory essay to his translation of *Beowulf*, Heaney directly addresses the role of his Irish-accented English and the function that this bent, colonized language might play in his understanding of Old English. He observes that he struggled for years with what he imagined was a harsh, binary split between English and Irish, only reconciling them when he came upon the Old English word *thole* in his translation and remembered it from his aunt's County Derry idiom. He later includes the Elizabethan colonial term

28 Niranjana, *Siting*, 165.
29 Niranjana, *Siting*, 38.
30 McGuckian was born Maeve McCaughan; she changed the spelling of her first name to the more Irish version after Heaney used it in his book inscriptions for her. See McGuckian, "Drawing Ballerinas: How Being Irish Has Influenced Me as a Writer," in *Wee Girls: Women Writing From an Irish Perspective*, ed. Lizz Murphy (North Melbourne: Spinifex, 1996), 185–203, at 195.

bawn (from the Irish *bó-dhún*, a fort for cattle), because "putting a *bawn* into *Beowulf* seems one way for an Irish poet to come to terms with that complex history of conquest and colony, absorption and resistance, integrity and antagonism, a history that has to be clearly acknowledged by all concerned."[31] Unlike Heaney, of course, McGuckian is a feminine subject engaged in a traditionally masculinist poetic discourse; she has long had only patchy access to the archive.[32] And, unlike *Beowulf*, McGuckian's original sources are not foundational to the construction of the literary canon. Instead, "How the Good Wife" translates Middle English texts that feature female speakers, are addressed to girls or women, and discuss the banalities of female life, such as comportment, groceries, dress, and postpartum suffering. Designed more to edify and inculcate than to delight, their language is often clichéd, as when the daughter in a medieval conduct poem is bid to remember that "many hands make lyght werke."[33]

The original Middle English "How the Good Wyf" is an anonymous poem that bids the daughter (and presumably the reader) in rhyming couplets to resist public misbehavior. In a hectoring voice, the poem's speaker catalogs all of the things a girl is not to do. The use of the possessive pronoun "my" suggests that the speaker of the poem is that of the "Good Wyf" herself, and that she is speaking to her own daughter.

> Be fayre of semblant, my der doughter;
> Change not thi countenans with grete laughter,
> And wyse of maneres loke thou be gode.
> Ne for no tayle change thi mode,
> Ne fare not as thou a gyglot were,
> Ne laughe thou not lowd, be thou therof sore.
> Luke thou also gape not to wyde,
> For anything that may betyde.
> Suete of speche loke that thow be,
> Trow in worde and dede—lerne this of me.
> Loke thou fle synne, vilony, and blame,
> And se ther be no man that seys thee any schame.
> When thou goys in the gate, go not to faste,
> Ne hyderward ne thederward thi hede thou caste,

31 See Seamus Heaney, "On Beowulf," in *Beowulf*, bilingual edition (New York: Norton, 2000), xxx.

32 McGuckian now teaches at Queen's University Belfast, and notes that this now provides her with "access to a pretty good library where I can get 25 books out for six months, whereas before I was getting six books for three weeks, and out of not very good libraries … Before I was starved and now I am kind of sated." See Alcobia-Murphy and Kirkland, "Interview," 196.

33 Shuffelton, ed., "How the Good Wife Taught Her Daughter," l. 154.

No grete othes loke thou suere;
Byware, my doughter, of syche a maner.
Go not as it were a gase
Fro house to house to seke the mase.[34]

The mother urges the girl to control her affect and thereby how she is perceived by others. She should be constant in her public comportment and not change her countenance with laughter (ll. 46 – 47). She should not widely gape her mouth (l. 52). Likewise, she should not change the way she behaves in response to anybody's good story, and should not carry herself like a giggling slut (ll. 49 – 50). In the TEAMS version of the poem, the archaic "gyglot" is glossed as "harlot," which is in frequent contemporary use.[35] "Gyglot" is also loosely etymologically related to "giggle," which offers an onomatopoetic source of ironic pleasure given the mother's admonition that the daughter avoid loud public laughter.[36] Too much joy in public will make people think you are a slut. Carrying yourself properly and refraining from open-mouthed laughter will also somehow prevent men from catcalling you, for when you are out and about, you must "se ther be no man that seys thee any schame" or ensure that no man will say shameful things (l. 57). Street harassment, in "The Good Wyf," is a giggling girl's own fault.

Just as her affect must be calmly neutral outside the confines of the home, so as to protect her sexual reputation, the daughter should also avoid public entertainment. These activities carry a sort of sexual and moral taint, as evidenced by the second appearance of "gyglote." The poem's first use of the term associates being a "gyglote" with having a changeable affect and with laughter, as well as possibly visiting a tavern. The second use of "gyglote" connects it with wrestling and cock shooting; it serves as just one of two misogynist terms used to demean female sexuality.

Ne go thou not to no wrastlyng,
Ne yit to no coke schetyng,
As it were a strumpet other a gyglote. (ll. 74 – 76)

---

34 Shuffelton, ed., "How the Good Wife Taught Her Daughter," ll. 46 – 63.

35 Urban Dictionary defines "harlot" as "a female capable of frequently having casual sexual relations with different partners and is completely undiscriminating in the choice of sexual partners, hence being appreciated by everyone she knows. Also known as a 'sex saint.'" See https://www.urbandictionary.com/define.php?term=harlot.

36 See *Middle English Dictionary*, s.v. "gigelot (*n.*)," https://quod.lib.umich.edu/m/middle-english-dictionary/dictionary/MED18531/track?counter=1&search_id=3156286. The *Oxford English Dictionary* notes the etymological link to "giggle," in its entry for the archaic "giglet | giglot (*n.*)," accessed March 14, 2020, www.oed.com/view/Entry/78243.

The girl should refrain from raucous, loud activities when she is out and about. She should avoid public drinking, as well as opportunities where gambling may take place. Even being a passive bystander to these sorts of activities can cause onlookers to question a girl's chastity. Adolescent sexuality must be bounded by a girl's own self-control—over her face, her emotions, her activities. To watch "wrastlyng" in a crowd is to be a whore.[37]

The association between femininity and public movement, affect, and sexual reputation exists in both the original and in McGuckian's version. However, McGuckian's poem replaces "gyglote" with the more contemporary pejorative "harlot." Where the original addresses a second-person subject and catalogs a series of prohibited behaviors, her translation names the subject directly as a precise third-person noun, "the harlot," who actively engages in the forbidden behaviors that the original merely lists.

> The harlot is talkative and wandering
> By the way, not bearing to be quiet
> Not able to abide still at home
> Now abroad, now still in the streets. (ll. 9–12)

This promiscuous woman is unable to be kept at home; she visits the green to check on her geese, and watches wrestling matches at the tavern. She does not tolerate quietness but heads out and about, living her life in all the chatty and gossipy ways that the original poem cautions against.[38] She might be understood as one of the "spirited and daring girls" described by Felicity Riddy, who "seem to have been the agents of social mobility" in their movement from small farms to cities.[39] Within McGuckian's poem, the harlot laughs and gossips at the public green, her movement calling into question that "prime bourgeois value: respectability."[40] Indeed the Middle English "Good Wife" can be read as "a text for the embourgeoisement of servants, in the interests not only of the girls, but of the respectability of the households in which they were employed,"

---

37 The MED notes that "strumpet" is associated with prostitution; a "strumpetis hous" was a brothel. See https://quod.lib.umich.edu/m/middle-english-dictionary/dictionary/MED43418/track?counter=1&search_id=3156286.

38 McGuckian was herself frequently housebound with four small children during the 1980s in Belfast. See Borbála Faragó, *Medbh McGuckian* (Bucknell, PA: Bucknell University Press, 2014), 14.

39 See her "Mother Knows Best: Reading Social Change in a Courtesy Text," *Speculum* 71, no. 1 (1996): 66–86; "spirited and daring" is found at 86; "social mobility" at 77.

40 Riddy, "Mother," 78.

according to Riddy.[41] The loud laughing girls are subjected to scorn and judgment from others who see them.

Multiple Margeries

For Middle English speakers, "harlot" was a masculine term, used to describe low level male servants or entertainers; it is only in the early modern period that it shifts to the feminized slur still in use today.[42] McGuckian's translation of "gigelote" as "harlot" is a translational point of departure, supporting the poem's notion of femininity as under siege. The harlot here looks after her geese, and in a crucial difference from the original, is not forbidden from public movement. Instead, she simply "goes" out to pursue her own interests, though not without dire consequences.

> She goes to the green to see to her geese,
> And trips to wrestling matches and taverns.
> The said Margery left her home
> In the parish of Bishopshill. (ll. 17–20)

Just as McGuckian replaces the original "gygelot" with the contemporary "harlot," so too does she translate the merry, unnamed girl to an actual medieval person, Margery Nesfield of York, in line 19. The link between the loud laughing girls of the conduct poem and Margery Nesfield's desire for freedom is elegantly compressed in McGuckian's poem. This quatrain offers a distinct shift in diction and tone, moving to awkward legalese. The "said Margery," like the wandering harlots and their loose sexuality, has left the confines of her home. Alcobia-Murphy misreads this moment, claiming that the source for "the said Margery" is *The Book of Margery Kempe:* "Margery Kempe had petitioned for a separation from her husband, Thomas, on the grounds of cruelty; however, his violence was deemed acceptable by the court because of 'her refusal to stay within the household.'"[43] Within the structure of McGuckian's poem, in which women who travel

41 Riddy, "Mother," 85.

42 *Oxford English Dictionary,* s.v. "harlot (*n.*)," accessed March 13, 2020, www.oed.com/view/Entry/84255.

43 See Alcobia-Murphy, "Nobody," at paragraph 14; he is citing Salih, "At Home," 126. The Nesfield case is detailed by P. J. P. Goldberg, which Salih makes clear, and can be found in P. J. P. Goldberg, "Fiction in the Archives: The York Cause Papers as a Source for Later Medieval Social History," *Continuity and Change* 12 (1997): 439.

are punished, this reading of "Margery Kempe" being victim of her husband's violence makes sense. It aligns well with the poem's overall configuration of medieval femininity as a role caught between a desire for freedom and the surveillance and violence that follows. Yet Margery Kempe's own historical *Book* reveals a far more complex relationship between bourgeois femininity, desire, and personal sovereignty. Margery Kempe is married not to Thomas but to John, a superlatively tolerant husband; he negotiates with her fairly, allows her to visit Jerusalem, and agrees to live separately from her. Margery Kempe's difficulties are with her own desire to pursue her spiritual purpose, which sets her at odds with her neighbors, the courts, and the church. While her wish for chastity is at odds with her husband's request that she pay the conjugal debt, he eventually consents to her determination to travel and he regularly defends her from public harm.

McGuckian's poem uses language taken directly from *The Book of Margery Kempe*, but does so to signal the return of the female figure to a domestic space. In particular, McGuckian deploys the end of the *Book*'s opening chapter, which describes Margery's first vision of Jesus and her subsequent return to her senses.

> And anon the creature was stabled
> In her wits as well as ever she was biforn,
>
> And prayed her husband as so soon
> As he came to her that she might have
> The keys to her buttery
> To take her meat and drink. (ll. 27–32)

Kempe's language serves as an epigraph for Salih's "At Home," in fact, and is more substantial than McGuckian's excerpt reflects. Confined to her bed, her hands tied so as to prevent her from continuing to engage in self-harm, Margery struggles to communicate effectively her return to mental health. Neither her servants nor her caregivers believe she is well. It is only John, "hir husband, euyr hauyng tendyrness & compassion of hir," who understands her and returns to her the pantry keys and thus her role as wife.[44] McGuckian's intertextual meshing of her sources necessarily results in a confusion between what her poem is saying about women's mobility, and what the primary medieval texts themselves actually say. Margery Nesfield was censured and beaten for leaving her husband. But Margery Kempe is freed from confinement at home by hers.

44 Quoted in Salih, "At Home," 124.

Within McGuckian's poem, the figure of "Margery" is both Margery Nesfield as well as "this creature." She is at once a combination of actual people as well as a complete fiction. This strange lack of verbal stability or authority is also reflected in the fact that *The Book of Margery Kempe* has a named author, but it isn't exactly Margery Kempe herself.[45] In fact, none of the primary sources used in McGuckian's poem have clear, stable authors. Voiced by women, recorded by men, the texts exist in a variety of versions. These popular vernacular texts directed at medieval women are part of a vibrant manuscript culture, one which Magnani and Watt argue is marked by "its disjunctures, non-linear processes of production and dissemination, pleasures found in errors, its complex and refracted networks of professional agents and readers, and the non-binary subject positions which it accommodates."[46] The multiple Margeries in these medieval and twenty-first-century poems who speak, resist, pray, orate, and recover seem to do so from within the strangely queer disjunctures that constitute medieval manuscript culture itself. Indeed, in his analysis of McGuckian's "How the Good Wife," Kenneth Keating has argued that McGuckian's use of anonymous late-medieval women's writing makes her much like "a medieval scribe" who in copying produces a new text that is "simultaneously the same and different" when compared to the original.[47] He lists the various medieval manuscripts in which McGuckian's source texts are found, noting in particular the multiplicity of versions of the late-medieval "Good Wife" poem. Because of this multiplicity, it's not possible to pin down which specific version McGuckian uses; instead, we might consider that this plurality of sources "underlines the destabilizing multiplicity of meaning" within McGuckian's poem.[48] Like a medieval lyric with many iterations and no clear author, the multitude of primary sources for McGuckian's poem "does not reveal a singular meaning but complicates the process even further."[49] However, while Keating lists these primary texts, he does not fully consider the role that Salih's "At Home" might play in McGuckian's access to them.

---

45 See for instance Lynn Staley, *Margery Kempe's Dissenting Fictions* (University Park, PA: Pennsylvania State University Press, 1994), in particular her first chapter, "Authorship and Authority."
46 Magnani and Watt, "Towards," 257.
47 See Keating, "Source Texts," 321.
48 Ibid.
49 Ibid., 320.

Laws about Pilfering

McGuckian's *poeisis* knits together multiple sources into a translational whole. From her source texts, she seeks out "images, striking conjunctions of maybe two or three unusual words, esoteric vocabulary" which she uses to make her own poem from the "poetry which is there, embedded in what people write and say, and what they themselves quote from."[50] McGuckian does not believe that her appropriation is necessarily negative for the original author, who desires that the work be read and "doesn't mind it being read and going straight into someone's head. If it's enshrined in the work of art, even in a truncated or bowdlerized form, still I think when I meet the people who wrote all the books I think they will forgive me."[51] McGuckian's practice gives the secondary work—which itself often uses and quotes from outside sources—a new aesthetic life.

McGuckian's *poeisis*, in the case of "How the Good Wife," is rooted less in various examples of conduct literature than in a single, historiographical essay about that literature. Her poem is almost entirely constituted by Salih's collation of primary documents in "At Home." Following Alcobia-Murphy's model, I have tracked McGuckian's use of "At Home" in "The Good Wife," identifying Salih's language and sources below in bold, in an attempt to recreate McGuckian's practice.

Lordship is the same activity
Whether performed by lord or lady. (Robert Grosseteste, *Household Rules for the Countess of Lincoln*, qtd in Salih, 128)
Or a lord who happens to be a lady, (Grosseteste, *Household Rules*, qtd Salih, 131)
All the source **and all the faults.** (Grosseteste, *Household Rules*, qtd Salih, 131)

A **woman steadfast in looking** (*Book of the Knight of the Tower*, qtd in Salih, 134) is a **callot**, (*How the Good Wife*, qtd in Salih, 135)
And **any woman in the wrong place**
Or outside of her proper location (126, Salih's own words)
Is, by definition, a foolish woman. (*The Book of the Knight of the Tower*, qtd in Salih, 126)

50 Alcobia-Murphy and Kirkland, "Interview," 201.
51 Ibid., 199.

The harlot is talkative and wandering
By the way, not bearing to be quiet
Not able to abide still at home,
Now abroad, now still in the streets

Now lying in wait near the corners (*Proverbs*, cited in Salih, 125)
Her hair straying out of its wimple.
The collar of her shift and robe
Pressed one upon the other. (*Ménagier*, qtd in Salih, 134)

She goes to the green to see to her geese, (*Ballad of the Tyrannical Husband*, qtd in Salih, 128)
And trips to wrestling matches and taverns. (136, Salih's own words)
The said Margery left her home
In the parish of Bishopshill,

And went to a house, the which
The witness 'does not remember,'
And stayed there from noon
Of that day until the darkness of night. (*Nesfield court case*, cited in Salih, 126)
Anon the creature was stabled
In her wits as well as ever she was biforn,
And prayed her husband that she might have
The keys to her buttery to take her meat and drink. (*The Book of Margery Kempe*, qtd in Salih, 121)

He should never have *my* good will
For to make my sister for to sell
Candle and mustard in Framlyngham, (*Paston Letters*, qtd in Salih, 127)
Or fill her **shopping list** with **crossbows**, ("shopping list" is Salih's language, 129)

Almonds, sugar and cloth. (*Paston Letters*, qtd in Salih, 129)
The **captainess**, (*Paston Letters*, qtd in Salih, 129) the **vowess**
Must use herself to work readily (Salih, 125)
As **other gentilwomen doon**, (*Paston Letters*, qtd in Salih, 127)
In the innermost part of her house,
In a great chamber far from the road. (*Ménagier*, qtd in Salih, 130)
So **love your windows as little as you can**, (*Ancrene Wisse*, qtd in Evans, "Vir-

ginities," 33)
For we be, either of us, weary of other. (*Paston Letters*, qtd in Salih, 127)

Every stanza is comprised of primary material—letters, poems, conduct treatises, spiritual autobiographies, court cases—directly taken from "At Home." There are also snippets of Salih's own language.[52] The final stanza contains an admonition from the *Ancrene Wisse*, which tells anchoresses to "love your windows as little as you possibly can," and is quoted in Ruth Evans's essay "Virginities," also contained in the *Cambridge Companion.*[53]

The poem mines Salih's sources, but it does not follow the trajectory of Salih's argument. "At Home" focuses upon "the vast majority of medieval women who wrote nothing more than family letters and household accounts, if that; who were not mystics; who apparently accepted the roles prescribed for them."[54] McGuckian compresses Salih's nuanced analysis of mundane, popular sources of women's writing and writing directed at women, focusing only on the claim that "the house is the privileged locus for medieval women; notionally this is where the good woman can be found, bustling about her domestic duties."[55] McGuckian's lyric is a feminist disquisition on social surveillance, and as Alcobia-Murphy argues, it is "alive to the ways in which the female subject is constructed and curtailed by masculinist ideology."[56] McGuckian tracks the "good wife's" trajectory from "within the innermost part of her house" (l. 32) into and through a series of public spaces that are "outside her proper location" (l. 7). This therefore not-so-good wife is "not able to abide still at home" (l. 11), but flits, like a pinball of desire, "now abroad, now in the streets, / now lying in wait near the corners" (l. 12–13), and is judged a harlot for her movement. Within the confines of the poem, this construction of medieval femininity stitches together disparate sources into a coherent whole. But it does not reflect the varied complexity of how that femininity is reflected in medieval conduct literature, as Salih takes pains to argue.

The women who write the letters, books, and household accounts analyzed in "At Home" are not monoliths. What is proper comportment for medieval women is continually in flux. They move between a variety of roles, perpetually

52 I am thankful for Salih's own eagle eye in catching these. See Sarah Salih, personal interview, March 14, 2020.
53 See Ruth Evans, "Virginities," in *The Cambridge Companion to Medieval Women's Writing*, 21–39. Alcobia-Murphy discusses this further in "Nobody," paragraph 12.
54 Salih, "At Home," 124.
55 Ibid., 125.
56 See Alcobia-Murphy, "Nobody," paragraph 26.

doing domestic labor, but as Salih notes, "the division between domestic and non-domestic does not match the modern one," given that the late-medieval household "was not only conceived of as a private sphere: it was both family dwelling and workplace."[57] To be at home, for a late-medieval woman, was not necessarily to be confined to privacy. Instead, the home was often the locus for artisanal commerce, and a married woman was responsible for managing employees, manufacturing goods, and selling products to the public. Margery Kempe's *Book* in particular troubles McGuckian's association of women with a stable, private, domestic sphere. Trained as an alewife and deploying a variety of business ventures, Kempe lives and moves within the world. More than this, her *Book* "represents a medieval woman whose saintliness is marked precisely by its distance from the secular model of good womanhood to which she had initially been trained."[58] Margery Kempe receives the keys to the buttery at the beginning of her spiritual autobiography, but her entire narrative charts the symbolic rejection of what those keys represent—staying home and managing a family. As Salih observes, Kempe refuses a life of proper housewifery in favor of pilgrimage, prayer, and abstinence and in this way actively resists masculinist ideology, staking out a life on her own terms.[59] Her *Book* and the conduct literature Salih examines are highly performative, demanding particular duties of women that they may or may not adequately sustain, yet as Salih argues "with performativity comes the potential for instability."[60] The women who speak in "At Home" may be constrained by their gender, but they are also able to claim fresh possibilities from within those constraints, as evidenced by the texts they produced.

McGuckian has argued that her mining of source texts is recompense for the postcolonial harm that she has suffered as an Irish writer. Angry at the "self-righteous tutors in Cambridge," who "lay down laws about pilfering," she notes that "fair exchange is no robbery and every word I take *back* from *their* shelves and their books and their imposed culture into *my* mouth and hand is to feed all those who died (but not spiritually) in the Famine and elsewhere."[61] As Alcobia-Murphy posits, McGuckian's anger at university tutors who reject "pilfering" stems from "feelings of linguistic dislocation and her need to use her literary precursors to effect a rebellion against what she considers to be a

---

57 Salih, "At Home," 127.
58 Ibid., 136.
59 Ibid., 124.
60 Ibid., 136.
61 Alcobia-Murphy, "Intertextual Relations," 280.

colonized language."[62] Yet this tit-for-tat exchange for what was stolen depends on an assumption that McGuckian's sources use their cultural and linguistic dominance in overt, obvious ways. The Cambridge tutors are the owners of shelves, books, "imposed culture," in this letter; they are hegemons, protecting an archive built on colonial oppression. Within McGuckian's *poeisis*, to take from this archive is a kind of heroism, an act of aesthetic and cultural restitution that memorializes the Irish past. However, neither Salih nor her essay, built of the words and experiences and documents of ordinary medieval women, stands in opposition to McGuckian's need for payback.

Salih's essay appears, of course, in a Cambridge volume and thus carries an imprimatur of authority and cultural prestige against which McGuckian positions her poetry. But Salih is not a Cambridge hegemon obsessed with "laws about pilfering." She is a feminist, mixed-race scholar who is herself a postcolonial subject,[63] and her essay illuminates not just the ways conduct literature forced women into their proper roles but also the ways that women resisted those roles. "At Home" charts the vernacular texts that describe women going about their daily lives—they buy sundries, obsess about their appearance, fight with their husbands, are hectored by their mothers to be more proper, recover from postpartum illness. Their voices are not the product of what men imagine women might sound like, à la Chaucer's *Wife of Bath*, but are instead the closest we might get to women's actual lived experience in all of its performative possibility. Salih's historicist analysis is an act of feminist reclamation. "At Home" skews the traditional academic focus away from famous, canonical men to zero in on those who have long been derided as irrelevant.

Medieval poetry famously steals and poaches and alludes, in gestures that at once self-deprecate and forcefully position the speaker within a broader canonical tradition. Consider, for instance, Chaucer's claim that he is but a maker compared to Petrarch's laureate skills, or Dunbar's cataloging of past masters in his "Lament for the Makaris." In this way the poet is able to humbly retract any faults in his poetry while also placing himself amidst the pantheon of other, important poets. McGuckian's poetry plays with and resists these patrilineal methods of making meaning, and "How the Good Wife" lives within the queer blurred space between historiography, translation, and postcoloniality. It is the lyric place where the past and the present rub shoulders and where no one author is governing the trajectory of the text, where women read and steal from one another, and where the act of stealing is a kind of retributive justice. It is important

62 Ibid.
63 Salih, personal interview.

to note, however, that retributive justice is organized around a binary system in which the oppressor criminal and the oppressed victim are stable, essential categories. In its focus on retribution, this form of justice resists complexity or ambivalence and often punishes harshly those who have done no wrong.[64]

On the last page of *Currach*, McGuckian offers thanks to the library staff of Queen's University Library, Belfast, and to the unnamed "authors and editors of the texts on which many [poems] have been based."[65] But it is Salih's work that has given us a palimpsest of medieval women's voices—the "gigelots" and scrutinized laughers, the girls watching the world from their windows, Margery Nesfield reported on by her neighbors, Margery Kempe's return to her senses, the housewives irritated by their servants—whose presence is woven into the very structure of McGuckian's poem. McGuckian's practice of collation allows for a kind of compressed sonorous possibility, a way of letting multiple voices speak in the present. It isn't clear, however, whether this practice is one of translation or of unacknowledged theft.

---

64 My thinking on retributive justice and its binaries has been greatly informed by the work of Sarah Marshall and Michael Hobbes, "The Victim's Rights Movement," August 16, 2019, in *You're Wrong About*, podcast, https://www.stitcher.com/podcast/michael-hobbes/youre-wrong-about/e/63258684.

65 She only names "in particular the research carried out in Patricia M. Crawford and Laura Gowing's *Women's Worlds in Seventeenth-Century England*." See McGuckian, *Currach*, 66.

Jonathan Hsy and Candace Barrington

Queer Time, Queer Forms: Noir Medievalism and Patience Agbabi's *Telling Tales*

The time of medievalism is anything but straight. Queer theorists have long explored how ways of knowing, feeling, and desiring diverge from heteronormative drives—and also how queer temporalities and lifeways evade linear and progressive models.[1] Within medieval literary and cultural studies, the queer scholarship of Carolyn Dinshaw has shown how "studying the Middle Ages" and interpreting modern forms of medievalism are both ultimately "about desire—for another time, for meaning, for life."[2] Inhabiting a similarly queer orientation toward medieval studies, Jonathan Hsy has emphasized how the vibrant field of medievalism studies—that is, the critical analysis of contemporary artistic and cultural adaptations of medieval materials—entails a versatile practice of "cognitive multitasking," a flexible "channel-flipping orientation toward time" that understands the cultural productions of the Middle Ages in their "own" historical circumstances as well as their divergent receptions throughout subsequent time periods.[3] From a different perspective, Candace Barrington has shown that contemporary retellings of medieval texts offer insight into the original texts by operating outside "the master narrative that both guides and hampers academic imagination."[4]

In this co-authored essay, we seek to explore how a multidirectional mindset (as Hsy describes) and an embrace of non-academic readings (as Barrington describes) allow medievalism scholars to incorporate heterogeneous places and times into a richer understanding of and affection for a medieval past—and to appreciate a dynamic ongoing relationship between the historical past and our own diverse and ever-changing present. We jointly accept Dinshaw's call for ex-

1 See J. Halberstam, *The Queer Art of Failure* (Durham, NC: Duke University Press, 2011); see also José Esteban Muñoz, *Cruising Utopia: The Then and There of Queer Futurity* (New York: New York University Press, 2009); and Kathryn Boyd Stockton, *The Queer Child: Or, Growing Sideways in the Twentieth Century* (Durham, NC: Duke University Press, 2009).

2 Carolyn Dinshaw, *How Soon is Now?: Medieval Texts, Amateur Readers, and the Queerness of Time* (Durham, NC: Duke University Press, 2012), 32.

3 Jonathan Hsy, "Co-disciplinarity," in *Medievalism: Key Critical Terms*, ed. Elizabeth Emery and Richard Utz (Rochester, NY: D. S. Brewer, 2014), 43.

4 Candace Barrington, *American Chaucers* (New York: Palgrave Macmillan, 2007), 160.

https://doi.org/10.1515/9781501511189-009

panding the scope of those traditionally identified with "expert knowledge production" beyond academics per se, by attending to the intellectual and artistic contributions of a modern group of Chaucer's interlocutors—contemporary poets—who offer "different ways of knowing and sources of knowledge, and different purposes and goals."[5] Reading Chaucer alongside one such poet, Nigerian-British author and spoken-word performance artist Patience Agbabi, allows us to avoid what Stephanie Trigg and Thomas Prendergast have identified as "a cautious professionalism that codes the Middle Ages as distant, remote and all but unreachable."[6]

Our collaborative essay explores how queer approaches to the time of medievalism, as well as medievalist scholarship grounded in queer diaspora studies, can inform the complex "queer time" of Agbabi's neo-Chaucerian poetry collection *Telling Tales* (2014). In acknowledgment of her own deep engagements with contemporary urban musical and performance genres, Agbabi calls her work a "remixed" transformation of all extant narratives within *The Canterbury Tales.*[7] Agbabi's "remix" is just one of the most recent contributions to a multifaceted range of modern Chaucerian poetic adaptations by Black and African diaspora women, each of whom reinvents the medieval poet's work "as a vehicle for exploring contemporary African diasporic identities"[8] and relocates the medieval Chaucerian storytelling context to a new time and place.[9] Jean "Binta" Breeze's much-anthologized "The Wife of Bath Speaks in Brixton Market" (2000) reincarnates Chaucer's character through versified Jamaican *patois*;[10] Marilyn Nelson, who uses iambic pentameter couplets throughout *The Cachoeira Tales* (2005), traces a rerouted African American "reverse diaspora" pilgirmage to Black regions of Brazil;[11] Karen King-Aribisala, whose novel *Kicking Tongues* (1998) incorporates prose and poetry and Nigerian Pidgin English vernacular, tells stories of trauma, migration, and recovery in post-independence Nigeria;[12] and Ufuoma

---

5 Dinshaw, *How Soon is Now?*, 38.

6 Thomas Prendergast and Stephanie Trigg, *Affective Medievalism: Love, Abjection and Discontent* (Manchester: Manchester University Press, 2019), 113.

7 Patience Agbabi, "Stories in Stanza'd English: A Cross-Cultural *Canterbury Tales*," *Literature Compass* 15, no. 6 (June 2018): 2.

8 Kathleen Forni, *Chaucer's Afterlife: Adaptations in Recent Popular Culture* (Jefferson, NC: McFarland, 2013), 106.

9 Candace Barrington and Jonathan Hsy, "Afterlives," in *A New Companion to Chaucer*, ed. Peter Brown (Hoboken, NJ: Wiley Blackwell, 2019), 15–17.

10 Michelle R. Warren, "'The Last Syllable of Modernity': Chaucer and the Carribean," *postmedieval* 6, no. 1 (2015): 79–93.

11 David Wallace, "New Chaucer Topographies," *Studies in the Age of Chaucer* 29 (2007): 3–19.

12 See Forni, *Chaucer's Afterlife.*

Overo-Tarimo, whose Nigerian Pidgin English play *Wahala Dey O!* (2012) incorporates dialogue and musical peformances, transplants Chaucer's *Miller's Tale* to contemporary Nigeria.[13]

If Agbabi is read alongside this heterogeneous range of cultural productions by Black and African diaspora women, her *Telling Tales* emerges as dinstictive—and not just because the author has identified in previous contexts as bicultural and queer.[14] With an ear attuned to Chaucerian polyvocality, Agbabi relocates her Chaucerian storytelling context to a multiracial contemporary Britain and, in the process, reassigns the racial and gendered perspectives of many of the narrators and their stories. Like her earlier collection, *Transformatrix*, which "focuses on language as infinitely malleable and constructive of new realities," her Chaucerian retelling transforms the past so that it can reflect the way Britain is now.[15] Despite the apparent dissimilarity between Chaucer's *The Canterbury Tales* and Agbabi's *Telling Tales* in length, language, and forms, the connection is recognizable. *Telling Tales* imaginatively recreates the pilgrimage ritual, moving from horseback and foot along the road between London and Canterbury to a Routemaster bus. Agbabi's multiracial and queer adaptation profoundly reorients Chaucer's *Canterbury Tales* for modern audiences, radically transforming the medieval poet's configurations of time, gender, and desire. Although Chaucer's text remains the "ground base" (to borrow Louise D'Arcens's term) for Agbabi's collection,[16] Agbabi's poems cede no authority to the fourteenth-century poems. Indeed, while Agbabi brings distant voices to the present via voices of England's performance poetry circuit, she invites professional medievalists to reconsider what we thought we knew about Chaucer, his tales, and his characters.

Our essay focuses on both the formal qualities and the queer dimensions of three poems within *Telling Tales:* "Unfinished Business," Agbabi's adaptation of Chaucer's prose *Tale of Melibee* (transformed into a mirror poem); "I Go Back to May 1967," her realignment of Chaucer's *The Clerk's Tale* (condensed into a free-verse, personal narrative); and "Joined-Up Writing," her rendition of Chaucer's

---

13 Ufuoma Overo-Tarimo, *The Miller's Tale: Wahala Dey O! A Nigerian Play Adaptation of Chaucer's Canterbury Tale*, ed. Jessica Lockhart, with Aleheh Amimi, Mussié Berhane, Mahera Islam, and Justin Phillips (Toronto: University of Toronto-Mississauga, 2018); see also Candace Barrington, "Global Medievalism and Translation," in *The Cambridge Companion to Medievalism*, ed. Lousie D'Arcens (Cambridge, UK: Cambridge University Press, 2016): 180–95.

14 Manuela Coppola, "Queering Sonnets: Sexuality and Transnational Identity in the Poetry of Patience Agbabi," *Women: A Cultural Review* 26, no. 4 (2015): 369–83.

15 Romana Huk, "Lyric Returns in Recent Black British Poetry," *Journal of British and Irish Innovative Poetry* 12 (2019): 5.

16 Louise D'Arcens, "From 'Eccentric Affiliation' to 'Corrective Medievalism': Bruce Holsinger's *The Premodern Condition*," *postmedieval* 1, no. 3 (2010): 301.

stanzaic *Man of Law's Tale* (converted into a crown of sonnets). These three retellings each use a poetic structure that loops back to its beginning (the final line being a verbatim or nearly word-for-word or sense-for-sense repetition of the first), and each poem through its very structure conspicuously fails—or rather, refuses—to submit to a linear, progressive model of time. Each of Agbabi's three poems features a marriage in trouble (one due to an act of violence against women, one due to spousal abuse, and the other due to racist xenophobia directed toward an African woman specifically). Not only do these works grapple with the complexity of affective, single-sex bonds and the dangers of heteronormative marriages, but each poem's narrative also reveals a complex racialized dimension to queerness. In these ways, Agbabi's poems use medievalism to explore nuanced desires that move across bodies, borders, and time.

To explore Agbabi's queer medievalism, this essay devotes one section to each poem. Each section is neither linear nor progressive but rather a constellation of close readings and meditations on the queer formal qualities of Agbabi's poetry, the sociopolitical implications of the poet's medievalism, and the layered understandings that arise through acts of reading and re-reading Chaucer's three tales. In this essay, we attend to how Agbabi queers Chaucer and his texts, which have long been used to support, justify, and legitimize centuries of racism, homophobia, and sexism.[17] Agbabi's poetry does not present *Telling Tales* as a modern corrective to a fourteenth-century "original" text, but rather as part of a mirroring, a circling back to rethink the medieval past and its presence in the present.

Queer *Melibee:* "Unfinished Business"

The mirroring structure of Agbabi's remix of Chaucer's *Tale of Melibee*, "Unfinished Business," creates a recursive chain of poetic translation and adapation that invites us to reverse the usual trajectory of adaptation study. That is, the essay takes the adaptation as the point of orientation for understanding or interpreting the original. In this reversed hermeneutics, the adaptation is no longer a

17 See Carissa Harris, "'It is a brotherhood': Obscene Storytelling and Fraternal Community in Fifteenth-Century Britain and Today," *Studies in the Age of Chaucer* 41 (2019): 249–76, and "Rape and Justice in *The Wife of Bath's Tale*," in *The Open Access Companion to The Canterbury Tales*, ed. Candace Barrington, Brantley L. Bryant, Richard H. Godden, Daniel T. Kline, and Myra Seaman (2017), https://opencanterburytales.dsl.lsu.edu/; see also Jonathan Hsy, *Antiracist Medievalisms: From "Yellow Peril" to Black Lives Matter* (Leeds: Arc Humanities Press, 2021), 1–3, 24–25, and 115–32.

secondary or "derivative" version of the original but a work in ongoing and perpetual dialogue with its counterpart. When we circle back and look at Chaucer's text, Agbabi's poem will provide the mirrors allowing us to see Chaucer's *Melibee* anew.

In writing about "Unfinished Business," we are returning to some of our own unfinished business. In 2015, we published "Remediated Verse: Chaucer's *Tale of Melibee* and Patience Agbabi's 'Unfinished Business'" in *postmedieval.* We had used as our base text a version of the poem that antedated *Telling Tales* and did not have affiliated with it an "author biography," part of a series of fictional biographies for each tale-teller that functions like Chaucer's *General Prologue* and appears at the end of the tale collection. Throughout the article, we had refered to "Mel" using masculine pronouns. We knew that "Unfinished Business" was a retelling of *The Tale of Melibee,* and that Chaucer's omniscient narrator describes Melibee as a "yong man ... mighty and riche" (7.967) who is grappling with the aftermath of physical violence against his "wyf" (7.967).[18] Agbabi's Mel is similarily considering how to respond to recent violence against "my wife."[19] When we read the full collection after our article had gone to press, we were disoriented to learn *Telling Tales*'s "Author Biographies" uses the phrase "*her* poem:" "Mel O'Brien was born in Belfast, raised in Chatham and teaches English at a secondary school in Gravesend, Kent. Her poem was inspired by *The Long Memory* (1953) starring John Mills, filmed in and around Gravesend."[20] Agbabi's use of the pronoun "her" for Mel exposed our own unthinkingly heteronormative reading practices. By ascribing her own version of *Melibee* to a woman named Mel, Agbabi profoundly transforms the gendered dimensions of the poem. Mel could be speaking as a woman responding to violence against her wife, or speaking in the persona of a man in the same situation. In either case, Agbabi's Mel speaks in first person ("my wife"), leaving the reader to determine how, or if, to ascribe any definitive gender identity to the "I" in the poem.

Agbabi's "Unfinished Business" is also innovative as one of the few renditions of *The Tale of Melibee* (either as an adaptation or a modernization, in prose or in poetry) in Present-Day English (PDE). Online resources indicate multiple modernizations, but (at the time we wrote this essay) all had dead links but one, a site that is part of a larger project to bring Middle English romances to the

---

18 Unless noted otherwise, all quotations and line numbers from Chaucer follow *The Riverside Chaucer*, ed. Larry D. Benson, 3rd ed. (Boston: Houghton Mifflin, 1987).
19 Patience Agbabi, *Telling Tales* (Edinburgh: Canongate, 2014), 4.
20 Agbabi, *Telling*, 18.

common reader.[21] Among print publications, Tatlock and MacKaye's *The Complete Poetical Works of Geoffrey Chaucer* (1912) provides the opening and closing paragraphs, with a bracketed note standing in for the missing lines: "*The greater part of the tale, consisting of the advice of Melibeus' wife and friends, is here omitted.*"[22] David Wright's prose modernization's page-length note explains why he's substituted a one-paragraph summary for the "wearisome" tale.[23] Subsequent printed modernizations have been even less generous, omitting the entire tale, a move also not uncommon in modern Middle English editions.[24] These omissions are allowed to go unremarked because *Melibee* is considered one of Chaucer's least inventive, most hidebound translations of an already tedious text.[25] Cast as dull and dreary by modern readers, *Melibee* has been seen as more of a commentary on the tale-teller—Chaucer himself—whose two entries in the tale-telling competition are failures.[26]

In contrast to this inglorious past, *Melibee*'s reincarnation bursts forth in poetic form as "Unfinished Business," a confident performance of everything that *Melibee* is not. Mediating between the medieval past and the present, the poem "Unfinished Business" visually manifests Agbabi's complex strategy of transformation. Transmuting Chaucer's prose into verse, she condenses over 900 lines of Chaucerian prose into 32 lines of verse: 16 (off-)rhyming couplets presented in two stanzas. Just as crucial is Agbabi's queer reconception of Melibee and "his wyf" as Mel and her/his wife. The verbose *Tale of Melibee* is radically converted through Agbabi's verse into a tight retelling that queers the form and content of the Melibean narrative.

Agbabi's sophisticated rerouting of the tale's reception history provokes a three-pronged question: what does it mean that Agbabi not only remixed the tale, but that she (a) made it among the shortest of her tales, (b) transformed

21 Richard Scott-Robinson, "Geoffrey's Tale of Melibeus and His Wife Prudence," *Old Tales Rebound* (2009): http://eleusinianm.co.uk/middle-english-literature-retold-in-modern-english/works-by-geoffrey-chaucer/melibeus.

22 John S. P. Tatlock and Percy MacKaye, *The Complete Poetical Works of Geoffrey Chaucer: Now First Put into Modern English* (New York: Macmillan, 1912), 112.

23 David Wright, *The Canterbury Tales: A Prose Version in Modern English* (New York: Random House, 1964), 127.

24 See Peter Ackroyd, *The Canterbury Tales: A Retelling* (London: Penguin, 2009); Sheila Fisher, *The Selected Canterbury Tales: A New Verse Translation* (New York: Norton, 2011); and Glenn Burger, *Chaucer's Queer Nation* (Minneapolis: University of Minnesota Press, 2003), 164.

25 Carolyn P. Collette, "Heeding the Counsel of Prudence: A Context for the 'Melibee,'" *The Chaucer Review* 29, no. 4 (1995): 416–19.

26 Lee Patterson, "'What Man Artow?': Authorial Self-Definition in the *Tale of Sir Thopas* and the *Tale of Melibee*," *Studies in the Age of Chaucer* 13 (1991): 117–75.

it into one of her collection's most accessible poems, and (c) marked it for notice by making it one of the most formally sophisticated and complex poems in the collection? One answer is that Agbabi has rewritten Chaucer-the-pilgrim's tale to be her own calling card, a suggestion re-inforced in the "Prologue (Grime Mix)" to *Telling Tales:* "Chaucer Tales were an unfinished business. May the best poet lose, as the saying goes."[27] By going beyond the tradition of reworking the tale to meet scribal needs or audience demands, she delivers a dazzling poetic performance that reinforces her place (as Canterbury Laureate from 2009–2010) among the poets in the Chaucerian lineage of England's poets laureate.[28] In as few lines as possible, "Unfinished Business" demonstrates that Agbabi's *business* is being a poet.

In many ways, a poet who appropriates and retells a Chaucerian tale resembles the "amateur"—or lover—of medieval literature that Dinshaw's *How Soon is Now?* holds up for analysis, in contrast to professionals who study, teach, and write *about* medieval literature. If, however, we remember that Agbabi is an established, Oxford-trained, spoken-word poet, then she more closely resembles the hybrid that Richard Godden describes: someone who studies Chaucer and writes poetry as a professional calling, not a weekend avocation, yet who nevertheless receives deep satisfaction from their engagement with the poet.[29] Building upon Dinshaw's description of "bricolage" (but eschewing both her term "amateur" and Godden's "nerd"), we see Agbabi's "remix" as "bringing whatever can be found, whatever works to the activity."[30] Agbabi's reconception of a canonical text "provides an opening of potential otherwise foreclosed" and "different ways of knowing and sources of knowledge."[31] By freely inhabiting multiple temporalities, she begins to exact "justice for past exclusions and injustice."[32] Agbabi not only writes a poem that brings a queer sensibility to a poem authored by the canonical, patricarchal, and misogynist "father" of English poetry, but she also profoundly rethinks time, affect, and justice in the process.

Agbabi's retelling of Chaucer's tale reminds us that one of the ways contemporary scholars have recalled the *Melibee* from the wastelands of tedium (an exile for which modern readers are primarily responsible) has been through po-

27 Agbabi, *Telling*, 2.
28 Seth Lerer, *Chaucer and His Readers* (Princeton: Princeton University Press, 1993), 95.
29 Richard H. Godden, "Nerds, Love, Amateurs: Reflections on *How Soon is Now?*," *Modern Medieval* 29 (March 2013): http://modernmedieval.blogspot.com.au/2013/03/nerds-love-amateurs-reflections-on-how.html.
30 Dinshaw, *How Soon is Now?*, 23.
31 Ibid., 24.
32 Ibid., 34.

litical readings. These interpretations generally emphasize the tale's affiliations with the "advice to princes" genre and end up arguing something along the lines that the *Tale of Melibee* "employs a marginal figure"—a woman—"to tell the king what he would not otherwise hear."[33] End of story. If, however, we consider what Prudence says about Melibee's "bisynesse," that it is to "geten hym a good name," a process that must be constantly renewed and repeated, then the tale's ending is really only preparing Melibee for the next iteration of getting his "good name." Prudence is not arguing for a "one-and-done" approach; instead, she is making a case for the behaviors that are the tale's distinguishing feature: doing and saying the same right thing over and over. As Prudence makes her case, right action doesn't look singular; instead, it appears as the multiple reflections in an infinity mirror.

"Unfinished Business" queerly occupies two kinds of time: mythic time of the Bible and quantifiable time of days, nights, and weeks. On the one hand, each can be seen as linear. Biblical time moves inextricably (yet mysteriously) toward the final moment of Judgment. Calendrical time marches forward, with nighttime following daytime, days following days, forming clusters of weeks, months, and years that progress along a timeline ticking forward. On the other hand, each kind of time can be seen as circular or recursive. Biblical time, with its allegorical prolepticism, merely repeats what has already occurred, either in historical time or in God's eye. The Bible provides a template for the cycle of holy-days and holidays, repeated weekly and annually. Calendars, too, turn back on themselves, with those weeks, months, and years forming recognizable, reiterable units.

"Unfinished Business" gestures towards Biblical time by comparing a rainstorm that happened on the night of the attack to the 40-day rain that destroyed the earth's terrestrial creatures while Noah, his family, and their menagerie waited out the flood in a boat. It simultaneously points to past events, and brings that past, with its threats of destruction, to the present. More persistently, the poem records the passing days and nights, marking them with "That night," "It's been a week," and "Tonight," words that in the first stanza would seem to bring us causally from the events that happened at night a week ago, to the present, tonight.[34] Within those days and nights, the Thames' tide's rise and fall is the only timekeeping feature that remains in place when the sequence of events reverse in the second stanza, taking us from "Tonight" to "that

33 Lynn Staley, *Languages of Power in the Age of Richard II* (University Park, PA: Penn State University Press, 2005), 39.
34 Agbabi, *Telling*, 86.

night" a week ago.[35] Defying either circularity or linearity, we see the speaker's knot of indecision caught in time's queer web.

Because they mark time's passge, the mirrored stanzas in "Unfinished Business" are reflections, not perfect reproductions, of one another. The word order in each line remains the same, yet their semantic functions and syntactical relationships are shifted in three ways: each line is punctuated differently; each line is now in a different sequential relationship with the other lines; and, each word and line has a relationship with the corresponding words and lines in the other stanza. These three shifts are visible at the poem's hinge:

> How can I forgive?
>
> How can I forgive
> none of them?[36]

In these three ways, the mirrored stanzas provide a new perspective on familiar terrain. Because Agbabi empowers her typographical marks to "dictate the message," and because the mirrored stanzas cause "none of them" to follow "how can I forgive?" in the second iteration, the first stanza wonders "How can I forgive?" and obversely the second stanza wonders "How can I forgive / none of them?"[37] As adjacent closing and opening lines of the two stanzas, the three lines moreover create a new relationship, their "repetition with a difference" suggesting the whirling thoughts that occupy Mel who determines what to do next. The reflected lines show us Mel's self-reflections on the unsettled matter of revenge, which end where they began: "[t]hat night, it rained so hard."[38]

Agbabi further queers time by refracting the tale through another narrative set in a third time but same place as "Unfinished Business," Robert Hamer's 1953 noir film "*The Long Memory*."[39] Set in shabby post-war Gravesend, the film isn't interested in who murdered whom or why. Instead, it asks viewers to consider the futility of revenge. The protagonist, Phillip Davidson, comes to Gravesend seeking revenge on those whose lies convicted him of murder and

---

35 Ibid., 87.
36 Ibid., 86.
37 Lee Clark Mitchell, *Mark My Words: Profiles of Punctuation in Modern Literature* (New York: Bloomsbury, 2020), 6; see also Agbabi, *Telling*, 86–87.
38 Agbabi, 87.
39 For a reading of the poem vis-à-vis Jonathan Nolan's story, "Memento Mori," and *its* film adapation, *Memento* (2000), see Candace Barrington and Jonathan Hsy, "Remediated Verse: Chaucer's *Tale of Melibee* and Patience Agbabi's 'Unfinished Business,'" *postmedieval* 6 (2105): 136–145.

sent him to prison for 12 years. He befriends an immigrant barmaid, Ilse, who provides the outsider's perspective. Her initial claim that "Perhaps it is not worth it to hurt people back" is first met by his repetiton of her first three words, "Perhaps it is." Eventually, when he has the opportunity to exact his revenge, he realizes that "I just can't be bothered." Not only is revenge unsatisfying —"Funny, when you come to the point, revenge isn't worth it"—but extrajudicial revenge so resembles the legal forms of retribution that it throws into doubt the whole notion of institutional justice. The other characters think Davidson's narrative has yet more chapters, and they offer to help him get "justice" through the courts. Ilse rejects that trajectory and imagines a cyclical pattern to their lives: "It's not justice we need ... He doesn't need anything you can do for him. He only needs to be left alone to come back to life again." Davidson's story is unfinished, but revenge will no longer drive the narrative forward. In Agbabi's poem, Mel's "unfinished business" is unfinished, not abandoned. Readers are left not knowing if the speaker will take revenge or forgive. The two choices hang in suspension. One thing we are certain of, though, is that Mel's narrative is also set entirely outside the juridical realm. With no mention of police, courts, or jail, her story exists in the extra-juridical world of personal revenge.

Even as our own analysis of "Unfinished Business" is circular, the reading process is by no means complete. Interpretation entails perpetual re-reading, a continued return with a difference. We could take queer readings of this poem even further to explore the implications of Agbabi's decision to make a gendered turn away from a speaking Prudence—whose words take up most of Chaucer's prose narrative—to pivot toward the male Melibee figure, refigured in the voice of a fictive woman poet. Agbabi's narrative reorientation not only multiplies the reader's possible perspectives on the marital couple but also destabilizes our notions of who is conventionally considered the "household protector." The wronged spouse meditates on the assailant's right to live: "None of them, even Joe, has the right to live" becomes "Even Joe has the right to live."[40] The speaker's use of a familiar first name only ("Joe") and evident ambivalence at the prospect of taking Joe's life suggest that a deep bond exists between Mel and Joe. Whether this is an ongoing bond of friendship, kinship, or enmity—or something else that Mel cannot, or will not, disclose—a complex affective connection sustains Mel's delay in avenging the wrongs done to a wife and daughter.

The unsettled queerness of "Unfinished Business" could also be read in conjunction with the work's allusive cultural reorientations. Agbabi relocates Chaucer's *Melibee* to the gritty environment of Gravesend, with the poem's atmospheric

---

40 Agbabi, *Telling*, 86.

imagery of torrential rains, intimate interior spaces, and desolate parking lots evoking cinematic tropes of film noir. In a posting on a blog maintained throughout her composition of *Telling Tales*, Agbabi observed that the pervasive "noir" aesthetic of her *Melibee* adaptation was influenced by the 2003 BBC adaptation of *The Shipman's Tale* (entitled "The Sea Captain's Tale"), a retelling of the story that is set exclusively among characters living within the South Asian ethnic enclave of Gravesend.[41] This TV adaptation by Indian screenwriter Avie Luthra explores both heteronormative and homosocial relationships in this Gravesend community, as well as the ethics of vengeance and destruction.[42] Agbabi's blog posting reveals her gradual and nonlinear process of adapting *Melibee* by "veering toward" a media-crossing fusion of 1950s British noir and twenty-first-century Asian British noir—in addition to the film *Memento* by the British-American Nolan brothers.[43] The unsettled "veering toward" a completed poem that recirculates a range of cinematic and cultural influences befits the recursive loops, and the queer desires, that sustain "Unfinished Business."

Queer *Clerk's Tale:* "I Go Back to May 1967"

If Agbabi is singular in her decision to update Chaucer's *Tale of Melibee*, she joins a host of translators and adaptors who have refashioned the story of Griselda that Chaucer adapted as *The Clerk's Tale*. In order to retell and comment on the perplexing, sad story of Griselda's persecution at her husband's hands, Chaucer relied upon at least two sources: Petrarch's *Historia Griseldis* in his *Epistolae Seniles* and an anonymous French translation, *Le Livre Griseldis*; these, in turn, find their source in the final story of Giovanni Boccaccio's *Decameron*, which can be traced back to folk legends.[44] Despite (or perhaps because of) the tale's focus on spousal abuse, the tale not only survives in most fifteenth-century manuscripts of *The Canterbury Tales*, but was a predictable selection when Chaucer's oeuvre was recrafted and modernized for nineteenth- and twentieth-century audiences. The tale even appears frequently in Chaucerian collections published

---

41 Agbabi, "Genre: Gravesend Noir ...," *Telling Tales* (blog), November 20, 2010, https://patienceagbabi.wordpress.com/2010/11/20/genre-gravesend-noir/.

42 Kathleen Coyne Kelly, "The Color of Money: The BBC 'Sea Captain's Tale,'" in *Chaucer on Screen: Absence, Presence, and Adapting the Canterbury Tales*, ed. Kathleen Coyne Kelly and Tison Pugh (Columbus, OH: Ohio State University Press, 2016), 218–29.

43 Agbabi, "Genre: Gravesend Noir ...."

44 Tom Farrell and Amy Goodwin, "*The Clerk's Tale*," in *Sources and Analogues of The Canterbury Tales*, ed. Robert M. Correale and Mary Hamel (Cambridge: D. S. Brewer, 2002), 101–67.

for children over the past two centuries. In varying degrees of bowdlerization and across an array of audiences, *The Clerk's Tale* has been among the most consistently anthologized of Chaucer's tales.[45] Throughout the centuries, generations of readers have wondered, "What on earth was Griselda thinking while Walter tormented her all those years? Why was she not like the 'noble wyves' which the *Lenvoy de Chaucer* exhorts to 'holdeth no silence' and to resist their husbands' abuses" (4.1183–1206)? Some, like Harry Bailey, have an easy answer: She was thinking about being a good, obedient wife, just the sort of model-wife he wished for his own "wyf at hoom" (4.1212d). Some, like the Clerk himself, have ignored that question and tried to re-orient the tale's focus by asking readers to see an allegory teaching us how "every wight, in his degree / Sholde be constant in adversitee" (4.1145–46), an allegory that just so happens to feature a cruel husband and beleaguered wife. Whatever their answer to Griselda's behavior, few readers have considered what Walter and Griselda's unnamed, unspeaking daughter was thinking. This unasked question becomes the premise for Agbabi's adaptation, "I Go Back to May 1967."[46]

As we have seen with the way "Unfinished Business" revists a Chaucerian tale through twentieth-century literary and cinematic tropes, the fictive narrator for "I Go Back to May 1967," Yejide Idowu-Clarke, insists we read her parents' marriage (as well as *The Clerk's Tale*) through the lens of Sharon Olds's similarly titled "I Go Back to May 1937."[47] By linking Idowu-Clarke's lyric retelling of *The Clerk's Tale* to Olds's poem set in 1937, fifty years in the past, Abgabi continues a second chain of appropriation that Olds's poem mediates with her echoes of Delmore Schwartz's "In Dreams Begin Responsibilities" (1937), a short story that imagines his parents' doomed courtship as a disaster film he helplessly watches in horror. Agbabi first signals her appropriation with her poem's title, different from Olds's by only one digit, and with the epigraph "After Sharon Olds."[48] Agbabi strengthens the bonds between the two lyrics by reusing Olds's opening phrase "I see," two words that move the narrators from one temporal zone (the present) to another temporal zone (the past) without erasing the narrators' knowledge of the ensuing years. The parallels continue for another two words: "I see them standing," with "them" being the narratorial daughter's parents. With that similarity established, Agbabi then weaves together the details from the narrative of medieval Lombardy's Walter and Griselda, the lines describing Olds's

---

45 Barrington, *American Chaucers*.

46 Agbabi, *Telling*, 47–48.

47 Russell Brickey, *Understanding Sharon Olds* (Columbia: University of South Caroline Press, 2017), 6.

48 Agbabi, *Telling*, 47.

inter-war California parents, and the most recent narrator's story of her parents set in another troubled time and place, post-independence Nigeria. This outright borrowing and the surprising parallels allow Agbabi to craft a queer, time-bending flow of transmission from trecento Italy to twenty-first-century Nigeria.

This queer flow of transmission, with Sharon Olds's time-bending narrative lyric as the most recent, provides a potent catalyst for Agbabi's transformation of the Chaucerian Clerk's exended account of a story "which that I / Learned at Padowe of a worthy clerk" (4.26–27) into a tight lyric voicing the daughter's perspective of family trauma. With the title and the opening words, Idowu-Clarke claims to witness what should be impossible to witness: the moment her parents meet for the first time. Its temporal doubling allows her to witness her own parents' courtship with a first-person fabrication based on first-hand experiences. Those experiences were not based on what the narrator could have physically encountered in 1997, but on how those past events irreversibly shaped (and continue to shape) her present. This feat of temporal displacement and imaginative reconstruction gives voice to a figure in *The Clerk's Tale* hitherto kept silent, Griselda's daughter. In Agbabi's version, Idowu-Clarke is made both daughter and the narrating "Clerk of Oxenford" (4.1), in keeping with Olds's precedent. This newly-voiced narrator uses borrowed material to craft her deeply invested yet highly mediated perspective in order to expose "patriarchal abuse, women's solidarity, [and] family dysfunction."[49]

Though Agbabi's fictive poet adopts Olds's practice of examining and re-examining the the vestiges of memory and the "ultimate effect these memories have on the adult speaker," Idowu-Clarke twists Olds's narratorial practice.[50] Whereas Olds's persona is interested in how past traumas affect the adult child, Agbabi's narrator is concerned with the mother's trauma, a vestige of the story's medieval source. The Nigerian daughter, watching from the advantage of her own adulthood, knows what her parents seem not to recognize: the bride is "not a bad woman, / he is not a good man," a sly resetting of Olds's lines—"she's the wrong woman, / he's the wrong man"[51]—in which the couple are wrong for each other, but not themselves necessarily bad. In Agbabi's account, the marriage is bad because he's a bad man, and the mother is the one who needs to be (but is not being) warned away from the impending disaster, as indicated by her direct address to the mother: "*you* are not a bad woman" (our emphasis). Though she cannot undo the violence the father inflicts on his wife, the

49 Brickey, *Understanding Sharon Olds*, 3.
50 Ibid., 4.
51 Agbabi, *Telling*, 47; Sharon Olds, *The Gold Cell* (New York: NY: Knopf, 1987), 23.

daughter repeats it in a verse narrative, and so prevents another act of violence: forgetting the unwarranted "trial" suffered by the mother.[52]

Olds also provides a model for rethinking the narrator's relationship to the lyric's events and her complicity. Instead of Chaucer's learned, disinterested male tale-teller, Agbabi introduces a highly educated daughter to bear witness to the family's dysfunction. Idowu-Clarke takes us to the place and time of the injury. Witnessing the trauma of her parents' marriage, she has neither the ability nor the desire to undo it, for her own existence depends upon the familial trauma. Indeed, the shape of her childhood and her adult life is determined by her father's singular, violent stroke. When he claims his wife's illiteracy makes her an unfit mother and threatens his authority, everything shifts, and the narrator presents herself as a beneficiary of his actions. Her exile from Oga's household grants her an education at "the best schools in the country,"[53] an education evidenced by the poem itself. In complete sentences with standard word order and standard vocabulary, the narrative creates a persona whose voice we can imagine as speaking with a carefully mastered received pronunciation. Her mother's trauma, therefore, was the means by which she became well-educated and ended up in the metropole. And though she might want to reach back to say "Stop," she knows that her own existence depends on her mother's suffering. Witnessing the moment when a catastrophe could be headed off, she offers to deploy her education to tell her mother's tale, mirroring her initial "I see" with "I will bear witness."[54]

Agbabi also takes advantage of Olds's pattern of identifying "emotional correlatives" between her personal grievances and such collective tragedies as the Holocaust.[55] A similar comparison between grand upheavals and the narrator's personal and familial traumas in Idowu-Clarke's tale is suggested by the titular date, "May 1967." In that month, newly independent Nigeria was on the brink of civil war between the military government and the Biafran secessionist movement. Noted for its brutality, the civil war became known in the West for its high rates of child starvation when Nigeria blocked food shipments to rebel areas. Without directly invoking the cruel civil war, the poem's geographical and temporal setting (as well as its links to Olds) invites us to consider the ways national and familial cruelty feed on one another. Furthermore, that local reverberation is undergirded by the destructive legacy of colonialism, which divested Nigerians of their birthright in exchange for a promised access

52 Agbabi, *Telling*, 47.
53 Ibid.
54 Agbabi, *Telling*, 47–48.
55 Brickey, *Understanding Sharon Olds*, 7.

to the West's material wealth, for which Oga's Cadillac provides a crass synecdoche. With these elements of Nigeria's postcolonial legacy—and without withdrawing Oga's responsibility—Agbabi frames Yejide Idowu-Clarke's family in terms of the many African women whose lives were turned upside down by local forms of patrarchy as well as by Great Britain's colonial enterprise. By imagining her narrator as a scholar who shuttles between Oxford and Lagos, Agbabi considers the tension between seeing emigration to the metropole as a dislocation and as an opportunity.

Ultimately, Agbabi's recreation of Walter's story and Griselda's story through the eyes of their daughter lets us divert our eyes from the "sensational spectacle that concentrates intense affectivity" on the mother's trauma[56] and onto the queer discomfort of the family's script.[57] Through her perspective, we are able to see anew that Walter's efforts to assert his patriarchal authority undermines the heteronormative nature providing the foundation of that authority. When the daughter is returned to her father's household, her mother would have been a stranger, and the ways of the household would not have been familiar to her. Instead, she would have re-entered and witnessed a childless household, apparently devoid of reproductive sexual relations. In the place of heteronormative formations would be incestuous formations created by Walter's compulsion to assert his patriarchal authority. Because Walter's sister (unnecessarily) becomes the mother of Walter and Griselda's children, and because he stages his marriage (albeit fake) to his daughter, he entangles himself in incestuous formations, all of which become most apparent when the family reunion is reconsidered from the daughter's perspective. Agbabi's retelling allows us to rethink Walter as a patriarch undone by his own excessive masculinity, a man whose zealous assertion of his dominance allows him to slip into becoming what he worked so hard not to be.

Queer *Man of Law's Tale:* "Joined-Up Writing"

In an essay entitled "Queering Sonnets: Sexuality and Transnational Identity in the Poetry of Patience Agbabi," Manuela Coppola examines Agbabi's pre-*Telling Tales* poetic oeuvre through an intertwining of queer diaspora and intersectional

---

56 Geraldine Heng, *Empire of Magic: Medieval Romance and the Politics of Cultural Fantasy* (New York: Columbia University Press, 2003), 217.

57 Sara Ahmed, *The Cultural Politics of Emotion*, 2nd ed. (Edinburgh: Edinburgh University Press, 2014), 144–51.

Black cultural studies. Coppola explores how Agbabi's poetry repurposes the gendered and cultural norms of the European medieval sonnet form—with its presumed male speaker and objectified blonde muse—to craft new poetic configurations of queer desire among Black women; and "by destabilizing safe assumptions about literary canons, race, sex and gender, Agbabi *queers* the sonnet form by challenging and reworking its conventions."[58] In the context of the queer crown of sonnets of "Joined Up Writing" in *Telling Tales*, Agbabi creates space for unsettled desires among women—in addition to situating these desires within a nonlinear recursive time of medievalism.

"Joined-Up Writing" most noticeably registers as a queer sonnet form through Agbabi's layers of gendered and racialized voicing. The poem is authored by a fictional female poet who herself has immigrated from Zimbabwe, and her poem is attributed to a fictive white British female speaker; the layering of voices in the sonnet sequence exposes the implicit and explicit forms of racism and queer desire that disturbingly structure British xenophobia. Agbabi's fictive narrator is "Memory Anesu Sergeant," whose author biography states that she is a barrister by profession who "[o]riginates from Zimbabwe" and "began writing seriously during maternity leave" and has published a book of poetry and "learns her poems off by heart and reads regularly on BBC Radio 4."[59] Such a fictionalized biography obliquely resonates with Agbabi's own experience as an established figure on the performance poetry circuit who incorporates her particular bicultural "English and Nigerian upbringing, in England and in Wales" into her work, exhibiting throughout her artistic and professional endeavors a "passion" to "counter [the] hegemony" of a field dominated by white men.[60]

While Chaucer's narrative is composed in rhyme royal stanzas, Agbabi crafts a crown of sonnets, with the final line in each stanza (each a complete sonnet) slightly reshaped to become the first line of the subsequent stanza. Chaucer's *Man of Law's Tale* has been richly assessed for its complex treatment of racial and religious difference on two concurrent geocultural fronts (Muslim Syria and pagan Britain, respectively), and its protagonist Custance—a noble Christian from Rome who is both virtuous and fair (in all senses of the word)—finds herself rejected by a foreign mother-in-law figure in both spaces. Cord J. Whitaker and Shyama Rajendran have explored how Chaucer's story invites modern readers to question its intertwining of medieval racial and linguistic ideologies, and

---

58 Coppola, "Queering Sonnets," 372 (emphasis in original).

59 Agbabi, *Telling*, 119.

60 Agbabi, "Stories in Stanza'd English," 3.

they divergently demonstrate medieval modes of rhetorical "othering" of entire groups of people along the lines of religion and geography.[61] In contemporary terms, Agbabi not only grapples with bodies in motion—the migratory positionalities of the diasporic subject—but she also exposes what intersectional Black feminists have called "misogynoir," a term initially coined by queer Black feminist Moya Bailey that conjoins "misogyny" with "noir" (the French term for "black") in order to name the interlocking social systems of race and gender that harm Black women in particular.[62] The term "misogynoir" has since garnered widespread use throughout discussions of race and gender in British contexts as well.[63]

Agbabi's poem reinvents Custance as Constance, an immigrant from Zimbabwe who settles in Britain, yet the story of Constance and her husband Ollie is told through the voice of Constance's white mother-in-law speaking in a Northern (Geordie) variety of British English. Elsewhere in her work, Agbabi characterizes this mother-in-law speaker as "a person … between classes [who] reacted with jealousy and racism when her son took a Zimbabwean wife."[64] Agbabi's unnamed narrator characterizes her African immigrant daughter-in-law, obliquely yet disapprovingly, as Black: "Constance was coloured, brown, / a name so long you'd sweat to break it down."[65] The disruptive conjunction of the phrase "coloured, brown," followed by the phrase "break it down" (with a reference to some lengthy but undisclosed "foreign" name) anticipates the emotional "breakdown" that the narrator invokes in the opening line of the next stanza. In this poem, Constance's "coloured, brown" body and her "foreign" name and origins effectively break down closed systems of white British insularity. The mother-in-law prefaces her remarks about Constance's Blackness by unconvincingly disclaiming her own racism: "Not that I'm prejudiced, some of my best/friends are foreign."[66] Nonetheless, the poetic speaker's repeated references to "Africa"—rather than naming the specific country of Constance's origin—sug-

---

61 Cord J. Whitaker, "Race and Racism in the *Man of Law's Tale*," in *The Open Access Companion to The Canterbury Tales*; Shyama Rajendran, "Undoing 'the Vernacular': Dismantling Structures of Raciolinguistic Supremacy," *Literature Compass* 16, no. 9–10 (September–October 2019): 1–13.
62 Moya Bailey and Trudy, "On Misogynoir: Citation, Erasure, and Plagiarism," *Feminist Media Studies* 18, no. 4 (2018): 762–768.
63 Eliza Anyangwe, "Misogynoir: Where Racism and Sexism Meet," *The Guardian*, October 5, 2015, https://www.theguardian.com/lifeandstyle/2015/oct/05/what-is-misogynoir.
64 Agbabi, "Stories in Stanza'd English," 5.
65 Agbabi, *Telling*, 22.
66 Ibid.

gest the narrator's inability to fathom Black Africans as anything other than monolithically foreign.

The racially evasive terminology that this mother-in-law employs deserves closer attention precisely for its painstaking avoidance of the term "Black" and proliferation of awkward circumlocutions. The conspicuously roundabout descriptors of "colored, brown" and "foreign" signal the mother-in-law's fear of openly uttering the word "Black"—her tightly-controlled rhetoric seeking to disavow, or disguise, the reality of anti-Black racism and misogynoir. The speaker's rhetorical diversions take on an especially resonant meaning due to the formal qualities of Agbabi's crown of sonnets. Its circular and interlacing structure takes the reader back to the beginning of the poem, endlessly circling around the emotional heart of this story: the mother-in-law's envy of Constance, who is "replacing" the mother, the proper object of her own son's devotion. By the end of the poem, the reader realizes the speaker has been left behind in Britain while Ollie and Constance have returned to her homeland abroad. Through geospatial and temporal movements and rhetorical distancing devices, Agbabi showcases how poetic adaptations effect racial reorientations as well as sociopolitical disorientations.

Agbabi's queer sonnets, when taken as a whole, enact a trenchant political critique. "Joined-Up Writing" not only attests to hostility toward, and rejection of, Black and immigrant women; the poem also reveals the harms that prejudice enacts upon British xenophobes in turn. The unnamed mother-in-law speaker in this poem embodies the corruptive effects of maintaining closed ideas of who properly "counts" as British, and Agbabi reveals how white resentment can coincide with undisclosed or inexpressible queer envy. The apparent mysteries of the mother-in-law's true desires and prejudices are thematized by the writerly career of her beloved son. In the opening lines of the poem, the speaker disjointedly and recursively reveals that Ollie is a famous author of detective fiction: "My son's a writer, aye ... Detective novels ... I wronged my laddie, Ollie, Oliver,/Oliver Robson. Have you heard of him?"[67] Through these opening gestures to the mystery novel and an obliquely confessed crime, Agbabi slyly suggests how a submerged genre of British noir coincides with this poem's open indictment of misogynoir. Agbabi constructs the crown of sonnets in order to invite the reader to re-read the entire work from the beginning and layer their interpretations of the story in the process. The circular form of the poem conveys the suspended animation and lack of progress associated with racism and misogyny, and it

67 Agbabi, *Telling*, 21.

challenges the reader to carefully consider any initial sympathy the poetic speaker might have garnered.

Inconclusion

We close this essay not with a conclusion but with an "inconclusion," acknowledging how all readings of texts are never complete and always open to recursive layering. The circular and recursive form of Agbabi's poetic adaptations showcases the queer time of medievalism and the queer form of adaptation. Across all three poems, women's vulnerability never overshadows women's strength. The darkly British "Asian noir" that obliquely informs Agbabi's "Unfinished Business" resonates with a distinctively British form of misogynoir in "Joined-Up Writing"; and bridging these two poems, "I Go Back to 1967" invites us both to consider the ways lyric voices can investigate public roles and transgress racial polarities, and to attend to queerly time-bending cultural flows of literary influence, imitation, and allusion. Each poem invites the reader to revisit their initial assumptions about the gendered positions or desires of fictive characters and to reconsider their own reactions to the texts through attentive acts of reflection and re-reading. Remixing Chaucerian tales with influences from contemporary screen narratives, from poetic interlocutors across disparate moments in time, and from "noir" genres, Agbabi's queer reconfigurations of gender, racial, and national positionings perpetually reorient and challenge their audiences.

David Hadbawnik

Speak Like a Child: Caroline Bergvall's Medievalist Trilogy

To raise a bilingual child is to accept a certain amount of linguistic estrangement. My son shares his language between me, an American, and his mother, a native Slovene fluent in English as well. From birth, his mother has spoken to him—for the most part—only in Slovenian, while I use English. Our son began to use words from both languages soon after he turned one year old and was speaking in sentences by age two. But there were unexpected developments. For one, he is still prone to portmanteau phrases, a mixture of both Slovenian and English: "Lahko night," he has said upon going to bed, and picking up on how I'd called one of his stuffed animals a "teddy bear," adapted this to "medo-bear" ("medved" is Slovene for "bear," while "medo" is colloquial for "teddy bear") when showing it to his mother, and also sometimes refers to a "polar-medo." "The code-switching has started," his mother said one evening as we were eating dinner, and I noticed that he kept approaching me at the table to say, "Ati, gimme some" ("Ati" means "Daddy"), while simultaneously using Slovenian to ask for tidbits from mama. In other words, he exists—at least for the time being, as I write this, a few months past his second birthday —in a weird, quasi-undifferentiated nexus between languages. What is his "mother tongue?" Which tongue predominates, and are they destined to battle each other in his thought and speech? Pulled between two cultural-linguistic spheres, will he feel estranged from one or both of them? These are questions that arise from the writings of poet and artist Caroline Bergvall, who contemplates the dilemma of the multilingual author.[1] In examining Bergvall's trilogy of works that engage with medieval material and languages, I begin with her 2009 essay "Cat in the Throat: on bilingual occupants," since exploring her ideas of multilingualism in writing helps pave the way to understanding how she persistently and increasingly inverts or "queers" the relationship between source texts and her own poetry.

Bergvall's essay begins by intriguingly suggesting, via postcolonial critic Gayatri Spivak, that the bilingual speaker should risk "spitting out" the "mother tongue" so as to "clear space." Bergvall writes, "Spitting out the most intimate and most irretrievable, the most naturalised source language, or so-called moth-

1 Caroline Bergvall, "Cat in the Throat: on bilingual occupants," *Jacket* 37 (2009), www.jacketmagazine.com/37/bergvall-cat-throat.shtml.

https://doi.org/10.1515/9781501511189-010

er tongue (this gendering always strikes me as deeply problematic), is a dare, it is dangerous, but it also starts a whole process of re-embodying and reappraisal of language's spaces." Embodying is key; what Bergvall attends to are the "semantic and somatic events" that "manifest as language." The vibrations, hesitations, actions, and reactions that go into forming "voice"—and even at times loss of voice. For the multilingual speaker, writes Bergvall,

> It is not about having a "voice" (another difficult naturalising concept), it is about siting "voice", locating the spaces and actions through which it becomes possible to be in one's languages, to stay with languages, to effect one's speech and work at a point of traffic between them, like a constant transport that takes place in the exchange between one's body, the air, and the world.

Following Spivak, she considers the case of Samuel Beckett, an Irish author who rejects the colonizing language of English in favor of French: "Fighting off one language with another language, transforming in the process both the spat-out source language and the adoptive language."

In other words, the speaker of more than one tongue becomes aware of the friction between them. And this friction is embodied through metaphors like "cat in the throat" (the French idiom) and "frog in the throat" (English), which both express the uncomfortable feeling of needing to "clear one's throat" before speaking. As Bergvall argues, what these expressions imply is a need to clear away the friction, the hesitation or roughness that keeps one from fully "articulated" speech, or—in the case of the multilingual speaker—the accent and other verbal ticks that might give one away. To not clear the throat is to risk "inarticulacy:"

> Cat is the tone in my speech, its accentedness, its autography. Cat is my hesitations, my speech's subjective accent, the tone in my speech, the stutter of my silencings, the explicit accentedness of its functionality. So what if I were to decide to talk with a cat in the throat?[2]

In short, what Bergvall seems to favor is a deliberate in-betweenness about language that, for the moment, comes naturally to my bilingual son. The whimsical possibilities for such a liminal stance—the code-switching, the linguistic bricolage—should be apparent from my observations above. But even as I recognize doors open to him, I'm also aware of the odd position his bilingualism puts him in, already. In situations in which people are speaking to him in English, I worry that he can't fully understand them. Naturally shy, I also wonder if he

2 Bergvall, "Cat in the Throat."

tends to refrain from talking and mingling with other kids, having noticed a difference in their way of speaking. Increasingly, as he comprehends more and responds in more complex ways, I seem to perceive a desire in him to lean this or that way with language. Bergvall's medievalist projects court such indeterminacy and instead lean away from the pull of one language over another.

I argue that Bergvall's poetry makes use of medieval forms of English—Chaucer's Middle English, as well as Old English and Old Norse—in order to give her some purchase on a sort of in-betweenness in language. As she writes,

> At the end of the 14th century, the spelling and fixing of Middle English was very much up for grabs. Chaucer's decision to write in a spoken Southern English idiom helped to confirm the richness and versatility of a linguistic region that was starting to strongly de-frenchify its cultural language, de-latinate its vocabulary's antecedents, and revalue its Anglo-Saxon glossary ... He made his choices from within the language's active maelstrom of influences and confluences. Everything about Middle English was a mashup on the rise.[3]

But Bergvall's approach differs from that of other poets who have looked to the past for linguistic "origins" or "authentic" English.[4] Bergvall aims to destabilize language and, if she does seek to recapture an "originary" moment in English, it is one of pre-articulation rather than authority. Her move to select and deploy Chaucerian English in "The Shorter Chaucer Tales"—the first sequence of poems in *Meddle English*—also places Bergvall in a tradition of poets who retroactively construct Chaucer in a certain image, drawing on, reinforcing, and altering cultural ideas about Chaucer the poet. Bergvall also stands alongside Patience Agbabi in infusing a fresh sense of orality to Chaucer's linguistic and tale-telling enterprise, "revising" Chaucer and his Middle English in a hybrid, performative blend of text and speech.[5] Further experiments in what her publish-

---

3 Caroline Bergvall, *Meddle English: New and Selected Texts* (New York: Nightboat Books, 2011), 13.

4 See, for example, Seamus Heaney, *Beowulf: A New Verse Translation* (New York: Norton, 2000). In the introduction, Heaney writes, "While I had no great expertise in Old English, I had a strong desire to get back to the first stratum of the language" (xxii). See also Edmund Spenser, *The Shorter Poems*, ed. Richard A. McCabe (New York: Penguin, 1999). Spenser was perhaps the first English-writing poet to articulate this desire, noting of the poem's "olde and obsolete wordes" in the introductory "Epistle" to *The Shepheardes Calender*, "sure I think, and think I think not amisse, that they bring great grace and, as one would say, auctoritie to the verse" (26).

5 Though Bergvall and Agbabi take quite a different approach; Agbabi is covered elsewhere in this volume. See "Caroline Bergvall: Close Listening with Charles Bernstein," June 11, 2015, in *PennSound*, MP3 audio, www.writing.upenn.edu/pennsound/x/Bergvall.php. See also Tom Orange, "Performing Authority: Gysin, Bergvall, and the Critique of Expressivist Pedagogy," *English*

er calls "a trilogy of works using medieval and contemporary sources and languages" include *Drift* (2014) and *Alisoun Sings* (2019), all published by Nightboat Books.[6] While Bergvall has been studied extensively by contemporary critics, she has only recently begun to draw the attention of medievalist scholars, another reason for a lengthy consideration of her project in this volume and this context.[7]

Deterritorialized Language

Before attending to Bergvall's poetry itself, it is helpful to flesh out some critical framework that helps explain why medieval poetry and language have been especially generative for her work. Bergvall's poetry seems to be roaming a broad field of language, feeling its way over the surface of words, making no distinctions between where this or that piece of diction comes from, high or low, here or there. While the poetry does seek purchase—a foothold here, there a place to rest a moment before moving on—it does not aim to "conquer" this field, to master it or even fully know it. This should be clear from the revealing section of "Notes" appended to the end of the second of Bergvall's medieval trilogy, *Drift*, in which the author describes doing copious research for the project, but at the same time feeling "lost:"

> The success of the first performance ... the audience's intense response ... the disturbance that is pushing a way into my life, all this leaves me in a total state of shock and openness. I come home and find that I have lost my sense of home. I come home to find that I have left my home.[8]

Studies in Canada 33, no. 4 (2007): 115–26. Orange writes of Bergvall's performance of one of Gysin's pieces, "Caroline Bergvall's work ... updates Gysin's work, not punitively but very much in homage: in addition to performing an utterly faithful rendition of Gysin's 'Come to Free the Words,' Bergvall has also composed and performed a piece that revises Gysin—one that recognizes Gysin's initial challenges to self and language while opening further lines of inquiry into the very nature of identity and writing" (120).

6 Caroline Bergvall, *Alisoun Sings* (New York: Nightboat Books, 2019).

7 Bergvall was invited to create "The Shorter Chaucer Tales," one of her first explicitly medievalist projects, by poet Charles Bernstein and medievalist David Wallace, both professors at University of Pennsylvania; Wallace has been a frequent interlocuter since then. See also Clare A. Lees and Gillian R. Overing, *The Contemporary Medieval in Practice* (London: UCL Press, 2019), 66–68. The authors write briefly about Bergvall's *Drift*. There will undoubtedly be more medievalist critical attention to Bergvall in the years to come.

8 Caroline Bergvall, *Drift* (New York: Nightboat Books, 2014), 135.

This sense of lostness is a regular feature of Bergvall's work, and it's one that Sophia Robinson, writing about a different piece (*Éclat*), strongly associates with a queer poetics: "Bergvall's text orientates us queerly in that we are encouraged to be lost, enter trapdoors, and linger in the between-spaces and doorways of the text. Our experience … is thus uncomfortable, and … we are the outsider on the inside." In that piece, which features diagrams that resemble housing floorplans alongside text, "Bergvall's poetics is also queered through this metaphor of the doorframe, in that meaning, through plurilingualism and innovative writing techniques, is never fixed but also 'between.'"[9] Refusing orientation and remaining in a state of uncertainty, even lostness, is both part of Bergvall's creative process and the effect created in her texts.

Turning back to Bergvall's statement on her process in *Drift*, her reaction can also be attributed to the highly charged subject matter of the piece, in which she constructs an "intertext" including the Old English "Seafarer," lyrics from pop songs, and "excerpts from human rights reports into contemporary sea migrants' disasters," also collaborating with visual artists and musicians for performances.[10] What for many artists might have signaled an encouraging starting point instead seems to have thrust Bergvall into a state of deeper and wilder searching. In further pages of the "Notes," she describes her continuing process with blistering candor, melding in reflections on her personal life that shape her struggles: "Total fumbling. The fog in my mind, my life, my heart … Being lost is a way of inhabiting space by registering what is not familiar, writes Sara Ahmed."[11] Despite "intense research," Bergvall admits she is "totally stumped," and to some extent it seems clear that the more Bergvall learns about the Old English poem, the harder it becomes to break free from it; she has to remind herself "this is not an exercise in translation, however closely I work with the original text. It is a template for writing. And for excavating language."[12] Plunging ahead into a sense of feeling lost appears to be a generative pattern for Bergvall; she describes a similar process in a prior medievalist project, *Fig*, which consists of 48 different translations of the opening of Dante's *Inferno:*

> [N]arratively, my piece is about being completely stuck and yet endlessly, imperceptibly, unreliably different. Methodologically, a lot of my intertextual and transhistoric pieces are

---

9 Sophie Robinson, "Queer Time & Space in Contemporary Experimental Writing" (PhD diss., University of London, 2012), 99.

10 Áine McMurtry, "Sea Journeys to Fortress Europe: Lyric Deterritorializations in Texts by Caroline Bergvall and José F. A. Oliver," *The Modern Language Review* 113, no. 4 (2018): 814.

11 Bergvall, *Drift*, 139.

12 Ibid., 143, 151–52.

> about finding a trick, a key, getting to a minimal point of maximal pressure through which a project can happen.[13]

Eventually, Bergvall becomes so lost with *Drift* that she arrives at a new "starting point," and looking for guides, turns to critic Édouard Glissant. Bergvall notes of Glissant that he "keeps medieval literature and its nomadic sociality always present and at work in his own wanderings."[14] Indeed, while the French-speaking Glissant focuses on postcolonial Creole in his elucidation of what he calls "the Poetics of Relation," he does mention the European Middle Ages as an analogous moment of language formation as the Romance tongues emerged from the shadow of Latin.[15]

There are a number of facets of Bergvall's work that clearly respond to Glissant. He writes, "Rhizomatic thought is the principle behind what I call the Poetics of Relation, in which each and every identity is extended through a relationship with the Other."[16] Later, Glissant describes the Poetics of Relation as being "against the comfortable assurances linked to the supposed excellence of a language. A poetics that is latent, open, multilingual in intention, directly in contact with everything possible."[17] There are no quick binaries against which Glissant develops this concept, though he does trace the way in which a great deal of Western literature is based on the wanderer who arrives in a new place as plunderer or conqueror, having a "preoccupation with identity" and establishing a "lineage."[18] He notes later that "[f]iliation is explicit in the Old Testament, implicit ... in the *Iliad*," also mentioning poems such as the *Odyssey*, the *Aeneid*, and the *Divine Comedy*, all of which are concerned with legitimacy (of groups, language) in different ways.[19]

Instead of orienting itself toward a stable identity, lineage, legitimacy, the Creole that Glissant values "leads from periphery to periphery ... it makes every periphery into a center; furthermore, it abolishes the very notion of center and periphery."[20] Such a process eschews the notion of "literary progression,"

---

13 Linda A. Kinnahan, "An interview with Caroline Bergvall," *Contemporary Women's Writing* 5, no. 3 (2011): 247.
14 Bergvall, *Drift*, 155.
15 Édouard Glissant, *The Poetics of Relation*, trans. Betsy Wing (Ann Arbor: University of Michigan Press, 1997), 69.
16 Glissant, *The Poetics of Relation*, 11.
17 Ibid., 32.
18 Ibid., 13.
19 Ibid., 50.
20 Ibid., 29.

wherein foundational texts lay the groundwork for national language, establish a lineage, and so on. Creole, in contrast, "renews itself in every instance on the basis of a series of forgettings," leading to "linguistic multiplicity" and "friction between languages."[21] In "Cat in the Throat," as noted above, Bergvall prefers to hold onto and even emphasize linguistic friction, finding the injection of Middle and Old English into her contemporary verse one generative way to do so.

Other critics writing on Bergvall, as well as the artist herself, have noted the importance of Deleuze and Guattari's concept of "minor literature" in elucidating her approach to creating texts.[22] Deleuze and Guattari write, "a minor literature doesn't come from a minor language; it is rather that which a minority constructs within a major language," and it consists of three characteristics: its language is marked by a "high coefficient of deterritorialization"; it is political; and "everything takes on a collective value."[23] To say that language is "deterritorialized" language, for Deleuze and Guattari, means that "common, dominant codes and conventions are treated as though they were foreign and dysfunctional." To put it another way, "as Deleuze states (channeling Proust), 'It is not a question of speaking a language as if one was a foreigner, it is a question of being a foreigner to one's own language.'"[24] Bergvall says, "I would say that writing began, in all seriousness, when I started writing in English, when I moved from my own languages of French and Norwegian to working in my third language, English," adding that the "bilingual invention" of a poet like Chaucer has been a helpful model in her work.[25]

Shorter Chaucer Tales

The first of Caroline Bergvall's "Shorter Chaucer Tales" is "The Host Tale", which "lists food and drink references in *The Canterbury Tales*" (161). Bergvall adds that it "first appeared in print in its current Middle English form in the Norwegian

---

21 Ibid., 69, 104.

22 See Caroline Bergvall, "Writing at the Crossroads of Languages," in *Telling it Slant: Avant-Garde Poetics of the 1990s*, ed. Mark Wallace and Steven Marks (Tuscaloosa: University of Alabama Press, 2002). See also Nathalie Camerlynck, "Cat in the Throat: Caroline Bergvall's Plurilingual Bodies," *Transnational Literature* 8, no. 1 (2015), http://hdl.handle.net/2328/35637; see also McMurtry, "Sea Journeys to Fortress Europe."

23 Gilles Deleuze and Félix Guattari, *Kafka: Towards a Minor Literature*, trans. Dana Polan (Minneapolis: University of Minnesota Press, 1986), 16–17.

24 Eugene B. Young, Gary Genosko, and Janell Watson, *The Deleuze and Guattari Dictionary* (New York: Bloomsbury, 2013), 197.

25 Kinnahan, "An interview with Caroline Bergvall," 238, 247.

literary journal *Vagant*" and that the editors "let it pass for contemporary Norwegian" (161). The poem is a collection of lines from *The Canterbury Tales* that refer to food and drink. Bergvall has spoken about the way in which this opening poem offered her a point of entry for the project as a whole, which had been commissioned for the New Chaucer Society's 2006 congress in New York:[26]

> How do you start on *The Canterbury Tales?* I was really thinking about memes or lateral variations of a particular theme. Food and drink of course is absolutely everywhere, and I thought it was wonderful ... that allowed me to read *The Canterbury Tales* through the diagonal motif, pull that out, and allowed me to go through them.[27]

Upon closer examination, the references to food and drink are a mashup—in other words, the lines are drawn from various tales according to some arrangement, not always in order but often skipping around. For example, the first four lines of "The Host Tale" are:

> The fruyt of every tale is for to seye;
> They ete, and drynke, and daunce, and synge, and pleye.
> They soupen and they speke,
> And drynken evere strong ale atte beste.[28]

The first two lines are from "The Man of Law's Tale" (II.706–7). The next two come from "The Reeve's Tale" (I.4146–47), with the phrase "hem to solace" excised from line three.[29] Assuming that Bergvall is using the tale order from *The Riverside Chaucer*, she has chosen lines that follow sequentially but from tales that do not. From that point, things become much more scrambled. Line five comes from "The Pardoner's Tale," lines six and seven from "The Shipman's Tale," line eight from "The Squire's Tale," lines nine and ten from "The Shipman's Tale," lines 11 and 12 from "The Man of Law's Tale," line 13 from "The Shipman's Tale," and lines 14–17 from "The Squire's Tale." Nor is the last-mentioned series of lines in proper sequence from the tale; Bergvall's poem reads, "But thus I lete in lust and jolitee [V.344] / I lete hem, til men to the soper dresse.

---

26 Bergvall, *Meddle English*, 161.
27 Caroline Bergvall, "In conversation with David Wallace and Orchid Tierney," November 4, 2014, in *PennSound*, MP3 audio, www.writing.upenn.edu/pennsound/x/Bergvall.php.
28 Bergvall, *Meddle English*, 23.
29 All citations from Chaucer, unless otherwise noted, are taken from *The Riverside Chaucer*, ed. Larry D. Benson, 3rd ed. (Boston: Houghton Mifflin, 1987). Based on the orthography of Bergvall's text, she appears to have used the same edition.

[V.290] / They ete and drynke, and whan this hadde an ende," [V.295]. Line eight of Bergvall's poem is from "The Squire's Tale" [V.297].

Listening to audio of Bergvall reciting this poem reveals her commitment to and facility with the sound of Middle English (ME), no doubt made easier by her background in Norwegian and French.[30] Bergvall says of ME, "It's a language which is within time but outside of time. So I work it like a type of weird trans-futurity. It's also meant to remind us constantly of the depth and thickness of the language we are speaking right now."[31] She adds that over many readings of this piece, "its humour is always very clearly received," and "the familiar motif of food/drink/party put the point across and bring[s] the historical text and its languages closer to home."[32] Bergvall's reading style is smooth and assured, as she carefully enunciates each syllable, though sometimes slipping into a more modern way of sounding words. Many of these effects are audible in Bergvall's reading of a passage that appears at the top of the third page of "The Host Tale:"

> And of youre softe breed nat but a shyvere,
> And after that a rosted pigges heed
> Milk and broun breed,
> many a muscle and many an oystre.[33]

Here, Bergvall is consistently accurate on the pre-Great Vowel Shift sounds, but she does not pronounce the schwa at the end of "softe," which would seem to be indicated by the line's meter. (Usually she does carefully pronounce schwas, even in lines in which the schwa is followed by another vowel sound.)[34] Her reading of "shyvere" takes three syllables, and in the next line she follows the pentameter perfectly. The fourth line, however, sounds as it would in Present-Day English (PDE), as Bergvall pronounces both "muscle" and "oyster" exactly as they are today. Clearly, everyone who attempts to recite ME does so with their own style, and our best guesses as to proper pronunciation are largely based on conjecture from documentary evidence. Bergvall is a seasoned per-

30 Caroline Bergvall, "Shorter Chaucer Tales (2006)," September 22, 2006, in *PennSound*, MP3 audio, https://www.writing.upenn.edu/pennsound/x/Bergvall.php.

31 Caroline Bergvall, "Terms of Exchange: Caroline Bergvall," interview by Greg Nissan, *BOMB*, December 13, 2019, www.bombmagazine.org/articles/caroline-bergvall/.

32 Caroline Bergvall, email message to author, July 27, 2020.

33 Bergvall, *Meddle English*, 25.

34 See Peter G. Beidler, *A Student Guide to Chaucer's Middle English* (Seattle: Coffeetown Press, 2011), 40–42. See also Helge Kökeritz, *A Guide to Chaucer's Pronunciation* (New York: Holt, Rinehart, and Winston, 1961).

former whose major works often debut on the stage, alongside visual art and music (this holds true for both "Fried Tale" from *Meddle English* and much of *Drift*).[35] This is not to say that the "slippage" in Bergvall's pronunciation as she recites Chaucer's English is entirely deliberate—it seems only natural for even the most practiced reciter of ME to occasionally drift into modern soundings—but such slippage does fit with the seeming aim of the project, to blur boundaries between languages and ways of speaking.

Another example from further down on the poem's third page illustrates sound slippage that joins ME with PDE.

> So that men myghte dyne.
> Bacus the wyn shynketh al aboute,
> And broghte of myghty ale a large quart[36]

Bergvall sounds the "g-h" in "myghte," but "dyne" sounds like modern "dine" (with schwa appended) rather than the "ee" one would expect in ME. Likewise in the next line, "wyn" sounds like modern "wine," while the "y" in "shynketh" is pronounced as "ee," though it should sound as in "lid." In the final line from the above, "broghte" has the "g-h" sounded out, while these letters are silent in "myghty," pronounced as in PDE.[37] This minute focus on Bergvall's vocalizing of ME—which I will briefly revisit below—helps illustrate her subtle but persistent "revising" of Chaucer's language, which emphasizes slippage and friction alongside other, more textual features.

By and large, "The Host Tale" naturally features lines drawn from "lower" characters on the pilgrimage, those who tend to indulge in an excess of food and drink or tell fabliaux-style tales that involve the same, such as the Miller, the Reeve, and the Cook. Or, it draws from those who preach against such excess, such as the Monk and the Pardoner (the latter of whom is, of course, one of the lowest of the low). The Reeve, with his intricate tale of a miller stealing flour from two university students, is frequently quoted, with two straight lines in the middle of page two of Bergvall's poem, interspersed with a line from the "The Pardoner's Tale," followed by another from the Reeve, and another several lines down:

> With whete and malt (I.3988)
> Both mele and corn (I.3995)

35 See Bergvall, *Meddle English*, 162, and *Drift*, 128.
36 Bergvall, *Meddle English*, 25.
37 See Beidler, *A Student Guide to Chaucer's Middle English*, 26, 35.

> be it whete or otes, (VI.375)
> For male and breed, and rosted hem a goos (I.4137)[38]
> ...
> Instide of flour yet wol I yeve hem bren (I.4053)

I focus on the Reeve here because, while not a drunkard like the Miller or Cook, he is yet one of the most heinous of the pilgrims, and perhaps not coincidentally the one most associated with regional, northern dialect.[39] The frequent appearance of lines from his tale in Bergvall's "The Host Tale" is emblematic of the way in which this opening poetic gesture sets a playful and humorous but also gritty tone for this Chaucerian experiment. It also hearkens back to a previous poet's channeling of the Host.

In the prologue to John Lydgate's the *Siege of Thebes*, composed around 1420, the monk depicts himself encountering Chaucer's pilgrims on their return from Canterbury and, at the Host's insistence, joining them and telling a tale. In so doing, Lydgate furthers an intertextual mode of engaging with Chaucer perhaps already implicit in the latter's poetry.[40] As Daniel Kline writes, through his ingenious device, "Lydgate acts out the fantasy of being written—being engendered—by Chaucer, his literary father."[41] With his imaginative recasting of the Canterbury group, Lydgate subtly reshuffles the social stratifications of the pilgrims—a collection that includes Chaucer, and thus necessarily comments on Chaucer the author as well. In Chaucer's *General Prologue*, after the long roll call of worthies and, notably, immediately following the pious Plowman who never actually materializes to tell a tale, we are presented with a list of "rascals" that includes the author.[42] It is this grouping from which Lydgate draws his

---

38 Interestingly, line I.4137 from "The Reeve's Tale" actually reads "For ale and breed," and there are no variations in *The Riverside Chaucer* or any other edition I could find that support "male."

39 See J. R. R. Tolkien, "Chaucer as a Philologist: *The Reeve's Tale*," *Tolkien Studies* 5 (2008); see also Robert Epstein, "'Fer in the north; I kan nat telle where': Dialect, Regionalism, and Philologism," *Studies in the Age of Chaucer* 30 (2008); and Joseph Taylor, "Chaucer's Uncanny Regionalism: Rereading the North in The Reeve's Tale," *Journal of English and Germanic Philology* 109, no. 4 (2010).

40 See, for example, Chaucer's encounter with classical poets in *The House of Fame* (1456–1506), itself derived from Dante's imagining of Virgil.

41 Daniel T. Kline, "Father Chaucer and the *Siege of Thebes:* Literary Paternity, Aggressive Deference, and the Prologue to Lydgate's Oedipal Canterbury Tale," *The Chaucer Review* 34, no. 2 (1999): 217.

42 Kline, "Father Chaucer," 222. These include the Reeve, Miller, Summoner, Pardoner, Manciple, and Chaucer (I.542–44).

own list of Canterbury pilgrims, mentioning the Cook, Miller, Reeve, and Pardoner.[43]

Lydgate's Host is an exaggerated version of Chaucer's that draws from much of the frame narrative of *The Canterbury Tales*. After the would-be pilgrim offers his name, in response Lydgate's version of the Host amplifies his preoccupation with the body—and underscores it with base, rustic language:

> "Daun John," quod he "wel broke ye youre name![44]
> Preiyng you soupe with us tonyght,
> And ye shal have mad at youre devis,
> A gret puddyng or a rounde hagys,
> A Franchemole a tansey or a froyse.
> To ben a Monk Sclender is youre koyse" (96–101)

As Erdmann and Ekwall note, Lydgate sprinkles the Host's vocabulary with "several colloquial or slang words, not admitted by Chaucer, referring to parts of the human body"; this unique vocabulary extends to the culinary terms found in the above passage.[45] Thus, we encounter, in the space of three lines, the non-Chaucerian words "puddyng," "hagys" ("haggis"), "Franchemole," "tansey," "froyse," and "koyse."[46] While Lydgate's character borrows some phrases from Chaucer's Host, the vulgarity of his speech is also exaggerated; he seems linguistically aligned with the lowest of Chaucer's pilgrims. It is almost as if Chaucer's

43 John Lydgate, *Lydgate's Siege of Thebes*, ed. Axel Erdmann and Eilert Ekwall, Early English Text Society, Extra Series 108, 125 (London: Oxford University Press, 1911–1920), ll. 28, 33.

44 The Host's use of "broke" ("brook") meaning "to bear a name well," was new to the fifteenth century but is now obsolete. See *Oxford English Dictionary*, s.v. "brook (*v.*1)." accessed August 18, 2020, https://www.oed.com/view/Entry/23753?rskey=iQTTvf&result=3&isAdvanced=false#eid/. See also Erdmann and Ekwall, *Lydgate's Siege of Thebes*, who note, "The expression is much older than the earliest examples in the *Oxford Dictionary*" (98). The OED's first citation is 1587; Erdmann and Ekwall cite earlier instances, including one from *The Tale of Beryn* (ca. 1450–1470), which describes pilgrims in Canterbury.

45 Erdmann and Ekwall, *Lydgate's Siege of Thebes*, 28.

46 Erdmann and Ekwall, *Lydgate's Siege of Thebes*, 28: "franchemole" is a sort of haggis; "froyse" a pancake; "tansey" a pudding; "koyse" means "body." See also *Oxford English Dictionary*, s.v. "coise (*n.*)," accessed August 18, 2020, https://www.oed.com/view/Entry/36038?redirectedFrom=coise#eid. Erdmann and Ekwall write, "The word was at home only in the colloquial or vulgar language of the time, and is used here by the Host in a depreciatory or contemptuous sense" (98). "Slender is your koyse" would also seem to echo the Host's words to the Monk in *The Monk's Prologue:* "This maketh that oure heires beth so sklendre / And feble, that they may nat wel engendre" (ll. 1957–58); the lines are omitted in Ellesmere, but included in Hengwrt.

Cook has been revived and melded with Lydgate's version of Harry Bailly.[47] An analysis of the remainder of Host's language in the prologue reveals Lydgate's skillful way of weaving in and amplifying Chaucerian effects so as to underscore the base language of the Host.

Having advised the monk on his diet, the Host adds a word on sleeping: "After soper / Slepe wil do non ille. / Wrappe wel youre hede with clothes rounde aboute! / Strong notty ale wol make you to route" (108–10). So far, so Chaucerian; "Rout" meaning "to snore" was quite common into the fifteenth century, with a number of citations from Gower, Chaucer, and Caxton, among others; it is not difficult to imagine Chaucer's Host offering such an admonition.[48] Characteristically, Lydgate greatly expands on it, however. First comes his famous imperative, "Spare not to blowe!" (fart); he then explains that "holding wind" might bring on "Collikes passioun," "And make men to greven on her roppys, / whan thei han filled her mawes and her croppys" (112–16). This passage again requires linguistic unpacking. "Collikes passioun" is a complaint of the lower intestines,[49] while "roppys" ("black pudding") and "croppys" ("face" or "maw") are terms not used by Chaucer.[50] Thus, the sense of the four lines is, "To hold gas, in my opinion, causes *collica passio*, which makes men agonize over their black pudding after they've filled their mouths and throats." This detailed concern on the part of Lydgate's Host with the monk's eating and sleeping habits goes well beyond the largely good-natured jibing in Chaucer's frame narrative.

Lydgate thus initiates a way of "reading" Chaucer—and particularly the Host of *The Canterbury Tales*—as especially concerned with drinking, eating, and other bodily functions, anticipating and reinforcing such associations for future authors, including Bergvall. The association of Chaucer with unbridled "excess" perhaps reached its *reductio ad absurdum* recently with a comment from actor Johnny Depp that his own substance abuse could be traced in part to the author:

---

47 See, especially, *The Cook's Prologue*, in which the Host chides Roger the Cook for his inferior wares and the Cook offers a veiled threat in response (I.4345–62).

48 See *Oxford English Dictionary*, s.v. "rout, (*v.*1)," accessed August 18, 2020, https://www.oed.com/view/Entry/168065?rskey=iet1IT&result=10#eid.

49 See *Oxford English Dictionary*, s.v. "colic (*n.* and *adj.*)," accessed August 18, 2020, https://www.oed.com/view/Entry/36168?rskey=W06kZW&result=1#eid. See also Erdmann and Ekwall's note on "collica passio" (98–99).

50 See *Oxford English Dictionary*, s.v. "rope (*n.*2)," accessed August 18, 2020, https://www.oed.com/view/Entry/167403?rskey=5E4Noy&result=2&isAdvanced=false#eid; the etymology is from OE "hrop" and appears to have survived in ME as a dialect word, meaning animal entrails. See also "crop, (*n.*2)," accessed August 18, 2020, https://www.oed.com/view/Entry/44776?rskey=azsilh&result=1&isAdvanced=false#eid, meaning "throat" or "maw."

"I have always been interested in the counter-culture and many literary heroes of mine, including Chaucer, who was an opium addict."[51] Chaucer's experiments with various linguistic "profiles" for pilgrims have proven generative for a number of later interlocutors, most notably Edmund Spenser, who seems to channel Chaucer in creating the strange and differential language of his collection of poets in *The Shepheardes Calender.*[52] Of course, hovering behind all of these experiments in poetic diction is the image of Chaucer as the "Father of English," which begins with Thomas Hoccleve and Lydgate soon after the former's death.[53] Like Lydgate—who seems to want to steer Chaucerian language towards the "aureate" diction that he inaugurates and employs elsewhere in his verse[54]—Bergvall does not rest with the "bodily humor" version of Chaucer, but strikes out in a number of surprising and challenging directions.

In the next several "Shorter Chaucer Tales," Bergvall begins to experiment with other methods of foregrounding "friction" in her working through ME, even as she more actively translates and adapts the tales themselves. "The Summer Tale" quotes from "The Summoner's Tale" and "The Pardoner's Tale," while "The Franker Tale" makes use of "The Franklin's Tale." But both also draw from disparate sources: news stories, poet John Ashbery's *Variations, Calypso, and Fugue*, and what is listed in the notes as "Presence of Francis Bacon in his studio"; together the poems act as a sequence that satirizes and critiques the pope.[55]

In the first line of "The Summer Tale," Bergvall writes, "Rome is the hem home of ice cream," thus introducing a sort of linguistic "drift" that will become

51 See Harry Howard, "How I Became a Hollywood hell raiser," *Daily Mail*, July 7, 2020, www.dailymail.co.uk/news/article-8498465/Johnny-Depp-trashing-hotel-rooms-Kate-Moss-drinking-Marilyn-Manson.html.

52 See David Hadbawnik, "The Chaucer-Function: Spenser's Language Lessons in *The Shepheardes Calender*," *Upstart: A Journal of English Renaissance Studies* (June 2014), www.upstart.sites.clemson.edu/Essays/hadbawnik_spenser/hadbawnik_spenser.xhtml.

53 See Derek Brewer, *Chaucer: The Critical Heritage*, vol. 1 (London: Routledge, 1978), 44–59, for numerous examples of Lydgate's praise of Chaucer's rhetorical skill and language. See also Joseph Mersand, *Chaucer's Romance Vocabulary* (New York: The Comet Press, 1939). More recent critics have complicated and further elucidated Chaucer's role in expanding English; see Christopher Cannon, *The Making of Chaucer's English: A Study of Words* (New York: Cambridge University Press, 1998), 195–210; see also Jonathan Hsy, *Trading Tongues: Merchants, Multilingualism, and Medieval Literature* (Columbus: The Ohio State University Press, 2013).

54 See Robert J. Meyer-Lee, *Poets and Power from Chaucer to Wyatt* (New York: Cambridge University Press, 2007), 55. Meyer-Lee writes, of "Complaynt of a Lover's Life," "Lydgate will 'redress his style' in order to suit a divine rather than erotic object of praise—specifically, by making it aureate" (56).

55 Bergvall, *Meddle English*, 161.

a regular motif as the project develops. The interspersed ME word "hem" means "them"—a term used quite frequently in Chaucer—and in reciting the poem creates a slight slurring or stuttering effect bumping against "home."[56] Speaking about the above-mentioned line in particular, Bergvall says, "It's pointing to a transferring process, so you immediately know we are in a linguistic situation where we might be helped through the variations that follow, but there are these disturbances."[57] Later in the same poem, Bergvall repeats the effect: "during a viage trip there this wyke week," doubling up semantic terms for "voyage" and "week." Such doubling is even more heightened in "The Franker Tale," which begins:

> Following tweye two breathing crises
> and with a tube placidly placed placed
> in his esophagus, the papal Pope in Rome
> ...
> when the seeds of death's deeth
> one by one finally popped in hym him.[58]

Bergvall's recitation of the poem heightens the sense of "disturbance" created by the intrusion of ME into these otherwise PDE phrases. In the second line, she makes "placed" into a homograph, pronouncing a soft "a" sound and both syllables in the first "placed"; "place" is a frequent term in Chaucer, derived from Old French, though he never uses the participial "-ed" form and does not seem to employ it as other than a noun.[59] On hearing Bergvall recite the line, it becomes clear that this older way of sounding "placed" was likely suggested by "placidly." Similarly, Bergvall draws out the slight but noticeable difference in sounding "death"/"deeth" and "hym"/"him." All of the effects mentioned above—the differential pronunciation, the doubling of terms, and so on—contribute to the vocal friction Bergvall welcomes into the work, which is both performative and comes across most clearly in performance. She describes it as:

> using a process of translation as a way to reinvent or recreate the final word so that by explicating different spellings, different words for the same words, or through homophonic translation, there's historical depth. It opens up the semantic field. It's a way of writing ... Rather than having a translator go from A to B, it becomes an AB-type thing. Translation

56 Bergvall, "Shorter Chaucer Tales (2006)." See also Norman Davis, Douglas Gray, Patricia Ingham, and Ann Wallace-Hadrill, eds., *A Chaucer Glossary* (New York: Oxford University Press, 1979) for more information on this and other Middle English terms from Chaucer.
57 Bergvall, "In conversation with David Wallace."
58 Bergvall, *Meddle English*, 31.
59 Davis et al., *A Chaucer Glossary*, 110.

> doesn't have a resting point neither here nor there. But it spans that stretch. It comes across so many interactions. There's no final mastery in translation because it's taken over by the performative one way or another.[60]

Both tales, as well as the concluding "Fried Tale (London Zoo)" channel a version of Chaucer that will be quite familiar to medievalists and even to many casual readers: as opposed to the "bodily humor" Chaucer, this is Chaucer the reformist. The perception of Chaucer as being on the side of economic, religious, and social reform begins early and shifts over time and according to taste, however equivocal the poet himself seemed in life and however "open-ended" his poetry, and Bergvall participates in recuperating Chaucer in this way.[61] Bergvall says that she was searching for "contemporary narratives" to work with as opposed to simply "applying Chaucer to contemporary concerns ... wondering, 'How can I tell a voiced story?'" In other words, instead of adapting or translating *The Canterbury Tales* to a contemporary national culture, Bergvall tells contemporary tales after the mode of Chaucer, showing her work every step of the way. Thus, the news stories that inform "The Summer Tale" and "The Franker Tale," a focus on the pope that she says "is about rape ... he's basically advising women not to have abortions although they've been raped." Notably, for Bergvall it's "because of his irritation with those religious institutions" that it seemed appropriate to "bring Chaucer into it."[62] She does not make explicit use of the many tropes involving rape that surround Chaucer and *The Canterbury Tales*, although these tropes hover behind the project as a whole.[63] She adds,

> Gender games and sexual violence are rife in *The Tales*. Gendered assumptions that implicitly perpetuate social violence on various body genres are rife in the public statements of many contemporary leaders. The composition of 'The Franker Tale' dealt with various Chaucerian and contemporary socio-sexual motifs.[64]

---

60 Bergvall, "Terms of Exchange."

61 See James Simpson, "Chaucer's presence and absence, 1400–1150," *The Cambridge Companion to Chaucer*, ed. Piero Boitani and Jill Mann (New York: Cambridge University Press, 2003), 260. Simpson writes, "Chaucer ... became the key literary counter in the radical reshaping of the English past necessitated by the English Reformation. In short, Chaucer became a Protestant and a champion of English insularity" (263).

62 Bergvall, "In conversation with David Wallace."

63 See "The Wife of Bath's Tale," "The Reeve's Tale," and of course Chaucer's own involvement with possible rape: "Chaucer and the Raptus of Cecily Chaumpaigne (1380)," in *A Companion to Chaucer and His Contemporaries*, ed. Laurel Amtower and Jacqueline Vanhoutte (Buffalo, NY: Broadview, 2009), 113–114.

64 Bergvall, "Short aside to 'The Franker Tale,'" *Jacket* 32 (April 2007), www.jacketmagazine.com/32/p-bergvall-franker-aside.shtml.

"Fried Tale" focuses on the global banking crisis and financial meltdown of 2008 and works from "The Friars Tale" in addition to a number of other sources. Bergvall says,

> I'd moved away from the papal situation to the bankers' crisis, which again carried a sense of hopelessness—there's a lot of that for me in writing these tales. Some of the hopelessness that I feel ... when you see Chaucer with his society and the way he's describing, the way people are also being put down, that was one aspect in the narrative that gave me permission.[65]

This last entry of "The Shorter Chaucer Tales" is certainly the most challenging both linguistically and narratively, as Bergvall gains confidence in a "fluid movement across radically different textual registers."[66] It is this entry in the series that clearly forms a blueprint of sorts for Bergvall's next medievalist work, *Drift*, which, as noted above, grows in large part from her emotional response to the migrant crisis, another "hopeless" global conundrum. What's striking in Bergvall's medievalist trilogy as a whole is how persistently and stridently political it is. Even in the dense thicket of linguistic concerns and language games—indeed, inextricable from them—the poems have something to say politically.[67] This element of Bergvall's poetics well accords with the second characteristic of "minor literatures:" "everything in them is political."[68] At the same time, this aspect of Bergvall's work, for both "Fried Tale" and *Drift* in particular, has been explored in detail by other critics.[69] I am more concerned, for the rest of this chapter, to trace the importance of Chaucer (his matter and language) to Bergvall's project, and follow the inventive paths forged thereby.

To follow the thread of linguistic invention as it progresses in Bergvall's project, I must focus on "The Not Tale," described as "a translation of a cross-section

65 Bergvall, "In conversation with David Wallace."

66 Richard Owens, "Caroline Bergvall her 'Shorter Chaucer Tales,'" *postmedieval* 6, no. 2 (2015): 149.

67 See Kinnahan, "An interview with Caroline Bergvall." Bergvall says, "Linguistically, I have taken my cue from contemporary slang as much as historical English and explicit Chaucerian vocabulary or syntax. This kind of bilingual invention is, of course, politically and culturally very important for a lot of today's writers who have a mixed or complex cultural makeup ... I sometimes say that Chaucer's English is the closest to my own language and to my own way of speaking" (247).

68 Deleuze and Guattari, *Kafka*, 17.

69 See Owens, "Caroline Bergvall her 'Shorter Chaucer Tales'" and McMurtry, "Sea Journeys to Fortress Europe," as well as Clare A. Lees and Gillian R. Overing, *The Contemporary Medieval in Practice* (London: University College London Press, 2019), 66–70.

of Arcite's extravagant and moving funeral in 'The Knight's Tale'."[70] In terms of both form and content, it bears a stronger resemblance to the appropriative "The Host Tale" than the others in the sequence, as it contains no other sources besides Chaucer and eschews any overt political stance. As David Wallace notes, "The Not Tale" "riffs on *occupatio*" and the piling up of negatives that constitutes the Knight's rhetorical strategy.[71] The portion of the poem to which Bergvall responds, I.2913–66, includes "the longest sentence in Chaucer's poetry," which runs for 49 lines.[72] Much of Bergvall's poem proceeds by condensing Chaucer, shortening both the total number of lines (what Chaucer describes in 54 lines, Bergvall reduces to 44) and the lines themselves. The poem begins:

> The great labour of appearance
> served the making of the pyre.
> But how
> nor how
> How also
> how they
> shal nat be toold
> shall not be told.[73]

The "stuttering" effect that Bergvall produces by repetition and doubling is here accomplished by simply trimming back, in spots, almost everything but Chaucer's parallel structure of negatives. She also modernizes Chaucer's diction here and there, translating and even perhaps mistranslating. Chaucer writes: "Heigh labor and ful greet apparaillynge / Was at the service and the fyr-makynge" (I.2913–14). By "apparaillynge," Chaucer no doubt meant "preparation."[74] Yet, "appearance" is not wholly unwarranted as a translation; that meaning is attested as current for the time period.[75] The word derives from Old French and perhaps Bergvall's knowledge of French informed her choice. By choosing this meaning, she participates in a reshuffling of Chaucer's diction of which Spenser, and even Chaucer himself, may have heartily approved.

---

70 Bergvall, *Meddle English*, 161.

71 Bergvall, "In conversation with David Wallace." See also Deanne Williams, "The Dream Visions," in *The Yale Companion to Chaucer*, ed. Seth Lerer (New Haven: Yale University Press, 2006). Williams writes, "*occupatio:* the space intended for description is filled ... with complaints of unwillingness or inability to describe" (263).

72 *The Riverside Chaucer*, 840.

73 Bergvall, *Meddle English*, 36.

74 *The Riverside Chaucer*, 64. See also Davis et al., *A Chaucer Glossary*, 6.

75 *Oxford English Dictionary*, s.v. "apparel (*n.*)," accessed August 6, 2020, https://www.oed.com/view/Entry/9510?rskey=RBd0r4&result=1&isAdvanced=false#eid.

As Cannon writes, while Chaucer is often credited as "fathering" English, he in fact took part in a method of language adaptation and formation—combining terms from French, Latin, and Old English—that was already well under way.[76] Spenser greatly expanded this method and applied it to Chaucer's language itself, as his experiments with "glossing" in *The Shepheardes Calender* show. Elsewhere, I have discussed Spenser's invented definition for the French-derived term "chevisaunce," by which Chaucer seems to mean a (perhaps underhanded) financial transaction; it appears in "The General Prologue" description of the Merchant (I.282) and three times in "The Shipman's Tale" (VII.329, 347, 391). Chevisaunce is misused by Spenser to cast the term in a prettier, more chivalric light. Spenser acknowledges having gleaned "chevisaunce" from Chaucer in the gloss to the "April" eclogue, but immediately shifts the definition. So influential and enduring is his coinage that poets continued using the "Spenserian" version of the word for hundreds of years afterwards.[77]

Bergvall's shift of meaning for "apparaillynge" (from "preparation" to "appearance") operates in an analogous way to Spenser's move, subtly changing the mood of the funeral description and shading into a kind of critique, certainly of King Theseus, who labors to maintain appearances, as well as, perhaps, the Knight's labored rhetoric and by extension Chaucer's. One further line in the poem accomplishes a similar thing: "nor what she spak, nor what was her desire," which is a word-for-word modernization (aside from "spak") of I.2944 in "The Knight's Tale." The line refers to Emelye, the female member of Chaucer's tragic love triangle. Emelye takes part in the funeral preparations, and the Knight characteristically describes her while disavowing description. Preceded by a series of truncated negatives ("Nor what / nor how / nor how"), Bergvall's version of the line emphasizes Emelye's almost complete lack of agency in the tale, the way in which she is seldom heard from and her desires never taken into account. These are subtle shifts in rhetoric and diction, but they anticipate the more extreme and often jarring effects we encounter in the final part of Bergvall's trilogy, *Alisoun Sings*.

76 Cannon, *The Making of Chaucer's English*, 72, 78, 82, 85.

77 See Hadbawnik, "The Chaucer-function." See also Edmund Spenser, "April," in *The Shepheardes Calender.*

Alisoun Sings

Bergvall reports of the protagonist of this project, modeled after Chaucer's "Wife of Bath:"

> I have written her in as an anarchist collectivist, a feminist, queered female polyamorous lover, a friend/fighter, a Lucretian in her gender attributions and a Bakhtinian in her politics of the many and dissenting pleasure ... It felt crucial to me to embed Chaucer's rich Alisoun in one's contemporary quest around future gender and collective struggle.[78]

Here, Bergvall points towards Bakhtin's concept of "Dialogic Discourse," the notion that every individual utterance, every instant of linguistic expression, must be considered along a continuum both temporally and socially. Bakhtin writes,

> From a truly objective viewpoint ... language presents the picture of a ceaseless flow of becoming ... there is no real moment in time when a synchronic system of language could be constructed ... And indeed, to the historian of language, with his diachronic point of view, a synchronic system is not a real entity.[79]

This explains the concept in terms of a history of language; but there is a social element as well. Bakhtin adds, "Not a single instance of verbal utterance can be reckoned exclusively to its utterer's account. Every utterance is *the product of the interaction between speakers* and the product of the broader context of the whole complex *social situation* in which the utterance emerges" (emphasis in original).[80] A nascent kind of dialogic approach to poetics (and indeed, a "Poetics of Relation," à la Glissant, or something akin to Deleuze and Guattari's principles of a "minor literature") is apparent in Chaucer and Spenser. Both stretch across time, space, and class to create a differential poetic diction that pushes boundaries and sets the stage for later experiments. Yet, for Spenser at least, this project was often explicitly programmatic, even nationalistic. In a famous and much-referenced passage from a letter to Gabriel Harvey, Spenser writes, "Why a God's name, may not we, as else the Greeks, have the kingdom of our

---

78 Caroline Bergvall, email message to author, July 27, 2020.

79 Mikhail Bakhtin, *The Bakhtin Reader: Selected Writings of Bakhtin, Medvedev, and Voloshinov*, ed. Pam Morris, trans. I. R. Titunik (London: Arnold, 1994), 32.

80 Bakhtin, *The Bakhtin Reader*, 41. See also Hadbawnik, "The Chaucer-function," which includes a discussion of Bakhtin in relation to Spenser's dialogic project.

own language?"[81] This question has often been heard as Spenser's announcement of his own national language project.[82]

Bergvall pursues no such project, radically updating Spenser's appropriation of archaic and dialect words to create an English that degenerates into a range of marginal voices, constantly anachronizing and undercutting itself, short-circuiting any sense of continuity or linguistic "mastery" a reader might feel as they go along. Instead of distinct pilgrims as in Chaucer or shepherds in Spenser, Bergvall's Alisoun melds with other voices, other speech families, and uncomfortably rubs against and crosses boundaries at exactly the moments one expects a rhythm to stabilize and carry one forward. Bergvall inverts or queers the usual relationship to an "original" English because instead of building on the prestige of ME—the deliberate archaism of a Spenser—she erects a "minor literature" that speaks important truths from the margins.

Largely written in prose, *Alisoun Sings* opens with a greeting from its namesake in the hybrid, "collective" voice Bergvall fashions for her, a greeting that operates as a sort of statement of purpose in terms of both language and content:

> Hi you all, I'm Alisoun. Some people call me Al. Am many things to many a few thyinge to some & nothing but an irritant to socialites and othere glossing troglodytes. I dig a good chat banter aboute. Sbeen a long time, some & six hundred times have circled roun the solar sun, everything were diffrent yet pretty much the same, sunsets were reddier, godabov ruled all & the franks the rest. Womenfolk were owned trafeckt regulated petted tightlye impossible to run ones own afferes let alone ones mynd nat publicly nat privatly, & so were most workfolk enserfed, owned never free, working working day 'n niht. Sunsets redder, legs a little shorter.[83]

Bergvall has said of this voice that it came to her initially as a postscript of sorts to the "Shorter Chaucer Tales" in *Meddle English*, one that took her a long time to find a rhythm with: "I tried on and off for years. I wasn't happy with it. It was unclear to me why. It's the toughest project I've ever written. But that voice is nearly the bully; it pushes and pushes me on."[84]

In part, it seems that the Wife of Bath's penchant for glossing—the great deal of scripture that Chaucer "translates and comments on through this unlikely

---

81 Edmund Spenser, "Letter to Gabriel Harvey, 1580," in *The Works of Spenser*, vol. 2 (London: J. and R. Tonson and S. Draper, 1750), 306.

82 Richard Helgerson, *Forms of Nationhood* (Chicago: Chicago University Press, 1992). Helgerson uses the phrase "The Kingdom of Our Own Language" as the title heading of his introduction and this question of Spenser's as an important introduction to his discussion of what he sees as a "generational project" to reinvent England/Britain during the 1590s (3).

83 Bergvall, *Alisoun Sings*, 1.

84 Bergvall, "Terms of Exchange."

woman preacher"—becomes both impetus and model for Bergvall in reviving and structuring Alisoun's voice for her poem.[85] Such a voice can seemingly address the vast weight of political, economic, and social devastation to which Bergvall responds (and do so with humor and levity).[86] Like Chaucer's Wife, Bergvall's Alisoun weaves in quotes and allusions, a practice that begins immediately and continues throughout the text. Alisoun makes reference to artist Marina Abramović, who "screamed until no voice & screamed some mo until the earth joined in";[87] this alludes to Abramović's 1978 performance "AAA-AAA."[88] Early feminist activist Emma Goldman is quoted, though the first time her words are partially translated into ME: "Tis on the homefront it beginne womenfolks development hir freedom hir independance come from and through oneself"; later, she is quoted verbatim: "in a world so crassly indifferent to the various gradations and variations of gender and their great significance in life."[89] Alisoun also offers a brief account of John Eleanor Rykener, who was tried in the late fourteenth century for sodomy, although no verdict was returned as, according to Alisoun, "they could not decide whether or not Eleanor is man or womman."[90] Indeterminacy of subject, and even sex, appears to be one of Alisoun's aims:

> Wat if I present as a crowd, a school of beings deep and elemental, wisdom aroused, skinsack seriously furrowed by time, genitals soft and enlarged from years of use & praktike, what if we be praised for the largesse of our vaginas![91]

85 See Theresa Tinkle, "The Wife of Bath's Marginal Authority," *Studies in the Age of Chaucer* 32 (2010): 67–101.

86 Bergvall, "Terms of Exchange." Of Alisoun's voice, she adds, "We're in a time where we are asking questions about social living in the face of political and capitalist devastation, environmental catastrophes, intense processes of migration that can only increase. I think that begs the question: How do we speak in such a way that we can be bothered to be listening as well? What is it that justifies the poetic and the literary form?"

87 Bergvall, *Alisoun Sings*, 3.

88 See Marina Abramović, "AAA-AAA (compilation version)," LIMA Catalogue. Available online: www.li-ma.nl/lima/catalogue/art/abramovic-ulay/aaa-aaa-compilation-version/8009.

89 Bergvall, *Alisoun Sings*, 6–7, 11. See Matthew Gindin, "Emma Goldman: Intersectional Before the Word Existed," *The Wisdom Daily*, April 2, 2018, http://thewisdomdaily.com/emma-goldman-intersectional-before-the-word-existed/.

90 Bergvall, *Alisoun Sings*, 12. Many critics describe Rykener as an early transgender person, a category Bergvall seems in agreement with, though at least one author insists Rykener was a transwoman; see Kadin Henningsen, "'Calling [herself] Eleanor': Gender Labor and Becoming a Woman in the Rykener Case," *MFF* 55, no. 1 (2019).

91 Bergvall, *Alisoun Sings*, 15.

Another passage takes this idea even further, by directly writing against or queering a portion of the Wife of Bath's "Prologue."

The passage from Chaucer to which Bergvall's Alisoun responds is one that characteristically draws from anti-feminist writings;[92] Chaucer adapts it from Jerome.[93] In Jerome's text, he admits that although the sexual organs were indeed created for more than urination, people should—if they are called to serve—nevertheless follow the example of Christ and refrain from using them for sex.[94] Interpreting Jerome, Chaucer's Wife of Bath says:

> Telle me also, to what conclusion
> Were membres maad of generacion,
> And of so parfit wys a [wright] ywroght?
> Trusteth right wel, they were nat maad for noght.
> Glose whoso wole, and seye bothe up and doun
> That they were maked for purgacioun
> Of uryne, and oure bothe thynges smale
> Were eek to knowe a femele from a male,
> And for noon oother cause—say ye no?
> The experience woot wel it is noght so. (III.115–24)

Chaucer's Wife takes a simpler line based on experience in arguing for sexual enjoyment, though some critics argue that she actually hews closely to religious orthodoxy, albeit with an irreverent twist.[95]

In Bergvall's text, just prior to page ten, Alisoun rhapsodizes, "How free of body heart & thought one is, how free of humours curses spells gosts putdowns and fears one be, how free to action labour love & politicks one be ... How free extenden all being in hire being, female male en melee."[96] Bergvall's Alisoun celebrates the freedom to "extend" one's being, not only for "female male;" her

---

92 See *The Riverside Chaucer*, 864.
93 Ibid., 866.
94 See Jerome, *Against Jovinianus*, book 1, section 36, trans. W. H. Fremantle, G. Lewis, and W. G. Martley, in *Nicene and Post-Nicene Fathers, Second Series*, ed. Philip Schaff and Henry Wace, vol. 6 (Buffalo, NY: Christian Literature Publishing Co., 1893); revised and edited for New Advent by Kevin Knight, www.newadvent.org/fathers/30091.htm.
95 See Tinkle, "The Wife of Bath's Marginal Authority," who writes that Alison "agrees [with] ... Jerome's main argument" (101). See also Warren S. Smith, "The Wife of Bath Debates Jerome," *The Chaucer Review* 32, no. 2 (1997): 129–45. Smith writes, "ultimately the Wife arrives at a humorously presented but reasonable, balanced and, in basic outline, even Augustinian view of celibacy and marriage which triumphantly defends a literalist interpretation of the Bible, against the mischief of its male *glossators*" (130).
96 Bergvall, *Alisoun Sings*, 9–10.

strange addition to the end of the statement demonstrates Bergvall's multilingual queering of Chaucer's Wife. At first glance, "en" looks like it could be an ME orthographical variation for "and," though it appears nowhere in Chaucer and seems more likely to be French, in which case it means "in" (or "by" or "into," etc.). But it could also be Dutch for "and;" given Bergvall's background in both languages, there is perhaps no reason to choose between them.[97] Since English draws from *both* French and Dutch for "mêlée" ("quarrel or mixture"), "en" is all the more appropriate here.[98] In this way, the friction between languages helps enact the process Alisoun describes and illustrates her point.

On the next page, starting a new section but following up on the above thought, Bergvall writes,

> Experience shows, continues Alisoun, everyone is spawned in 3D yet pruned in 2D, every singled ones of us are wooed groomed for specific agenders in this flatland & never be anyoon free of its games & curses. Folk be arranged one typer pair, an army for nought, a science of zeroes & ones, detach apply the repetitive blocks of exes, whys and zebras & 'member ne give a fig takes for king that which bulges roundly and for queens that which holds in place squarely, strictest twopronged situation, its a structure for industry innit, a logic of global trading & worship, from bedrooms to boardrooms, aye what a wastage of good opps & positions![99]

Bergvall calls "Experience shows," "a Chaucerian line that Alisoun uses. Experience grounds her knowledge in the world; that's why she's been strong. One aspect of the work is rethinking gendering as an imprisoning mechanism, then riffing off toward liberatory forms."[100] In both language and logic, Bergvall pushes the Wife of Bath's argument to a further extreme, pointing out how people are "groomed" for gender roles, peppering her concluding exclamation with idiomatic turns of phrase ("give a fig" … "innit") and lamenting the "wastage" that results from this "global" "structure of industry." In a sense, Bergvall takes Chaucer's Wife of Bath global, both in terms of language and gender politics, "scaling up" her medievalist project in ways that grow increasingly capacious and precarious—moving toward the former while risking the latter.

---

97 See "en," *The Oxford-Hachette Concise French-English Dictionary*, ed. Marie-Hélène Corréard and Valerie Grundy (New York: Oxford University Press, 1995); see also "en" (accessed August 17, 2020), *Cambridge Dutch-English Dictionary*, https://dictionary.cambridge.org/dictionary/dutch-english/en.

98 See *Oxford English Dictionary*, s.v. "mêlée (*n.*)," accessed August 17, 2020, https://www.oed.com/view/Entry/116086?redirectedFrom=melee#eid.

99 Bergvall, *Alisoun Sings*, 10.

100 Bergvall, "Terms of Exchange."

Ben Jonson's famous statement that "Spencer, in affecting the Ancients writ no language," points neatly toward the risk involved in a "deterritorialized" approach to creative diction, one fashioned out of "nonsinging."[101] Jonson, of course, is critiquing Spenser (and other poets) in the name of a secure, proto-nationalist poetic diction in English—a different version of Spenser's own "language kingdom." Yet, as Deleuze and Guattari ask, "How many people today live in a language that is not their own?" They continue,

> This is the problem of immigrants, and especially of their children, the problem of minorities, the problem of a minor literature, but also a problem for all of us: how to tear a minor literature away from its own language, allowing it to challenge the language and making it follow a sober revolutionary path? How to become a nomad and an immigrant and a gypsy in relation to one's own language?[102]

For Kafka, they write, the solution was to "steal the baby from its crib" and refashion German into a hybrid language infused with various tongues in Kafka's Eastern European milieu;[103] Bergvall persistently shows the way towards a similar approach in English.

---

101 See S. P. Zitner, "Spenser's Diction and Classical Precedent," *Philological Quarterly* 45, no. 2 (1966): 360–371 at 360.
102 Deleuze and Guattari, *Kafka*, 19.
103 Ibid.

Index

https://doi.org/10.1515/9781501511189-011